Lamentable Intelligence from the Admiralty

Lamentable Intelligence from the Admiralty

Chris Thomas

NONSUCH

For

Daphne, Candy and Sabrina, three generations of '*Vanguard* descendants'

First published 2006

Nonsuch Publishing
73 Lower Leeson Street
Dublin 2
Ireland
www.nonsuch-publishing.com

British Library Cataloguing in Publication Data.
A catalogue record for this book is available from the British Library.

ISBN 1 84588 544 9

Typesetting and origination by Tempus Publishing Limited
Printed in Great Britain

Contents

List of Illustrations

Foreword

The sinking of HMS *Vanguard* never achieved the notoriety of those other Victorian warship disasters, the *Captain* and the *Victoria*. When this second class ironclad sank without fatal casualties she left no one grieving, and did not imperil the Empire. It was an accident of seamanship, not a design flaw or a failure of judgement by one man. No government minister was implicated, no-one famous was involved, even the technical lessons it taught were fairly mundane. So, for historians of the Royal Navy and of naval architecture, this event merits little more than a passing reference. And there it would have rested, unchallenged and unnoticed, had Chris Thomas not been inspired to re-open the case. That he did so from a family history background, his wife being descended from two of the survivors, merely reminds us that history is not the sole preserve of the professional. This is a very professional book, based on a thorough review of the extant archive, the discovery of fresh material and above all fresh questions. The real tragedy is one of a good officer crushed by the weight of the system, a story that that still resonates today. The question of blame in military accidents is one that continues to fascinate and trouble the public to this day, the Chinook crash at the Mull of Kintyre only the latest high profile case where the system seems to have failed those involved. While a handful of officers carried the blame, rightly or wrongly, the seamen of the *Vanguard* were also involved, many of them found their lives altered, their futures changed. This book is their story, and also that of the Victorian world that greeted the news.

Chris Thomas has produced an important addition to our knowledge of the Victorian Navy. He offers an insight into the lives of the officers and men who controlled the world with a handful of small warships, and of the system that ran the service. That this Victorian Battleship lies on the bottom of Dublin Bay will remind some of the long years Ireland spent under British rule, but others might wish to reflect on the considerable contribution made by Irish sailors of all ranks to the history of world's most successful fighting force. The better we understand our past, the better equipped we are to meet the future. 'Lamentable Intelligence' gives us a priceless insight into the world of our Victorian forbears, and reminds us that the past is always open to re-examination.

Andrew Lambert
Laughton Professor of Naval History
King's College London
September 2005

Chapter 1

'*Time is a great story teller*'

'Is maith an scéalai an aimsir' - from a Dublin sugar wrapper

'To listen to the narrative of stirring adventures connected with maritime life; to dwell upon the incidents which attend them until I almost seem to have shared in the perils of the hour; to repeat those hair-breadth escapes and thrilling tales of Father Neptune's dominions to an eager audience of lads and lasses, is as good a substitute for actual sea-life as a maimed, weather-worn tar can hope to enjoy.'

Thus did Mrs Jessie Margaret Saxby begin her collection of tales of lost ships, published in 1891 under the grand title of *Breakers Ahead; Or, Uncle Jack's Stories of Great Shipwrecks of Recent Times: 1869 to 1880*. It was a fertile period for wreck devotees. Mrs Saxby was able to put 32 stories into the mouth of 'Uncle Jack', from the loss of the *Deutschland*, about which Gerard Manley Hopkins had already written more eloquently, to 'A Brigantine wrecked on the East Pier of Swansea'. Two pages of her book describe the loss of 'one of our best ships of war', HMS *Vanguard*.

A hundred years later I sat in the Public Record Office in Kew, West London (now one part of the National Archives), puzzling over the fact that two of my wife's great-grandfathers, both Royal Navy sailors, had apparently been transferred together from HMS *Vanguard* to another ironclad on the same day in 1875. A visit to the National Maritime Museum, housed in the wonderful assembly of buildings that includes the Royal Naval College and Inigo Jones' Queen's House at Greenwich, provided my answer, in a laconic entry in Conway's *All The World's Fighting Ships*: 'HMS *Vanguard*: Sunk in collision with *Iron Duke* 1st September 1875, rammed accidentally in fog in Dublin Bay'. A few minutes later I discovered on the Library shelves the richly coloured narrative of Mrs Saxby, and my imagination began to run riot. A vision emerged of two desperate seafarers, struggling in freezing waters, on the verge of being overwhelmed by the merciless power of the deep – Mrs Saxby had entered my soul. But as I read more the picture became much less romantic. There was no thrashing about in the sea (which was actually not very cold at all), since all hands had shown exemplary discipline. It was peacetime, the ships were on a leisurely summer cruise, the accident had no undertones of enemy action or evil intent, no lives were lost; it was just sudden fog and split-second decisions taken with unfortunate consequences. This sort of thing occurs all the time. Still in the twenty-first century hugely expensive pieces of state-of-the-art fighting equipment are lost as the result of a moment's carelessness. It was just a very ordinary happening that hit the headlines for a while and then faded from the public memory.

Yet reading further it became clear that there was desperation, but of quite a different kind. People were hurt, and the damage to human souls lasted much longer than the headlines. Inevitably there was a Court Martial. There always is some kind of enquiry into such accidents, and often it takes the form of a judicial trial of the main protagonist. In 2002 the destroyer HMS *Nottingham* hit a rock east of Australia, and her Captain, Richard Farrington, was reported in *The Guardian* of 10 July 2002 as saying 'It is inevitable. The sun comes up in the morning, you run your ship aground, you get court martialled.' For Farrington the expected retribution came quickly. He knew he and his crew had made inexcusable errors. In the loss of *Vanguard* matters were nowhere near so clear-cut. The men subjected to trial were the crew of the ship that sank, not the one that ran into her – logically enough for the Admiralty, whose attitude was that if a ship was lost, her commander must answer for it. Upon this, which to the non-military mind must seem less than fair, was piled more and more injustice, administered in an atmosphere of pig-headedness and ineptitude that made a mockery of the great traditions of the Service in whose name it all happened. At the centre of all was Captain Richard Dawkins, a respectable man in early middle age, with three decades of experience in his profession, a clutch of campaign medals and an exemplary record. On him fell the full wrath of the Admiralty, and he was destroyed by the experience. For a while, as the nature of the Court Martial decisions dawned on the public, he won sympathy from a wide range of supporters; but nothing could move the Admiralty, and in the end he gave up the struggle and gently vegetated in the Devon countryside, while the world moved on.

This, then, is the story of the sinking of a ship, but also the story of a group of men thrown together by the circumstance of their calling, and working together as true professionals up to and well beyond the point when their ship foundered under them. A group within which there was real respect and indeed affection, in which every man played his part as well as he could, and inevitably a group of which none was unaffected by the experience. In particular the young Lieutenants, in their 20's and eager to make an impression in their chosen career on a smart ship of ultra-modern design, seem to have been hit harder than others; within a couple of years a significant number of them were dead or had disappeared. Above all this is the story of Captain Richard Dawkins RN, a sensitive and able man thrown aside by his employers, perhaps as a scapegoat, perhaps just as one dispensable unit of manpower among too many.

Vanguard was a special ship, one of a cascade of new designs in the second half of the nineteenth century – all of them special in some way – and I have tried to sketch the background of warship development into which she fitted. The subject is treated in much more detail in various books mentioned in the Bibliography, many of which are accessible to the layman, and give a thrilling account of new ideas, maverick personalities, and developing industrial muscle all contributing to the creation of the most formidable instrument of war ever seen – the twentieth century battleship. Now, of course, even the battleship is no more. It is a pleasing coincidence that the very last and greatest British battleship to be built was called *Vanguard*.

The story of the sinking has been told many times, fully in publications aimed at the specialist in military or naval history or naval architecture or those who like to read about disasters at sea, and more briefly in almost every history of the warship. These are all technical descriptions of what happened, its relevance to ship design, and so on. This book focuses on the people who were touched by the incident, including the grandees, among them the veteran Vice Admiral Walter Tarleton, the eminent naval architect Edward Reed, and the Hon George Ward Hunt MP, First Lord of the Admiralty; then the officers such as Captain Henry Hickley of *Iron Duke*, Commander Charles Young of *Achilles* who was just hitching a lift aboard *Vanguard*, and the irrepressible Lieutenant Stephen Thompson. Further down the social scale, the ratings including my wife's great-grandfathers, Henry Gaden and Francis Norton, and those unlucky enough to be thrust into the limelight of the Court Martial, such as Ordinary Seaman Michael Murphy, describing what he thought he saw from his lookout post on the starboard cathead. Service records and contemporary accounts illuminate these personalities, and I have had invaluable help from a small number of people who are descendants of, or otherwise related to members of the crew of *Vanguard*, *Iron Duke*, and *Warrior*, the archetypal ironclad that led the First Reserve Squadron on that day in September 1875. Finding these good folk (more than thirty of them) involved writing letters to the Press in the United Kingdom and Ireland, advertising in magazines devoted to family history and allied subjects, and following up leads on the Internet. Besides this there is always sheer serendipity. Having written to the Devon Family History Society to ask if I might put a note in their Journal about my quest, I was delighted to hear from the Chair of that excellent association that her late husband was also the great-grandson of a Marine on the strength of *Vanguard*. Indeed it was the same lady, Maureen Selley, whose innocent email set me on the road towards writing this story. In February 2001, she wrote 'When you have time, you really MUST write the full story ...'

The third quarter of the nineteenth century was a good time for many people. Britain in the 1850's was the richest country in the world, and went on getting richer. The comprehensive defeat of Napoleon had taken war off the agenda, and in the unaccustomed atmosphere of lasting peace there was time to devote to sorting out domestic problems and developing new ideas. Prosperity and security at home meant that Britain could maintain a lofty disengagement from any foreign quarrels. Paramount now was the development of trade world wide, and the consolidation and exploitation of the empire. The mechanisation of industrial processes had profound social effects with which Gladstone's new government had to deal when they came to power in 1868. Young men, who for generations had worked on the land, began to drift into the cities, where the new work was, and living conditions inevitably deteriorated with overcrowding. Cholera became a burden regularly borne, affecting places like Devonport and Kingstown, the two ports most associated with *Vanguard*'s short life. The 'ordinary people' began to find a voice, and Parliament had to accept the need to allow that voice to be heard in government. The historian Trevelyan summed up the political situation thus:

> 'The parliamentary aristocracy under the first three Georges had developed British maritime power to the point where Nelson left it; had lost one overseas empire and acquired another; had completed the reconciliation of Scotland and perpetuated the alienation of Ireland; and had guarded the arena for the early stages of the Industrial Revolution, but without any attempt to control its social effects, or any foresight of its political implications'.[1]

Gladstone got down to business with vigour and determination. Within a few years a national system of primary education had been established and the universities opened to all faiths. The army and the civil service had been reorganised and made more efficient, the franchise extended, and the legislators worn out by such a flurry of activity to the point where Disraeli could call them a 'range of exhausted volcanoes'. Bringing his Conservative government to power in 1874, Disraeli had a sound basis on which to introduce legislation to make life longer and more bearable for those in towns and cities. The second Public Health Act made local authorities responsible for public health measures, and specified basic standards on the handling and disposal of sewage, the inclusion of lavatories in new housing, cleaning the streets and the effective distribution of clean water to households; and the Artisans' Dwellings Act bestowed powers to clear slums. Both Acts were given Royal assent in 1875, the year *Vanguard* was lost.

In England, then, 1875 dawned with the promise of even better conditions and ever-increasing prosperity. Overseas, in so far as Britain had any interest other than in her Empire, the usual problems grumbled on. In January Alfonso XII landed at Barcelona and was recognised as King, after a coup d'état restored the monarchy and ended the ephemeral First Spanish Republic. In the summer the people of Bosnia-Herzegovina rebelled against their Turkish occupiers, and *The Times* carried almost as many column inches about their situation as it did at the end of the following century about fighting in the same place on a much greater scale. The Suez Canal was of more direct concern; having at first seen the canal as a dastardly French plot, the British government decided it was worth getting involved after all, and by November 1875 Disraeli had secured agreement with the Khedive to purchase 40% of shares in the canal company, giving Britain a controlling interest. In France the year saw the first performance of Bizet's *Carmen* at the Opéra-Comique, to less than universal acclaim. It ran for 37 performances, but Bizet died in June as the curtain fell on the twenty-third. American minds seemed to be becoming more philosophical. 1875 was the year that saw the foundation of the Theosophical Society by Mme Blavatsky, and the publication of Mary Baker Eddy's *Science and Helath and the Key to the Scriptures*, the essential Christian Science text.

The British press had plenty of home-grown excitement to write about. There were the abortive Arctic voyages of Sir Allen Young in *Pandora* – a ship apparently fitted out at the expense of the redoubtable Lady Franklin, who had still not given up hope of finding her husband, Sir John, lost in the search for the North West Passage thirty years before. Lady Franklin herself died in 1875. There was the incredible achievement of a chunky 27-year-old Army Captain called Matthew Webb, who at 1 o'clock in the afternoon of 24 August 1875 dived off the Admiralty Pier in Dover, covered in porpoise grease, and emerged dripping on to French soil at 10.41 am the next day, the first man to swim the English Channel. He had managed to swim 40 miles rather than the 22 of the direct crossing, having been driven off course by strong currents. During his 22 hours in the water he had been sustained by a good English diet of beef tea, brandy, coffee and strong old ale.

In 1875 Britain was immensely proud of her achievements and not a little self-satisfied. Her hallowed institutions – Parliament, the Church, the Law, the Army and of course the Royal Navy – were beginning to be undermined by improving standards of health and education and the increasing expectations that went with them, and consequently those in high places reacted strongly to any questioning of traditional values. People in general 'knew their place', and few spoke out about the crushing effect that so tightly structured a society could have on individuals who happened to be in the wrong place at the wrong time. At the beginning of September, something happened that for a time rattled the doors of the Admiralty, exposed the flaws in their well-worn system of duty and responsibility, but still allowed hard-working, loyal servants of the Crown to be unjustly stigmatised. *Vanguard* sank, and Captain Richard Dawkins lost his ship, his status, and almost all his reason for living, while others equally to blame walked away unscathed.

At the same time, half a million pounds worth of modern warship had been lost. To put this loss in context, I now turn to the development of the iron steamship as a weapon of war.

Chapter 2

'HMS Teakettle'

The arrival of the iron warship

We are accustomed to thinking of the twentieth century as a period of intense, break-neck development. My father was born the year before the Wright Brothers achieved the first controlled flight in 1903, and died the year in which Neil Armstrong set foot on the Moon. In the thirty years remaining of the century the computer technology that guided Apollo 11 had shrunk in size to become an integral part of the workings of my watch and my washing machine. We tend to forget that the previous century had seen equally huge development, on a scale and at a speed never experienced before. The Battle of Trafalgar was a magnificent display of beautifully crafted 'wooden walls' deployed to their optimum by a brilliant commander, whereas at the Jubilee Review at Spithead in 1897, the Navy's ships were utterly different – dark, menacing, metal beasts with poor vestiges of the masts that had been the glory of their predecessors. For offic-ers and crew the terminology might seem to have changed little, but the environment and the job would have been unrecognisable and terrifying to Nelson's men.

The Industrial Revolution moved faster and further in Britain than anywhere else. One spur was coal. With the rapid depletion of timber stock, a fuel famine threatened towards the end of the eighteenth century, and was solved by the cutting of a network of canals to transport coal throughout the country. Coal was put to good use in the smelting of iron, and within 40 years the production of iron increased tenfold[2]. British industry adapted gradually, often painfully but inexorably to the use of new materials, new energy sources, new machines such as the spinning jenny and the power loom, improved trans-port links, a new organisation of work within the factory system, and the introduction of scientific techniques to the manufacturing process. British skill, British industrial muscle and British inventiveness seemed at a peak. Writing in 1867, the pioneer feminist Frances Power Cobbe (distantly related to Captain Dawkins of *Vanguard*) could already list 'The steam-engine locomotive by land and sea, steam applied to printing and manufacture, the electric telegraph, photography, cheap newspapers, penny postage, chloroform, gas, the magnesian and electric lights, iron ships, revolvers and breach-loaders of all sorts, sewing-machines, omnibuses and cabs, parcel deliveries, post-office savings banks, working-men's clubs, people's baths and wash-houses, Turkish baths, drinking fountains and a thousand minutiae of daily life, such as matches, Wenham ice, and all the applications of india-rub-ber and gutta-percha ... '[3] Naturally the Navy was in a position to take full advantage of what was available. Thus within a few decades wooden hulls changed to iron (and later steel), sail gave way (reluctantly) to steam, solid shot was replaced by explosive shell, and the stately pavane that had been Naval warfare was transformed by a welter of new ship designs. In this chapter I shall set *Vanguard* in her place among so many new things.

Again, we have been used to most major developments in military hardware appearing as a reaction to imminent or actual war; but during much of the nineteenth century the nation was at peace - the Pax Britannica, of Palmerston's enduring phrase. Much of what was new appeared as a result of developments elsewhere. Since Britain quite evidently ruled the waves, there was no need to make changes in the well-tried military machine unless a competitor nation got in first. When that did happen, Britain had the resources, the technology and the industrial capacity to go one better quickly. That of course carried a direct cost, in that although the Navy Estimates imposed firm control over shipbuilding and its associated expenditure, the Navy's budget more than doubled between 1849 and 1861, from £6.2 to £12.5 million[4]. Just as significant was the longer-term cost implication; every launch of a ship with successful new architecture or technology meant that the remainder of the fleet was immediately obsolete.

The first major development, chronologically, was the introduction of the steam engine. The Admiralty were naturally cautious about the new motive power, and determined not to introduce it until it had been proved. A steam-powered paddleboat had navigated the Saône near Lyons as long ago as 1783, and in 1802 the first commercially successful steamboat began operations on the Forth and Clyde Canal. It was not until 1816 that the Navy ordered steam dredgers for use in its ports. On the strength of their performance a few paddle-wheeled steam tugs were introduced, to handle sailing ships inside the harbour while being unaffected by the wind. Gradually the new form of propulsion made inroads, hampered by the teething troubles of all new machinery, and also by the prevalence of the paddle wheel. The large wheel housings amidships reduced considerably the number of guns in the broadside armament, and presented a tempting target to the enemy. The wheel was also vulnerable to heavy seas from the beam, and added to wind and water resistance, as well as giving the designer a multitude of problems in relation to the optimum positioning of the paddles in the water. In the 1830's however a variant on a very old invention appeared: the screw propeller. This promised greater manoeuvrability, more space for guns, and a less vulnerable propulsion unit, below the surface of the sea. The Admiralty subjected it to exhaustive tests, culminating in a splendid and slightly absurd demonstration by the small steam sloop HMS *Rattler* in April 1845. *Rattler* was tethered stern to stern with the paddle-driven HMS *Alecto*. *Alecto* set off first, but five minutes later *Rattler* was pulling her rival backwards at a rate of 2.8 knots, despite her vainly turning paddles[5] (Richard Dawkins, the ill-fated Captain of HMS *Vanguard*, served aboard *Rattler* from 1849). But the Navy did not undertake a wholesale conversion of its fleet from sail to steam. The first steam-powered ships of the line were ordered only in 1848, following a French decision to build vessels of this type. *Agamemnon,* the first steam line-of-battle ship, was launched at Woolwich in 1852, and her trials were successful enough to foreshadow the end of the sailing vessel as an instrument of war.

The coming of steam and the increasing size of warships naturally caused an upheaval in the dockyards; besides the need to provide for repairs and replacements for steam engines, Devonport Yard discovered that even when the chain cable and a great deal of ballast had been removed, it was still not possible to dock the 90-gun second-rate HMS *Albion* because there was not enough water. This led to the development of a new Yard at Keyham, at which 'it is proposed to construct two floating basins about six acres each, with entrances 80 feet wide, laid at a depth sufficient for the largest steamer to enter and depart at all times of the tide; there are to be three large docks besides the lock, which is to be constructed as to answer the purpose of a dock when required. There are to be complete engine and boiler workshops, with the requisite tools and storehouses for fitting-out and repairing large fleets of steamers; the whole establishment will cover a surface of about 72 acres.'[6] Faced with such costly developments, which were repeated elsewhere, the Admiralty's caution is understandable.

Equally understandable was the attitude of many old seamen to the very idea of a ship driven by steam. Ships were meant to be beautiful and graceful, but all that machinery was dirty, covering the gleaming deck with coal dust. It produced intolerable heat, it stank of oil. The need to make space for engines and equipment upset the traditional arrangement of cabins and decks, and above all it was ugly. All the skill and art of riding a ship in harmony with the wind and tide appeared to have gone overnight. Barnaby[7] quotes Admiral Belcher, whose contribution to a debate on rudder design was that steering was only a matter of 'trim'; properly trimmed one could 'run the flying jib-boom into the eye of a needle … The idea of steering even a boat, by force of rudder is utterly repugnant to the feelings of all good seamen'.

It is easy to assume that such attitudes led to the retention of masts and sails on steam-powered ships. Beeler[8] relays the warning of Rear Admiral Sir John Gilford: too great a reliance on steam, he said, 'induces carelessness on the part of those who would act differently if they were trimming or working the sails and ropes of a vessel not under steam … This constant steaming … produces ignorance in the rising young officers of all ranks'. The real reason for retaining a spread of sail was more practical. Steam engines ran on coal, and to carry adequate stocks of coal involved sacrificing more space as well as adding weight, with consequent effects on handling. The earlier simple expansion engines consumed fuel at a startling rate, and even when compound engines were introduced later in the century there were few coaling stations in the distant parts of the Empire that Britain was supposed to protect. Ballard[9] says that 'Fires were required under all boilers to move at even 10 knots, and when that was the case no ship in the fleet could in practice rely on her coal lasting for more than 120 hours steaming … In so far as its steaming capabilities were concerned, therefore, the battle fleet of 1870 was little more than a home guard'. Sails remained necessary, and British designers took trouble to retain good sailing qualities in steamships, in contrast to the French, for whom handling characteristics under steam were more important, with sails a necessary back-up. This difference in approach explains why British ships often had a mechanism to hoist the screw propeller out of the water when not in use, on the assumption that propeller drag would hinder good sailing. There were other problems for the designer. For instance, where to put the funnel? There seemed to be no position that did not foul the main or mizzen mast. Then there was the omnipresent rigging, that got in the way of experimenting with new gun positions – of which we shall hear more later.

In the middle of all this came the next development: iron hulls. The first iron ship preceded the development of the screw propeller, and iron construction was well under way in Birkenhead by 1830. The merchant navy had built up considerable experience with steam and iron, Brunel's *Great Britain,* launched in 1845, being one of the more dramatic examples. The Admiralty again experimented, but, as in the case of steam, seemed to see no need to adopt a radical and expensive method of shipbuilding when the world still trembled at the might of the wooden fleet. The dockyards had large stocks of timber (although its cost had escalated by 1860 as a result of the Russian War, which had taken up great quantities of high quality wood), and the shipwrights were skilled in timber construction only. The factor that changed their minds was the development of the explosive shell, introduced by the French in the late 1850's. Solid shot, fired from muzzle-loaded guns in a broadside, could make a mess of rigging and superstructure as well as men, but did not sink ships; not one English ship had been sunk at Trafalgar. Shells, however, especially when elongated and fired from a rifled gun-barrel, were much more dangerous.

The beginnings were not auspicious. In 1840 tests were carried out using a 73-ton steamboat called *Ruby.* Her hull was thin iron, and as might be expected, the shots went straight through both sides, in the process scattering lethal splinters throughout her interior. This, combined with further tests on specially constructed targets, led Captain Chads of HMS *Excellent* (then the gunnery school) to report that 'from these circumstances I am confirmed in the opinion that iron cannot be beneficially employed as a material for the construction of vessels of war' [10]. Part of the problem was that wrought iron was strong but brittle, and thus unsuitable on its own, as Captain Chads correctly noted. Iron construction came to a standstill, and the French publicly declared themselves against it in 1847. Nevertheless, they were concerned about the effect of Russian shell-fire on their wooden hulls during the Crimean War, and experimented with 'floating batteries' built of wood sheathed in 4 inches (10 cm) of iron; under Russian bombardment at Fort Kinburn in 1855 they suffered no penetration by shells. The plans had been shared with the British, since both countries were on the same side in this particular war, and the Admiralty had ordered five similar vessels, but they were not ready in time to be tested in battle. They were in any case dreadful under both sail and steam, and had to be towed all the way to the Crimea. On the basis of this experience however France, reverting to her traditional competition with Britain, took a decisive step. On 4 March 1858 the French navy laid down three wooden frigates (warships with a single covered gun deck) that were designed to have iron plates hung round their sides, intended to protect against both shot and shell. The combination of wood and iron proved to be the winning formula.

The French designer responsible was Stanislas Charles Dupuy de Lôme. Born in 1816, he soon proved himself to be a brilliant naval architect. He was behind the building in 1850 of the *Napoléon,* a 90-gun steam line-of-battle ship, and in 1857 was rewarded for his skills by being appointed *Directeur du Matériel* of the French navy. He is described as 'tough and with an equable temperament'[11], and later in life became a Director of the shipping line *Messageries Maritimes* and other companies, designing high-speed liners, and ventured into another medium by designing dirigible airships. One such, powered by men rather than an engine, made a number of flights in 1872 but could not achieve sufficient speed to be viable. He planned a cross-channel service with ships that could carry railway trains, and towards the end of his life finalised drawings for a submarine, which was constructed after his death by his colleague Gustave Zédé and became the first operational submarine in the French Navy. He died in 1885 at the age of 68, having made an immense contribution to French naval development, and, as a consequence, to the British fleet as well.

Dupuy de Lôme's best remembered achievement was *Gloire,* the first of the ironclad frigates to be completed. She was laid down in March 1858, launched in November 1859 and completed in August 1860, a 36-gun frigate of 5,360 tons, built of wood clad with a belt of iron 4½ inches (11.5 cm) thick from stem to stern (two of her sister ships were to be of similar construction, and the fourth, *Couronne,* was iron-built – the sole such hull that Dupuy de Lôme could build, because French industry could not cope with such structures in iron). Archibald[12] says that 'In fact all that M Dupuy de Lôme achieved in 1858 was to hang iron plates round a half-built wooden two-decker, to be called the *Gloire,* which he "razeed", that is, cut down a deck'; but in doing so he set the ironclad revolution on its way.

Crude though it might have been the very idea of France possessing a warship that might be invulnerable to shot and shell set the British Naval establishment by the ears. De Lôme's counterpart in Britain, Sir Baldwin Wake Walker, Surveyor of the Navy, immediately commissioned Isaac Watts, his Chief Constructor, to design an armoured corvette. Early 1858 also saw a change in government, when Lord Derby formed the first administration to be called 'Conservative'. In June Walker wrote to the First Lord of the Admiralty, Pakington, with an opinion that is quoted in almost every book about nineteenth century ship design:

> 'Although I have frequently stated that it is not in the interests of Great Britain
> – possessing as she does so large a navy – to adopt any important change in the
> construction of ships of war which might have the effect of rendering necessary
> the introduction of a new class of very costly vessels, until such a course is forced
> upon her by the adoption by foreign powers of formidable ships of a novel char-
> acter requiring similar ships to cope with them, yet it then becomes a matter not
> only of expediency, but of absolute necessity … This time has arrived'.[13]

The result was that the Board earmarked funds for the construction of an armoured screw frigate, 'a wooden steam man of war to be cased in wrought iron 4½ inches thick', and Isaac Watts came up with the design for *Warrior.* His concept however was not of a wooden hull covered in iron, but an iron hull lined with wood. In other respects his design met the Navy's need to go one better than the French; she would be larger, faster, better armoured and more heavily armed. *Warrior* was laid down on 25 May 1859, launched on 29 December 1860, and completed on 24 October 1861. She was far in advance of any other warship then planned. Archibald claims that she was 'the biggest advance on previous warship designs made in the history of naval warfare, and the biggest ever to be made until the building of the first nuclear submarine'[14]; Ballard commented that 'When the *Warrior* and the *Gloire* left the slipways, all war values had to be reckoned on a perfectly clean slate'[15]. *Warrior* was 380 feet (116m) long; her armoured belt extended for three-fifths of this length and was backed by eighteen inches (45cm) of teak. The armour protected the broadside guns; she had been designed to carry fifteen 68-pounders, but during her construction the 110-pounder breech-loading rifled gun firing conical shell had become available, so she carried 10 of them as well as 26 68-pounders, all on the gun deck and mostly within the armoured belt. *Warrior* was beautiful and terrible, and still is; she can be seen in restored glory at Portsmouth Historic Dockyard.

A ship of this size, carrying such a weight of armament, could not have been built in wood. The arrival of steam power had already made it necessary to make ships bigger in order to carry the machinery and coal, but trees are simply not tall enough or rigid enough, and beyond a certain length a wooden ship would sag in the middle, even in calm weather. A new wooden vessel needed four years on the stocks to ensure that it was properly seasoned, and wood rots after some time at sea, while iron should have longer life. Iron construction brought the bonus of being able to build in watertight compartments, which was not possible in wooden ships, and should have lessened the likelihood of sinking after being holed below the water line. That this did not always apply became very evident when *Vanguard* was lost.

In all, the combination of steam and iron provided many opportunities that sail and wood did not, but not without a cost. In money terms, *Warrior* cost £377,292, while the wooden frigate *Undaunted*, launched the same week, cost £105,000. There were further problems. Ironclads still relied on sail for longer voyages, but none of them sailed well, and some were regarded as unmanageable under sail. The huge weight of iron around the ships' sides gave rise to problems of stability that could be solved either by increasing the beam, which would mean a loss of speed, or lowering the freeboard (the distance between the upper deck and the water level). Any great reduction in freeboard required the abandonment of the traditional arrangement of two or three decks of guns, each of a different calibre - hence *Warrior* was built with a single gun deck – and that in turn meant increasing the length. Yet another difficulty arose from the effect of so much iron on the performance of the ship's compass, which at first was so great that iron ships could not operate out of sight of land. The Admiralty spent much thought and effort on this in the 1830's, and eventually a system was devised for compass correction.

The steam and iron revolution set off a flurry of new ideas, to take advantage of the new materials and methods while accommodating new developments in armament, which in turn led to fundamental changes in naval tactics. For centuries ship design had evolved gently and surely. Now everything seemed to be happening at once, and no sooner had a new idea been put to the test that something happened to nullify its advantages. For instance, when she was completed *Warrior*'s armour was impervious to attack by any gun then in service, but this state of affairs did not last long. As early as 1862 armour 5 inches thick was pierced in gunnery tests, and before long the Admiralty was being warned that every ironclad in service would be vulnerable to shells fired from a distance of 800 yards, the distance at which ship-to-ship combat was expected to take place. According to Beeler, 'Every time the Admiralty essayed to build a ship impervious to the state-of-the-art ordnance of the moment, it served up a challenge to Woolwich and private industry to develop a larger and more powerful gun'[16]. Guns were developing at a tremendous rate. From the cast iron smooth-bore gun firing solid shot, developed the rifled, muzzle-loaded gun made of wrought iron, and then the breech-loader. Ballard notes that 'So rapid was the increase in size when once wrought iron ordnance was adopted that within ten years five new calibres were introduced, each greater than the one before, and the weights of individual pieces increased six fold'[17]. The 7-inch Armstrong breech-loaded gun, firing a 110lb shell, was adopted in 1860 as the Navy's principal heavy gun, but teething problems led to a reversion to muzzle-loading for a while. It became supremely important to design the warship as an effective platform for these modern guns, and thus came about the plethora of new shapes under construction. In view of the pace of development the Admiralty abandoned its customary practice of building groups of ships to one design, so that of the armoured ships built in the 1860's, thirteen were individual in design, and ten more were built in pairs[18]. It would be thirty years before the collection of what one writer called 'bizarre and ill-assorted designs' settled into some kind of stability once more.

Designing to make best use of guns was intimately bound up with battle tactics. For as long as any sailor could remember, warships had holes in their sides out of which guns pointed when needed, and a squadron lined up stem to stern and discharged its guns at the enemy from a safe distance, giving rise to the terms 'broadside' and 'ship of the line'. A French observer wrote in the mid seventeenth century:

> 'Nothing equals the beautiful order of the English at sea. Never was a line drawn straighter than that formed by their ships; thus they bring all their fire to bear upon those who draw near them … They fight like a line of cavalry which is handled according to rule, and applies itself solely to force back those who oppose; whereas the Dutch advance like cavalry whose squadrons leave their ranks and come separately to the charge'[19].

This approach led to stalemate as often as outright victory. The fleet's successes were frequently achieved by commanders who took advantage of the 'small print' that said pursuit of an enemy vessel was allowed if he were on the run. Despite this apparent rigidity, great commanders could be flexible. The supreme example was Nelson, who at Trafalgar took this to the ultimate, using British superiority in gunnery in a series of individual battles. *Warrior* was built with her guns arrayed broadside. But now ships were faster and stronger, and could attack from any angle, which meant that guns should be able to fire ahead and astern as well as from the sides. But this raised fundamental questions about how naval battles might be fought with the new equipment, and uncertainty about this was another factor that contributed to the 'profoundly disparate collection of vessels, including a few of the most manifestly unsuccessful designs in the annals of naval architecture'[20]. *The Times* observed in 1873 'We do not know what to build, because we do not know how we shall fight our future naval battles'[21].

Three main types of ironclad design emerged during these chaotic years. The broadside ironclad was exemplified by *Warrior* and her smaller companions. Next came the central battery ship, and then the turret designs. Each had its advantages and disadvantages, its protagonists and detractors. The Admiralty had been well served by a series of talented 'Surveyors', as the chief designer was known during the first half of the nineteenth century. Captain William Symonds, who retired from the post in 1847, had introduced the first steam line-of-battle ship. Symonds was the first Surveyor not to be a naval architect. His first design was the 80-gun *Vanguard*, laid down in 1833; like his other designs she sailed well but made a poor gun platform. Sir Baldwin Walker, mentioned earlier, succeeded him. Among the designers Walker supervised was Isaac Watts, who himself acquired the title Chief Constructor at the age of 63 following a reorganisation in 1860. Watts had decades of experience in dockyards, culminating in his appointment as Master Shipwright at Sheerness in 1847. To him the Navy owed all its frigate type broadside ironclads, both those built in iron and wooden ships covered with iron.

Watts retired in 1863, and the Admiralty appointed the 33-year-old Edward James Reed. Reed was apprenticed at Sheerness, trained at the Central School of Mathematics and Naval Construction and returned to Sheerness as a draughtsman; but soon got bored and resigned. He went into private practice, occasionally submitting designs to the Admiralty Board. One such, involving plans to convert wooden hulled ships into ironclads, led to his being taken on to help design and construct *Pallas* and *Bellerophon*. The latter was the last of the broadside ironclads, launched in 1865. In 1853 he had become editor of *Mechanics Magazine,* where he learned to write persuasively and took every opportunity to attack what he saw as the Admiralty's deep conservatism. In 1860 he was one of the moving spirits in the establishment of the Institution of Naval Architects. Edward Reed was an inspired and creative designer, but could be opinionated and difficult. Nevertheless he willingly acknowledged the contribution of his colleagues to successful designs. Beeler characterises him thus:

'Possessed of an exceedingly caustic tongue, the chief constructor also actively relished controversy and argument, and while many – though by no means all – of his contemporaries were willing to acknowledge his professional brilliance, many more doubtless wished it was accompanied by a somewhat less acerbic personality'.[22]

Reed's principal contribution to the development of the ironclad was the central battery. Since guns had become larger in calibre, a warship needed fewer of them, and the area of the hull needing armoured protection could be lessened. This led to the emergence of the central battery, essentially an armoured box amidships. This arrangement still did not meet the requirement for fore-and-aft-fire, so Reed designed a variant in which part of the gun-deck projected out from the ship's side, providing gun positions from which fire could be directed towards the bow and stern. The *Audacious* class (*Vanguard* and her sisters) of 1869, of which more later, was the first design to have the central battery on two decks. Part of Reed's preference for the central battery format may be ascribed to his wish to retain masts and sails. In 1873 he wrote in *Naval Science* that:

> 'It was always our intention to furnish the *Devastation* and other similar ships with the means of setting a purely supplemental, but nevertheless considerable, spread of canvas' and later explained that in his view 'an object of the greatest importance in a National Navy is to make the officers and men expert seamen, and as this object is better attained the longer the time spent under sail alone, the comparative length of voyages performed by ironclads is not itself a disadvantage, but the contrary'.[23]

Reed's most visible competitor for the Admiralty's attention was Captain Cowper Phipps Coles, a gifted amateur of mercurial personality, some ten years older than Reed. More so than Reed, Coles had no doubts whatever about his own abilities, and used every trick available to the Victorian gentleman to push his ideas as hard as possible. He was the third son of a Hampshire clergyman and joined the Navy as a boy cadet. The 1850's saw him in action in the Crimea, where to get round the problem of shallow coastal waters he constructed a raft of casks and spars, which he called the *Lady Nancy*, and installed on it a 'long 32' gun. The device actually worked, destroying many Russian stores, and having cunningly ensured the presence of a 'press correspondent' aboard his ship, Coles got all the publicity he could have wished for. The raft idea went to the Admiralty, who liked it and gave orders to go ahead with constructing several, but the war ended before they could be used. The end of hostilities gave Coles time to develop his next great project, the armoured revolving gun turret. The idea had been Brunel's originally, based on the railway turntable. Coles became obsessive about it – in 1859 he submitted a design for a ship with 10 turrets - and thus began a battle over ship design that occupied ten years.

The turret was of course the right answer to the problem of gun deployment, but Coles seemed blind to the impracticability of installing turrets on decks cluttered with masts and rigging. When the Admiralty, advised at the time by Watts and other experienced naval architects, rejected his plans, he used his talent for publicity to win over the public, the press and the Prince Consort. Prince Albert was impressed enough to write to the First Lord in support of turret ships. Naturally enough, when the Admiralty gave way and ordered the construction of a warship designed by Watts and with turrets designed by Coles, it was christened the *Prince Albert*. At about this time occurred the famous clash in American waters between the tremendously armoured *Merrimac* and the Confederate floating battery *Monitor*, which was essentially a big turret on a submerged hull, like a mature version of Coles' Crimean raft. *Merrimac* could not dent *Monitor's* turret, and while the contest was inconclusive *Monitor* was felt to have got the best of it.

Coles' arguments had a considerable boost, and he rode the wave of approval enthusiastically. He gave lectures, wrote to newspapers, and published pamphlets, endeavouring to show that Reed's central battery design was far inferior to his turrets.

Tests on *Prince Albert* and another turret ship, *Royal Sovereign*, went well, and with the co-operation of Admiralty architects Coles submitted a design to be directly compared with Reed's ironclads. The Admiralty committee commissioned a vessel to be designed by Reed but to incorporate the ideas of Coles. Coles demanded changes in Reed's design in order to give the guns a greater field of fire, but which would threaten stability; however the committee preferred the experience of the professional to the enthusiasm of the amateur, and *Monarch* was laid down in 1866 in accordance with Reed's plans. Coles shrewishly wrote to the press that *Monarch* 'did not represent his views of a seagoing turret ship or one which could give his principles a satisfactory and conclusive trial'[24]. Eventually the Admiralty gave in to pressure from public opinion and allowed Coles to build a vessel to his own design. The result was HMS *Captain*, laid down by Lairds of Birkenhead in 1867. Coles insisted on a freeboard of no more than 8 feet (2.4m), minimum width of beam, and a huge spread of sail on the tallest masts in the Navy. By the time of her completion in 1870, the freeboard had reduced to 6½ feet because of the weight of armour and equipment, and some concern was expressed about her stability. Reed raised objections, but was overruled by the First Lord. *Captain* put to sea in the early months of 1870, came through her trials well, and joined the Channel Squadron. The young Lieutenant William Hathorn, in a moment of enforced idleness at Portsmouth, paid her a visit. He afterwards wrote to his mother:

> 'There is not much duty for us to do aboard here, so I very often pass the time away cruizing about the Dockyard – I have been all over the 'Captain', 'Monarch' & the troop ship 'Himalaya' – the 'Captain' is commissioned to day, I do not like the look of her'[25]

Meanwhile in July 1870 Edward Reed had resigned, probably tired of unjustified and badly informed criticism. Brown[26] records that 'while at the Admiralty he had designed twenty-five ironclads, two armoured gunboats, twenty cruisers, twenty-eight gunboats and twenty coastal gunboats, costing in total some £10 million … he had instigated, directed and encouraged major improvements in every aspect of design procedures.' His departure was described as a national disaster. Two months later came a more personal disaster. On 6 September *Captain*, with her designer on board, was standing up well to strong winds off Finisterre. After dark the wind freshened and the weather worsened significantly. By midnight the Channel Squadron was battered by a gale. When day broke and the squadron reassembled, *Captain* was missing. She had simply been blown over by the sea and wind, and sank, taking with her all but 17 of her crew of 490. The commanding officer, Captain Hugh Burgoyne, VC, was lost, and so was the midshipman son of Hugh Childers, the First Lord of the Admiralty, as well as the designer himself, Captain Cowper Phipps Coles.

William Hathorn's reaction stands for all in the Service: the news came by telegram when his ship *Columbine* had only recently parted:

'from the most powerful <u>Fleet</u> in the World, which included the <u>ill-fated</u> "<u>Captain</u>" whose loss we have since heard of … This dreadful intelligence has dismayed everyone here – I knew nearly all the Gun Room Officers – nearly all the Sub Lieuts passed through the "Excellent" & "College" with me. Nav Sub Lt Tregaskis was a great friend of mine aboard the "Octavia". Murray was an old chum of mine aboard "Britannia". Goldsmith was a "Britannia", Station and College mate of the best sort – Gordon was another. Capt Cowper Coles CB has died nobly & I think should be exempt from all abuse.'[27]

The terrible confirmation of his misgivings was not lost on Reed, who made good use of his freedom to give vigorous answers to the criticism that had been directed against him while in office. He later became a Member of Parliament, and was a persistent gadfly to the Admiralty, especially over the question of whether bow and stern of ironclads should be armoured. In his view it was madness not to protect such areas. In the meantime the Admiralty had established a 'Committee to examine the Designs upon which Ships of War have recently been constructed', known thereafter as the Committee of Designs, in an attempt to make sense of the disparate elements of design over which there had been so much discord. Their hope was to get beyond the situation implicit in the conclusion of the Court Martial on the loss of *Captain*:

'The *Captain* was built in deference to public opinion expressed in Parliament and through other channels and in opposition to the views and opinions of the Controller of the Navy and his Department'[28].

But the acrimony lingered. The First Lord, Childers, who had lost his only son in the *Captain* incident, put the blame squarely but illogically on Reed and Sir Spencer Robinson, the Controller of the Navy, and this led in 1871 to Robinson receiving a dressing-down from Gladstone. He was not offered a second five-year term in office. Barely a month later Childers too had to resign, on grounds of ill-health.

Following Reed's resignation his brother-in-law, Nathaniel Barnaby, took over, at first temporarily labelled 'President of the Council of Construction', then in 1872 Chief Naval Architect, and eventually in 1875 under the new title of Director of Naval Construction. Barnaby came from a family of shipwrights, and was first apprenticed at Sheerness in 1842. He had worked under Reed for some time and had been closely involved in Reed's projects. He seems to have been a very different person from his predecessor. Brown says that he had 'a strong conviction of the moral worth of his work; views which are difficult to summarise but the two short quotations which follow give an idea of his approach. 'Lasting good is only evolved in this world through strife and bloodshed' and 'Righteousness must come before peace'. He is said to have written a hymn'[29]. He was fifteen years in the post, and retired on grounds of ill health in 1885. To him went the credit for the very last masted ironclad, *Temeraire*, launched in 1876. But he had also been very much concerned with the design of *Devastation*, primarily a Reed design but modified by Barnaby, which was the first major warship that carried no masts or sails, and because of the lack of bow and stern superstructure could fire in any direction from its two turrets. Laid down in 1869 and completed in 1873, *Devastation* marked the true end of the era of the sailing warship.

Throughout this time one element of ship design had support from almost all quarters: the ram bow. The ram had a long history in naval warfare, but does not appear to have sunk enough ships to justify the enthusiasm shown for it in the 1860's. The battle of Lissa in July 1866, at which much of the Italian fleet was destroyed, some by ramming, seems to have boosted the fashion for the ram. 'The dramatic picture of the *Re d'Italia* disappearing at one blow, while so much gunnery had hardly accomplished anything, drove out all power of rational analysis'[30]. The power of steam and the assumed impregnability of iron conjured up visions of sea battles in which instead of lining up and bombarding the enemy, the fleet would steer straight for them and let fly from all angles, not least endeavouring to hit them square amidships and send them to the bottom by ramming below the waterline. Tactical thinking thus began to consider line abreast, angular or echelon formations. The ram was integral to this new approach. One of the Recommendations of the Committee on Designs in 1871 read:

'The importance of ramming in future naval warfare is likely to be so great that in designing armour-clad ships particular attention should … be paid to the best methods of resisting it'[31].

A textbook of tactics asserted that 'the ram is fast supplanting the gun in import', and many of the current designs assumed the primacy of the ram. In 1868 Reed found himself designing a vessel specifically intended as a ram, but *Hotspur* when launched proved to be unsuitable for fleet duties, and was confined to coastal defence.

Thus it was that a projection at the bow below the waterline became a standard element in ironclad design. By 1867, the Admiralty considered that the Navy's needs would best be met by building ships of moderate size, and in order to keep pace with the French decided to revert to previous practice and order the construction of four ships to the same design. Edward Reed took as a basis his designs for the five-year-old *Resistance* and *Defence*, and drew up plans for four central battery ironclads with improved power, armour and armament, intended to handle well under sail as well as steam. They would be the first to be driven by twin screws, and of course incorporated a ram bow. At the time Chatham Dockyard, the only Naval yard capable of iron construction, was fully occupied with *Monarch* and *Hercules*, so the orders for the first two of the quartet, *Audacious* and *Invincible*, went to Napier and Son's Clyde shipyard. The last, *Iron Duke,* was the only one built at a Naval yard, Pembroke, where she was laid down in 1868, and the third to be built was laid down at Laird's in Birkenhead in 1867. She was to be named *Vanguard*.

Chapter 3

'Did you ever wash when you went to sea?'
Life aboard an Ironclad for officers and men

The Officers

In Hanoverian times far fewer occupations than today were dignified with the title 'profession': the Church, the Law, medicine, the Army and the Navy. Victoria's reign brought more opportunity and the possibility of betterment: architects, engineers, civil servants, accountants, artists and others all acquired a hitherto unimaginable status. For centuries the hereditary nobility and the country gentry had effortlessly held the primary place in the social order, but now it became possible to achieve higher status by one's own efforts. Lord Palmerston, the Liberal Prime Minister, speaking in 1865 at the prize giving of the South London Industrial Exhibition, was reported as saying:

> 'The medals distributed today have inscribed on them the names of a great number of men who, starting from very small beginnings, attained, by their talent, their industry, their perseverance, and their good conduct, the very highest positions of social merit and distinction. .... Look at your Army, your Navy, your Law, your Church, your statesmen. You will find in every one of those careers men who have risen to the highest points, who have either themselves started from the smallest beginnings, or whose fathers began with nothing but their talents, their industry, and their energy to aid them.'[32]

Alongside this arose the concept of the 'Gentleman', ill defined but immediately recognisable to the average Victorian. One could not make oneself a Gentleman; one had to be acknowledged as such by one's peers. The title embodied so much that we now think of as Victorian values: morality, selflessness, courage, self-control, independence, and responsibility. These qualities were not restricted to any particular class, and writings of the period contain many humbler characters who display all the characteristics of the Gentleman. Besides these, contemporary society valued above all respectability, which became perhaps the sharpest social divider.

'All gentlemen could be called respectable … All respectable men wanted to be called gentlemen, but few were chosen … There was room for any number of respectable people; … but the gentleman idea was an elitist one … most would-be gentlemen, therefore, had to rest content with respectability, and make the most of that; priding themselves, perhaps, on respectability of a superior, solider style.'[33]

There can be no doubt that to serve as an officer in Her Majesty's Navy conveyed respectability and the status of gentleman, and the social attitudes associated with these concepts illuminate the behaviour of the actors in our story. The Navy was a highly fashionable profession, and 'up to about 1880 most naval officers came from the same mix of the population that had supplied them for the previous four centuries: moderately educated men from middle-income families, or impecunious branches of well-off families, with a leavening of sons of 'old naval' clans with a long tradition of service, and a further seasoning of those who had worked up by sheer activity, ability and application.'[34] Padfield says[35] that as late as 1850 half of officer recruits came from professional homes, and the rest from the gentry or aristocracy. Indeed in the early years it had been necessary to obtain the patronage of an influential personage to get into the navy at all. Even while serving it was more than helpful to a young lieutenant's career to cultivate senior officers. There is no direct evidence to suggest that any of the protagonists in the *Vanguard* incident overtly benefited from patronage, other than the relationship between Captain Richard Dawkins of *Vanguard* and Admiral the Hon. George F Hastings, described in Chapter 6. Even though Hastings had a family link with Dawkins, it looks as if he was not able to help him advance his career in any significant way.

An example of patronage during service may be detected in the service records of Captain Henry Hickley of HMS *Iron Duke* and Lieutenant Pierre Gervais Evans. Hickley took command of *Audacious,* sister ship to *Vanguard* and *Iron Duke*, in September 1873, and a couple of months later the young Evans came aboard for his second posting as Lieutenant. When Hickley transferred to *Newcastle* in March 1874, he took Evans with him; so he did later that year when he moved to *Endymion*, and finally the two transferred together to *Iron Duke* in July 1875. None of the other officers of *Audacious* followed this route, and it could be safe to assume that Hickley had decided to take this promising lad under his wing. Again, as we shall see, things did not work out as either of them might have hoped.

In the twenty-first century, the United Nations convention on the rights of children contains a protocol that young people under the age of 18 may not be engaged in hostilities. The Royal Navy in 2003 had 'a few hundred sailors under 18 … Britain is the only European country which has regularly sent 17-year-olds into combat zones and remains alone in recruiting below the age of 17'[36]. 150 years earlier, it was the norm for boys to join the Navy around the age of 14, and thus did most, if not all, of the officers and crew of the First Reserve Squadron. The Commander of the First Reserve Squadron on the day of *Vanguard's* sinking, Vice Admiral Sir Walter Tarleton, had himself enlisted at the age of 12 years 4 months. This was of course an age when child labour was only just beginning to be regulated. Employment of children under the age of 10 underground in mines had been banned in 1842 (raised to 12 in 1860), and there was a growing feeling in the newly powerful middle class that education was better than sending a child out to work, at least until the age of 9 or 10. But it was still necessary for many families to make use of whatever earning power was available, at as early an age as possible. Those on the threshold of their teenage years were thus quite late starters in the business of making a career.

Training took place on board ship, the 'young gentlemen' working alongside the seasoned crew, learning every detail of rigging and gun drill, often at the rope's end. Discipline was rigorous, and ensured that those who stayed the course were fit to handle any conditions at sea. Academic schooling was not neglected, and each ship had a Schoolmaster on its strength (on *Vanguard* this post was held by William J Little), but the job was unpopular and classes often skipped. After a couple of years the Captain was empowered to rate his trainees as Midshipmen, in which capacity they would serve until they had completed six years' seatime and could take the examination for Lieutenant. With the rank of Midshipman came some responsibility, and the chance to use judgement and initiative, often relying on the experience of the ratings under his command. The excess of officers did sometimes mean an extended wait before actually obtaining a commission as Lieutenant, but working closely with the crew gave Midshipmen invaluable experience. In the second half of the nineteenth century training arrangements for naval officers improved significantly. The old three-decker *Britannia* was moored in the River Dart and fitted out for officer cadets. After a few decades of tough instruction her reputation was such that she moved ashore and became the Britannia Royal Naval College, run on the lines of a British Public School.

The improved training regime meant being examined in seamanship, navigation, gunnery and other essential skills. That it was no formality is illustrated in the letters of Lieutenant William Hathorn of *Vanguard*. Aged 20, with six years' service, Midshipman Hathorn anxiously awaited the time when 'I pass in Seamanship next week on Wednesday & then join the 'Excellent' to go through the usual training and passing in Gunnery, after which I go to the College to pass in Navigation &c, the Service allows me 3 months to pass the 'Excellent' & College'[37], after which he would at last be granted leave to visit the family. But next week he wrote furiously 'I went up to pass this forenoon when to my disgust the 'Captains' would not examine me on account of my not having a Baptismal Certificate & said "I was to write home for it at once" and that they would examine me on Wednesday next.'[38] Next Wednesday came. 'The day is beastly wet, I have passed & taken a very good <u>Second</u> Class Certificate dated 28th July 1869 … The examination lasted over 2 hours – when I went in I had the knowledge of confidence (which perhaps I carried a <u>leetle</u> too far). The "Captains" were very <u>grumpy</u> from beginning having come onboard in a heavy shower of Rain which did not stop till Noon when they thought they could get to their Ships in comfort, and then told me that if I had answered their questions on Fleet Manoeuvring they would have given me a First – (I have never sailed with a Fleet, & to while the bad weather time away, that was their <u>hobby</u>).'[39] He was looking forward to the gunnery training, but the examination experience was no better. 'The late gunnery examination has <u>plucked</u> me – do not mourn for it was a case of ill fortune ... The examination was unusually severe & people also say unfair ... There were <u>four</u> Examining Officers (Gunnery Lieuts) & each of them have a different method of marking ... It was my misfortune as well as a few others to be examined in "Heavy" & "Revolving" Gun Drill by one of a most unfair nature, he was hot tempered, abusive and altogether a most annoying fool. ... I go up again on the 24th ... As you may imagine it has been a hard blow to me – besides having to stop onboard for another 4 weeks at hard <u>manual</u> drills (6 hrs a day) – I lose 3 months time & my pay is stopped from henceforth till I serve again after having gone through the College.'[40] Making allowance for the young Midshipman's amour-propre, it is evident that the process of passing the Lieutenant's Certificate was no walkover.

The 'Young Gentlemen' had a hard but protected life on board. Punishment was severe, and some senior officers, frustrated at lack of promotion, would lash out with the 'colt' – a piece of rope with a hard knot at the end – whenever they thought a youngster deserved a thrashing (or even for no good reason). At odd moments the midshipmen and Volunteers could relax in the Gun Room, lit with unpredictable tallow candles, and at night retire to their hammocks, slung on a lower deck, each above his sea chest containing all his possessions, and his washing basin. Winton says that in ironclads 'the officers' accommodation was generally very poor, with small, badly lit wardrooms, and cabins opening out of them, with no daylight except through small hatchways two decks above'[41], but Admiral Ballard points out that in the *Audacious* class of central battery ironclads, to which *Vanguard* and *Iron Duke* belonged, 'the design presented several novelties rendered possible by the small requirements of armament space consequent on mounting only three guns a-side on the main deck. This left such ample room for berthing allowance on that deck that the officers' messes and cabins could all be brought up from what might have been correctly described as the basement position which they occupied in all the older armoured ships. The period had at last arrived when officers lived in the enjoyment of full daylight and ventilation; with a wardroom hatch opening direct on to the quarter deck instead of through a deck intermediate, and cabins having square ports high enough above water to remain open sometimes even at sea ... Cabin candles were now no longer needed in the daytime.'[42] As to that washing basin, there may well have been little in the way of regular ablutions. Padfield[43] quotes Admiral Lord Fisher's memories thus:

'We never washed, because if you spilt a drop of water by your sea chest in which was a basin holding a pint of water, you had to dry holystone the deck, a holystone being a bath brick, and you rubbed the sand into the deck till the wood was spotless white! When the first bathroom was introduced into one of Her Majesty's Ships I heard the First Sea Lord myself say to the Second Sea Lord [scandalised by the innovation] "Did you ever wash when you went to sea?" "No," replied Sir Sidney Dacres. "No more did I," said Sir Alexander Milne.'

Padfield suggests that such tales should be taken with a pinch of salt, but water was certainly a precious commodity, not to be wasted on fripperies.

Young gentlemen who came from the same stratum of society shared values and attitudes, and life aboard seems in many ways to have been like what other young gentlemen got up to at boarding school, with petty tyrannies and boisterous horseplay; Padfield describes the rough and tumble of games on the quarterdeck. Ashore in foreign parts, they indulged in the activities they were used to at home, especially what we now call 'country pursuits'. Richard Dawkins in the journal of his days as a junior officer writes many times about the joys of hunting and shooting in various Mediterranean locations. Many officers kept such journals, which might be the only record available to them when they came to write their memoirs.

Promotion was erratic, and for those without influential patrons depended on being quick-witted, thick-skinned, enterprising, and self-confident. At their worst these qualities could produce thoroughly unpleasant commanding officers, but for the majority the necessity to work closely with and depend utterly on a heterogeneous collection of colleagues at all levels resulted in decent and fiercely loyal officers. When iron ships began to appear, their modern facilities and capability aroused even more enthusiasm. Captain Phipps Hornby, on a visit to *Black Prince* (*Warrior*'s sister ship) in Liverpool in the 1860's, found that 'the men in the ironclads are so disgustingly proud of their ships that they will allow them *no* faults'[44]. Thus united against the world outside the ship, between decks the stark stratification of Victorian society still ruled. Despite Palmerston's verbal sketch of a new elite able to drag themselves up by their own bootstraps, those who did so were not always regarded as equals by the old upper class. In particular this appears to have applied to engineer officers. The new technology required new knowledge and skills, to the extent that the trained and experienced engineer might know more about the workings of the ship than his Captain; but to be accepted as in the same 'club' as his fellow officers was much harder. Engineers were given warrant officer status, but in the early days engineer officers messed separately from the fighting officers. It was not until 1883 that any engineer officer other than the Chief Engineer of a battleship was permitted to mess in the wardroom. The eminent marine architect Edward Reed commented as late as 1877 that an engineer was 'a snubbed, subdued, subordinated man, with a dozen officers put above him to look down upon him'[45]. Later in the story we shall meet Captain Algernon Heneage, of impeccable upper-class lineage, who refused to remember the names of any of his engineers, instead calling them by the name of the first Chief with whom he had served. Gradually however engineers became accepted, and David Brown, a naval historian writing in the 1990's, has commented that 'Overall, there are strong indications that stories of prejudice against steam and engineers in this period are much exaggerated'[46].

Besides the Engineers, there were numerous other specialised warrant officer groups: Boatswains, Carpenters, Gunners, Paymasters (the old Pursers), and of course to care for body and soul, Surgeons and Chaplains. These were all very clearly junior ranks, despite the essential part that each played in keeping the ship afloat, and were not to be mentioned in the same breath as the fighting officers. There is a telling story among the memoirs of Henry Capper, who joined the Navy in 1869. On promotion to the warrant officer rank of Gunner, he went to be measured for a new uniform, only to be told that these naval outfitters 'did not make uniform for warrant officers, as such garments on their "finished rack" would be seen by senior officers and would be very likely to cost them the loss of their customers'[47]. Above all these lesser breeds came the fighting officers: the Captain, the Commander, and up to five Lieutenants. Each Lieutenant would have a specified area of responsibility, while the Commander acted as second in command and chief executive, making sure the ship was properly maintained, the men well drilled, the procedures effective, and so on. At the apex of this pyramid came the Captain, totally in command of his floating empire, living in relatively luxurious solitude in his cabin at the stern of the ship, protected by a marine guard, greeted with the ceremonial boatswain's pipe when he came aboard, not to be addressed directly unless he spoke to you first – a position of absolute power (within Admiralty regulations). In such circumstances the personality of the Captain set the tone for the whole ship, and her success in war or peace depended on whether he was capricious or caring in his treatment of his officers and crew. The potential to make life a misery for all and sundry was, according to some accounts, fully realised in a few cases, but all the Captains who were involved in the *Vanguard* incident seem to have been efficient, effective and solicitous of the welfare of their crews.

Once having reached the rank of Captain, an officer slotted in to the automatic promotion sequence that ought to take him through the Admiral ranks, provided he remained alive and behaved himself. As we shall see, Captain Dawkins of *Vanguard* was automatically promoted to Rear Admiral despite not being given any further command following his Court Martial, but when he eventually retired at the age of 50 his record was marked 'not qualified for Flag rank' – his perceived misdemeanour meant that in retirement, unlike Captain Hickley of *Iron Duke,* he did not automatically advance to Vice Admiral and Admiral. But becoming a Captain did not necessarily mean a string of satisfying commands. This was peacetime, and apart from technical innovation there was no pressure on the Admiralty to build new ships and keep older ones combat-ready, so the Navy became a greatly overcrowded profession. Richard Dawkins' first command as Captain was HMS *Zealous,* from which he signed off in January 1870, and it was not until October 1873 that he was appointed to his next ship. This 33-month gap he filled by getting married and producing two children, but it was a period of enforced idleness; there simply was no ship available for him to command. It appears that at one stage 9 out of 10 Captains were unemployed and on half pay. The phrase 'half pay' is not strictly accurate. Padfield says[48] that a Lieutenant on £129 or so a year could get £90 a year when on 'half pay', but to maintain the status of a 'gentleman' required at least £150 a year. Clowes[49] gives a table of officers' salaries that shows hardly any change between the rates paid in 1857 and 1900. A Captain in 1857 could be paid as little as £450 or as much as £701 per annum. In 1900, depending on seniority and the type of ship, command allowances could raise the maximum to £930. By my calculations in 1875 Captain Dawkins was receiving £821 a year. A Vice Admiral was paid £1,460, and at the top of the tree the Admiral of the Fleet had basic pay of £2,190. Generously, in 1900 the various levels of Admiral received from £250 to £500 as commutation in lieu of the retinue of servants which had been allowed in 1857. By contrast the Midshipman had to make do on £31 a year, and the naval cadet £18, less, says Clowes, a deduction of £5 if receiving instruction. Naval cadets in the *Britannia* received no pay. Well, they had bed and board provided; what more could they need?

There were other officers aboard a warship besides those of the Royal Navy: the officers of the Royal Marine detachments. The 'sea soldiers' had been in existence for two hundred years, since King Charles II authorised the creation of the Duke of York and Albany's Maritime Regiment of Foot in October 1664, the first regiment to be formed specifically for service afloat. In 1804 an Order in Council led to the formation of artillery companies, and by the time of our story two branches of the Marines existed in parallel: the Royal Marine Light Infantry (known as 'Lobsters' from their scarlet tunics) and the Royal Marine Artillery ('unboiled lobsters' in their blue tunics). The Corps was not fully amalgamated until 1923. In Nelson's day, according to the Royal Marines official website[50], 'A first rate Royal Navy warship ... mounted 100 or 90 guns and carried a complement of over 150 Royal Marines. This consisted of four officers (Captain, 1st Lieutenant, two 2nd Lieutenants ...) The Royal Marines acted as sharpshooters, sentries, boarding parties and gunners, along with deck and sailing duties, as ordered by the ship's captain.' Captain Dawkins had good experience of the effectiveness of naval brigades at the capture of Canton in 1857, and in 1875 *Vanguard* carried one Captain RMLI and two Lieutenants, one from each branch, and 115 NCOs and privates out of her total complement of 351 (Royal Marine ranks were equivalent to those of the Army rather than the Navy). At sea however there was little advantage in possessing the Queen's Commission as a Marine officer. You had no authority other than over your own contingent of Marines, who while performing normal duties on board were under the command of the ship's Captain anyway. You had no say in the running of the ship, and much of the time you had no responsibilities and hardly anything to do. Boredom must have been the chief enemy of a Marine officer in the 'long peace'.

There was yet another category of officers and men. The First Reserve Squadron, with no battles to fill its time, was allotted the task of giving support to the Coast Guard. Thus aboard the Squadron's ships for the duration of the summer exercises there were a few officers of the Coastguard: Chief Officer, Chief Boatman and Commissioned Boatman. *Iron Duke* was carrying 210 Coastguard officers and men on 1 September 1875. During the previous month *Vanguard* had at one time as many as 10 Chief Officers of Coastguard aboard, but all, together with their men, had been disembarked to their Irish stations before the final voyage. If anything, their status as members of the Naval Reserve was lower than that of the Marine officers.

Among those disembarked were a number whose descendants are today trying to preserve their memory. John Henry Paul was one such, about whom his grandson George Paul has given me much fascinating information. Born in Torpoint, Cornwall, in 1842, John Henry came of a long line of naval folk. His great-grandfather Oliver Paul, born at Leghorn (Livorno), was Yeoman of the Powder Room on HMS *Temeraire* in 1766, and subsequently worked his way up the Bosun's list. His first son, John Henry Paul, served throughout the Napoleonic War and was awarded the Naval General Service Medal, when introduced some 40 years later, for action off the coast of Egypt (1801) and in the battle of San Domingo in 1806. John Henry's son Henry Paul signed on as a Boy 1st Class in 1831 just before his sixteenth birthday, and served in the Pacific and Caribbean, retiring in 1851. John Henry Paul followed the example of his three forebears, signing on in 1857, so that by the time he joined *Vanguard* he had several years' experience on many oceans. He was now a 'fleetman', as the Coastguard men were known, and on 24 August 1875, when the First Reserve Squadron anchored in Belfast Lough, John Henry was sent off to his 'respective station' – in his case, Burr Point coastguard station on the Ards peninsula, south of Belfast. He remained in Ireland until the end of his service in 1884, and his children were born there. By the time of his death in 1912, at the good age of 71, he had returned to the little corner of Cornwall that he came from, and is buried in Antony churchyard. His family's naval connection did not end with him, and in George Paul's six-generation family tree there are no less than sixteen people, including John Henry's eldest son and granddaughter, who joined the Royal Navy.

Another fleetman who just missed being involved in the sinking of the *Vanguard* was Elias Rendall, who had earlier been a Stoker aboard her. Elias was a Devon lad, born in Pilton near Barnstaple and brought up in Tiverton, and was 36 in 1875. He had rendered some years exemplary service by then, earning various good conduct badges. He had married Mary Ann Nott at Sampford Peverell in 1866. Their first child was born in Tiverton, but the following three were all registered in Wexford. His home coastguard station was Arthurstown in that county, and he left *Vanguard* on 31 August to return to Arthurstown. Then began a sad period in his life. In 1880, four weeks before the birth of their fourth child, Mary Ann, Elias' 8-year old son John fell off the harbour wall in Arthurstown and drowned. Elias and his family went back to England as soon as Mary Ann was born, and lived in London, where he became a commissionaire at the office of the GPO. But this new life was abruptly shortened. Elias died in 1885 at the age of 46, and his wife followed him only nine weeks later. The orphaned children were brought up by a maiden aunt in Tiverton. Fred Burnett of Salcombe Regis, who told me the story of the Rendell/Rendall family, is the grandson of Louisa, the third child of Elias and Mary Ann.

Boatman Richard Thomas Edgcombe had also been serving on *Vanguard* while she did guard duty at Kingstown, but had left the ship some time before the events of 1 September. He signed on at the age of 19 in 1856, and retired two years after the sinking of *Vanguard*. He died in 1901 in Westlake, south Devon. His three sons, Richard, Oliver Henry, and William Sydney all followed him into the Navy. Ordinary Seaman Richard Edgcombe (junior), while serving aboard the sloop *Kingfisher* in 1888, became involved in an incident when nine German traders were murdered in Vitu State on the east coast of Africa. A field gun crew was landed, with significant effect. Richard was subsequently awarded the East and West Africa Medal with Vitu Clasp. Later in 1893, off the coast of Tripoli, Richard's ship HMS *Edgar* helped to rescue survivors when the battleship *Camperdown* accidentally rammed *Victoria,* an echo of what was to happen to *Vanguard.* William Sydney Edgcombe served on HMS *Algerine* at the Boxer Rising in 1900. In the next generation, William Sydney's son, Able Seaman Torpedoman William Richard Edgcombe while serving on the 'S' Class destroyer *Scorpion* took an active role in the battle of the North Cape, when the German battle cruiser *Scharnhorst* was attacked and sunk by units of the Home Fleet on Boxing Day 1943. Torpedoman Edgcombe's daughter married Quentin Morgan of Newport, South Wales, who told me about her forebears.

To these may be added the 30-year old Boatman Thomas Crocker, born in Plymouth and recently signed on for his second ten years of service, transferring to the coastguard at the same time. He was based at Arklow. His great-grandson Paul Hanna (of Chicago) told me that Thomas married an Irish girl and was later awarded a gallantry medal by the Board of Trade. Finally, Commissioned Boatman John Sweet, great-grandfather of Janette Courtney of Australia, who was 37 in 1875 and based at Ballygally. John's father and two brothers were also Coastguards, and one brother was later Harbour Master at Donaghadee. Having retired in the early 1900's, John Sweet lived on to the age of 92.

These examples, kindly provided by present-day descendants of *Vanguard* people, illustrate what a wealth of experience there was in the body of coastguard men carried by the ships of the First Reserve Squadron. As with Henry Gaden, my wife's great-grandfather, seamen who signed on for a second period of ten years' service had the option of joining the coastguard service. The service was popular with naval men, because pay was good, and they could live at home with the families that most of them had acquired by this stage in their careers. A new Naval Regulation of 1831 said, in part, that 'the vacant situations of Boatmen will be filled up, from time to time by Seamen, as Ships of War are paid off; of which the Captain or Commanding Officer shall select a given number ... of the men whom he shall judge to be entitled to fill these situations, and who may be desirous of entering this Service.' The names were to be submitted to the Admiralty (in duplicate, of course) with a certificate which read:

> 'These are to certify that A.B. ...... has served under my orders .... years. That he
> has been sober, attentive, and obedient to command, and is a healthy, active and
> good Seaman, not more than 30 years of age, nor under 5ft 5in high, and is in all
> respects fit for the situation of Boatman in the Coast Guard Service.'[51] (In 1856
> the maximum age became 37, with at least 8 years' sea service)

Thus did the Admiralty ensure for itself a Reserve of high quality, experienced seamen. At the same time, the guard ships, during their annual exercises, benefited from this experience. The disadvantage however was that after the fleetmen had returned to their stations, each ship was left with a young and relatively inexperienced crew, which in *Vanguard's* case amounted to barely three-quarters of her complement.

Another thing which emerges from the stories of these seamen is the tendency for old sailors to gravitate to the English West Country, where most of them would have started their naval service. The 1881 Census records for Devon contain plenty of names from the muster roll of *Vanguard* and her companion ships.

The Ratings

The much feared 'Press Gang' had fallen into disuse after 1815, though it remained a legal procedure, and most seamen joined the Navy as volunteers, at as early an age as the officers under whom they were to serve. Originally a seaman signed on for the duration of a ship's commission, to be paid off when that assignment ended, and left to find a job on another vessel. In 1853 the Navy introduced the concept of 'continuous service', under which a boy signed on for 10 years once he had reached the age of 18. Thus Henry Gaden, a Devon lad, signed on as a Boy 2nd Class in HMS *Implacable* on 21 October 1862. Henry was actually 15 years old, but for some reason his mother Elizabeth gave his date of birth as August 1848 instead of 1847 when she signed the formal letter giving her consent:

> 'I hereby certify that my son *Hy Gaden* has my full consent (being himself willing) to enter Her Majesty's Navy for a period of ten years Continuous and General Service from the age of 18, in attition *[sic]* to whatever period may be necessary until he attains that age, agreeable to Her Majesty's Order in Council dated 1st April '53, and the Admiralty Regulations of the 14th June '53 relating thereto.
> Witness our hands at *Devonport* this *20th* day of *October 1862*
> Date of boy's birth *18 August 1848*
> Parent's signature *Elizabeth X her mark Gaden*
> Boy's signature of consent *Henry Gaden*'

The document is written in good clear script, and the words I have italicised were added by different hands. It is not unusual for the period that Elizabeth, the daughter of a stonemason, was unable to sign her name, but that her young son could sign his. Winton records[52] that many of the long-serving seamen were illiterate, and the newly recruited Boys were able to earn a welcome few extra pence by reading and writing letters for them. Henry at 15 was 4ft 8inches (1.42m) tall and weighed 78lb (35kg), with light hair, a fair complexion and blue eyes[53]. In 1866 the Navy thought he had reached the age of 18 (he was actually 19), and he was able to sign on for his first ten years of service. By then, after a few years' exposure to the Caribbean and Indian Ocean wind and sun, his complexion was described as 'Dark'! Henry joined the crew of HMS *Vanguard* in February 1875. In 1876 he committed himself to another ten years, and eventually retired at the age of 47. This was the pattern for most of his contemporaries.

Another *Vanguard* crew member, Robert Thompson, was almost ten years younger than Henry Gaden, having been born in Bagnelstown, County Carlow, in 1856. Orphaned early in life, he was brought up by friends of the family. His grandson, Derek Paine, writes[54] that he 'was well looked after and enjoyed his childhood. He spent his free time playing on Bray Head and Sugar Loaf and often spoke of picking blackberries, mushrooms and primroses when in season. He attended Windgates School ... [and] received a basic but sound education, which greatly helped him in later life. Three weeks after his sixteenth birthday, he walked to Kingstown (Dún Laoghaire) where there was a recruitment centre for the Royal Navy.' His Royal Navy record show that on 2 May 1872, aboard HMS *Vanguard* in Kingstown harbour, his guardians signed the appropriate papers, and two weeks later he was on his way to join the training ship HMS *Ganges* at Falmouth in Cornwall.

HMS *Ganges*, whose teak timbers today form a wooden cross outside Guildford Cathedral, is famed for being the last sailing battleship to round Cape Horn, a feat she attained on 17 October 1857. She was converted into a training ship in 1866. It was common for numbers of Irish boys to train on Ganges. The ship's log for 18th December 1872 records that the Captain sent 25 Irish boys (most probably including Robert Thompson) on shore leave for Christmas. An article in the *Falmouth Packet* dated 30 November 1872 said that:

'recently entered boys frequently suffer from the sudden change of diet, especially boys from Ireland. They have been accustomed to a diet almost farinaceous, they have good appetites and when presented with meat and pudding, they find it more than they can digest.'[55]

Robert Thompson's Continuous Service Record notes: 'Height: 5ft 6in. Hair: Light Brown. Eyes: Blue. Complexion: Ruddy. Wounds, Scars, or Marks: Scar on left elbow. Trade: Farmer.' In his first week aboard *Ganges* 'he witnessed one of his fellow boys receiving 24 cuts (lashes) as punishment'. In February 1874, still a Boy 2nd Class, he stepped aboard *Vanguard* again. During eight months on the ironclad he was promoted to Ordinary Seaman 2nd Class on his eighteenth birthday. He left *Vanguard* in October 1874 and joined HMS *Penelope*, for an eighteen month stint which included the First Reserve Squadron's cruise round Ireland. *Penelope* developed engine problems that prevented her from proceeding on the final leg of the cruise, so that when *Iron Duke* hit *Vanguard*, *Penelope* was well on her way to Harwich. Two years later Robert Thompson's naval career took him across the world, serving for a number of years in the Far East including surveying the coasts of Korea, China, Japan and South Africa, while also visiting Shanghai, Vladivostok, Nagasaki, Sarawak, Sydney, Ceylon (modern Sri Lanka), Aden, Mauritius, and the isolated islands of St Helena and Ascension in the South Atlantic.

Awarded the Royal Navy Long Service and Good Conduct Medal in 1892, he eventually took retirement with the rank of Petty Officer 1st Class after 22 years' service on 15 ships. He had only just got married. He joined the Royal Fleet Reserve, from which he was retired on age grounds at the age of 50 in 1906. He worked for an insurance company in College Green, Dublin before finally retiring to Greystones with his wife Mary and five children. Until his death at the good age of 90 he lived in a house called *Glencoe* on the North Beach, facing directly out towards the Kish Lighthouse, near the spot where 'his ship' *Vanguard* lies to this day. Derek Paine, Robert Thompson's grandson, can recall him regularly sitting on the wall outside the house, binoculars in hand, looking at the passing ships and often pointing out to sea to the spot where *Vanguard* sank and telling tales of his life in the Navy. 'He recalled vividly how he and his fellow crew members would sometimes pass the time, catching sharks in tropical waters, by throwing a rope overboard with a meat hook and a slab of meat on it. On one occasion, they opened up a shark and found the remains of the hindquarters of a mule, complete with shoes'.

Derek Paine also has family connections with Thomas Curling, who served as a member of *Vanguard*'s crew in 1873/4. In 2001 Derek wrote 'I can sit at my kitchen table and look at the Kish Lighthouse, near where the *Vanguard* lies. My house is on the south side of Bray Head, which is marked on [Navigating Lieutenant] James Thomas' chart'[56] (see illustration). Gary Paine, in the next generation, works in London's Docklands, about as far away as possible, culturally, from the peace of Greystones.

The newly regularised system of recruitment was supplemented by more formalised training. Boys spent a period aboard a training ship and had practical experience at sea. On HMS *Vanguard* the job of instructing the Boys was taken very seriously. Captain Dawkins was anxious during the Court Martial to demonstrate this, and asked a leading question of Commander Tandy, who replied that the young seamen 'were instructed under the boatswain and day boatswain's mate, and questioned by me, and they were exercised aloft by me and the officers of the watch'[57]. This followed evidence given by a young recruit (George Cooper) who had been in a seagoing ship for eight months, but who admitted he did not know how many yards there were in a cable, and thought there were 32 points between right ahead and right abeam. But then such book-learning was hardly the most exciting part of learning seamanship; much more fun was being 'exercised aloft', as Tandy put it. Even in steam-powered vessels it was imperative that all hands were drilled in the business of setting and trimming sails, which could be thousands of square feet in area. Every day there would be drill evolutions, twice a day while at sea. To a deep-dyed landlubber like myself the skills that teenage boys mastered 'aloft' are terrifying to contemplate. They scampered up rigging and ran out along yards with apparently total disregard for safety. It was appallingly dangerous. In a decent wind a yardarm could whip like a fishing rod, and men regularly lost their lives by falling from aloft (as did Ignatius Nolan on *Vanguard* in Belfast Lough at the end of August 1875), but it was a matter of immense pride, shared by Captain and crew, that theirs should be the most crisply handled ship. Other training activities such as cutlass drill appear regularly in *Vanguard*'s log. On reaching the age of 18 Boys were promoted to Ordinary Seaman, whereupon opportunities existed for specialising in trades such as signals or gunnery. Some became stokers, who were paid half as much again as their colleagues in recognition of the conditions under which they worked. It was their job to keep the furnaces fuelled, and to separate ash from clinker, all in the blazing heat and deafening noise of the poorly-lit engine-room and stoke-hole. Coal-dust and smoke pervaded the whole ship, offending against the traditional Naval passion for spit and polish, but only the stokers experienced the full impact of the 'fire down below' – except, that is, when the ship took on coal, an operation in which everybody was expected to give a hand.

The Master at Arms, known as 'Jonty' (possibly from the French 'Gendarme'; on *Vanguard,* James Waldren held this rank) was responsible for discipline on the lower deck, and infringements were rarely treated leniently. In the 1860's the Admiralty attempted to impose order on punishments by requiring a record to be kept for each seaman, and gradually practice moved away from flogging towards confinement. Cells were designated on warships for this purpose. Flogging in peacetime was suspended in 1871, and in wartime in 1879 (technically, it has not yet been abolished). The ships' logs show that the crimes most likely to be punished by flogging were drunkenness and insubordination. In a time of peace, with warships manned to 'maximum intensity', it could soon become tedious to repeat the same routines every day, and with the utter lack of privacy perhaps a bit too much to drink was excusable. A sailor's life had however improved immeasurably since Nelson's day, when one writer has described it as 'abominable'. There was, for one thing, more living space. The splendidly restored *Warrior* in Portsmouth Historic Dockyard shows how hammocks were slung and mess tables erected in the restricted space between the guns, as had been normal on broadside vessels. On central battery ships like *Vanguard* and *Iron Duke* the few guns were concentrated in the battery, and the crew messed forward of the battery on the main deck, with plenty of room for hammocks. But there were still a lot of people in a confined space, with not too much ventilation, and the combined effects of limited washing facilities and a restricted diet produced a rank atmosphere that horrified some ships' surgeons. The few latrines were normally placed at the 'Head' of the ship, at first no more than a plank over the leeward bow, which must have been awkward and uncomfortable even in the calmest conditions.

The seaman's day began early, and followed a rigid pattern, something like this[58]:

03.30	Coil up ropes
04.00	Scrub decks
05.45	Re-set sails
06.00	Stow hammocks
06.30	Breakfast
07.15	Cleaning tasks
09.00	Prayers
09.30	Drills
12.00	Dinner

13.25	Roll call
13.30	Drills
16.15	Supper
17.00	Quarters
19.30	Stand by hammocks
20.30	Rounds

The routine varied only on a Sunday. The requirement to attend church parade meant a hectic scramble to get the decks cleared, breakfast eaten, and one's best uniform on in time for the Captain's meticulous inspection of not only the men but also every corner of the ship. The crew could be left standing for two hours while this went on, and then be made to attend divine service that often lasted more than an hour, which might mean a cold dinner. No wonder the men generally loathed Sunday mornings. Scrubbing the decks and burnishing the brass may have been insisted upon in order to stave off boredom on long cruises, but such chores did also foster considerable pride among a ship's company in keeping her smarter than any other vessel. William Hathorn wrote from HMS *Forte* of being anchored off the mouth of the Hooghly: 'Here we remained for 4 days making the Ship look "Ikie" as the sailors call it.'[59]

The Navy recognised that its men needed three square meals a day to maintain the energy necessary to stoke boilers or swarm over the yard-arm, but what could be provided was inevitably monotonous. It is interesting to see what stores *Vanguard* was carrying when she sank (see Annex 3). Fresh meat and vegetables appear on the list because the First Reserve Squadron were in home waters and had just taken these supplies aboard at Kingstown, but on longer voyages they would soon have disappeared from the table. Breakfast generally consisted of cocoa or chocolate and 'Biscuit', described as 'Kneaded cakes of flour that were baked with the least quantity of water possible and then stored, as a bread substitute, on board'[60]. On 1 September 1875 *Vanguard* was carrying 12 tons (over 12,000 kg) of 'Biscuit'. At sea dinner at noon consisted of a pound of salt beef and a pound of salt pork alternating, with pease soup or suet and raisins, and more biscuit; then at supper time tea and yet more biscuit. There was of course also the midday rum ration, though this had been significantly reduced since the days when half a pint (300ml) was the norm. The ration was halved in 1825 and again in 1850, and the evening distribution abolished. Beer and lime juice were available, and sailors could supplement the unending salt meat by catching fish. Padfield reckons[61] that this diet provided some 2,900 calories a day. Today's supermarket food labels say that the recommended daily intake for an adult male is 2,500 calories, but our lifestyle is infinitely less active.

Uniform was introduced for ratings only in 1857, replacing the variously coloured ready-made clothing sold by the purser. Blue had become the commonest colour by the middle of the century, largely because indigo dye was readily available from India and was generally colour-fast. The Navy List for 1875 includes the following among the prescribed uniform for Petty Officers, Seaman and Boys:

'Blue cloth jacket – To be made of navy blue cloth, double-breasted, with stand and fall collar, sleeve sufficiently large to go easily over a duck and serge frock, to reach the hip, with an opening at the cuffs on the seam, with two small black buttons, one inside breast pocket on the left side, and seven black horn crown and anchor buttons seven-tenths of an inch in diameter, on each side, according to a pattern. Blue Cloth Trowsers – to be made of navy blue cloth, of the ordinary naval pattern, fitting tight at the waistband, with two pockets and a broad flap, and stained bone buttons.

Hat – To be black or white, according to climate. The hat to be four inches high in the crown, three inches wide in the rim, and seven inches across the crown, and made of sennet, covered with brown holland painted black, with a hat ribbon bearing the ship's name; and in warm climates the same hat uncovered. A chin-stay to be attached to the hat.'

The uniform also included 'frocks' in duck or white drill and blue serge (an upper garment that tucked into the trousers), duck trousers, a pea jacket, a cap 'to be worn *at night*, and at sea when ordered' a black silk handkerchief and a woollen comforter 'to be of a dark blue colour'. There is no mention of footwear. The Victorian sailor generally went about in bare feet, for the best grip on the wooden decks.

Below decks the men naturally had to make their own amusements. After supper there was a time for making music and dancing. The great corpus of sea shanties comes mostly from an earlier time; by 1875 the cheerful and suggestive songs from the music hall were more likely to be heard. Games were played on deck, some of them very physically demanding. One wonders how they managed it after a hard day's work on 2,900 calories. In port things were different, and those allowed ashore made free with the local attractions. In 1861 the police in Portsmouth reckoned that there were 1,791 known prostitutes in the town, or nearly one in fifty of the whole population[62]. Such liaisons had their consequences, but the Contagious Disease Act of 1864 required prostitutes to submit to regular health checks. As a result the rate of sexually transmitted disease in the Navy reduced sharply. There were increasing efforts to provide more suitable entertainment for sailors on shore, such as the Sailors' Reading Room in Kingstown, described in the next chapter, and the work of the indomitable Agnes Weston. She was deeply religious and concerned for the welfare of the less fortunate, and began by writing to soldiers in foreign service and sailors at sea. In 1872 at Devonport she witnessed the behaviour of aimless men released from their ships, and took it upon herself to work tirelessly for the National Temperance League. In response to comments from bluejackets that 'they wished they had a public house without the drink', she opened the first of her Sailors' Rests the year after *Vanguard* sank. More than a century and a quarter later, the splendid organisation she founded still provides welfare and support for the seagoing community. It is fair to say that the majority of sailors at this time, settled in a stable career path, were sober family men, and 'Aggie's' was a safety net for the less fortunate.

Fortunate or otherwise, the Victorian sailor had little enough pay to support a family. An Ordinary Seaman, according to Clowes[63], received £22 16s 3d (just over £22.80) a year, or about 1s 2d (about 6p) a day, which might be adequate for a man on his own, with all found while on board, but hardly sufficed to support a wife and children. Nevertheless this did not seem to deter them. Of the many crewmen whose descendants have kindly provided me with information, most got married in their 20's. Ordinary Seaman Robert Thompson, who served on *Vanguard* until 1874, was nearly 40 when he married, the year before his retirement from the Navy, but seems to have been an exception. What might have made some of these steady, reliable men go wild in port could have been the system of paying them in large sums at long intervals. At one time it had been the practice to pay the men off only at the end of the ship's commission. In the 1870's payday came more often, but then only every six months while the ship was at sea. Apparently pay parade on board *Warrior* was a monthly event, which may be because she spent so much time in her home port.

To sum up the British 'Jack Tar', I can do little better than borrow a quote from *Martello Tower* (FC Norman):

'If you understood how to manage him, he would do anything he was asked to do – whether he could or not! He would make brooms, milk the cow, play at cricket, march, fight, run, dance, sing, play the fiddle, smoke a pipe, drink a glass of grog (or more!) and mind the baby. That he had his weaknesses and shortcomings cannot be denied, but take him all in all he was a splendid fellow! – and I expect we shall never see his like again.'[64]

Far left: Philip Le Quesne

Left: Philip Lecane at the sight of the *Vanguard* wreck.

Chapter 4

'Our magnificent Ship'

HMS *Vanguard*

Construction of the third of the four *Audacious* class sister ships began on 2 November 1867 at Laird's yard in Birkenhead. She was to be named *Vanguard*. 'Instead of choosing such names as the *Victory* or the *Valorous*, it might be as well to christen vessels as the *Faulty* or the *Timorous*,' said *Punch*[65], reflecting on the apparent unseaworthiness of Naval ships after a series of unfortunate incidents that included the 1875 sinking. Fighting ships, despite the convention of being called 'She', always seem to need names that imply something virile and warlike. There are only so many words of that kind in the language, so they get re-used over and over again. Thus there had to that point been six RN vessels named *Vanguard*, and following the loss of 'our' *Vanguard* there have been three more. For the full story of all but the most recent, the most readily accessible source is *Nine Vanguards*, by Lieutenant-Commander P K Kemp RN, published by Hutchinson in 1951. In 1946 the Commander of the newly completed ninth *Vanguard* wrote an equally full history, but it is less easy to find. The seventh *Vanguard* thus carried the weight of reputation of several illustrious predecessors, at which we now take a glance.

The first Naval vessel to be christened *Vanguard* was built by Matthew Baker at Woolwich and launched in 1586, a galleon 108 feet (33m) long rated at 500 tons, and carrying 32 guns. 'Low and snug in the water, and more like a galleass'[66]. She represented the very latest development in ship design and armament, ready to be launched against the Spanish, who were at the height of their powers. In July 1588, after months of frustrating patrols in the Straits of Dover, *Vanguard* was summoned to Calais along with Sir Henry Seymour's squadron, and became engaged in the battle of Gravelines. Philip of Spain's fleet proved less invincible than intended, and *Vanguard* came through undamaged. She was then given a rest off Sheerness for some six years before being refitted for action as Frobisher's flagship in the eastern Atlantic, but he suffered a mortal wound in the fighting off Crozon. She rejoined Howard and Raleigh for the attack on Cadiz, and was involved in the long series of skirmishes with Spain until 1600. Between then and 1615 she underwent one or possibly two comprehensive refits, emerging 150 tons heavier and with 40 guns. In this guise she took part in an expedition against Algerian pirates, and a strange episode in which she was ordered by Charles I to embark French troops for some unspecified task; the officers and crew did not like this idea, and together engineered a mock mutiny. Eventually towards the end of 1627 her service came to an end. There were insufficient funds to pay off the crew, so low had naval management sunk since the days of Drake and Frobisher.

In one respect the Navy under the Stuarts practised good housekeeping. The next *Vanguard* was largely constructed from the timbers of her predecessor. She was a Second Rate of 731 tons, launched in 1631, carrying 56 guns and a complement of 390. By this time dishonesty and inefficiency were rife in the running of the Navy, and conditions on board were dreadful. It is perhaps understandable that many vessels, *Vanguard* among them, went over to the Commonwealth cause. In 1651 animosity towards the Dutch blew up into full-scale war. *Vanguard* took part, some of the time under the command of the splendidly named Captain William Haddock (later Vice-Admiral), distinguishing herself in the battle of the Kentish Knock. The tactics used on this occasion are an interesting contrast to the precise line-of-battle described earlier. According to Commander Lamb, 'The naval tactics of those days were an elephantine version of the 'dive and zoom' of the fighter aircraft of today: the fleet with the windward gage bore down on, and charged through, the enemy line firing briskly; both fleets would then work up to windward and, when one was in a suitable position, it would repeat the procedure on the other'[67]. Later under Captain Mildmay she served in an action off Dungeness which led to defeat for the British, but then helped set the record straight in 1653 at the battle of Portland. In this engagement she acted as flagship for General Monck, a cavalry officer for whom this was his first experience of war at sea. Impatient to get at the enemy, he is said to have drawn his sword and given the order to charge. Perhaps because of such recklessness she lost her captain and 30 of her crew on that day. There was more fighting with the Dutch until 1654, whereupon *Vanguard* limped home extensively damaged, to see no more action for 11 years. The Dutch declared war again in 1665, and *Vanguard* was at sea once more. The following winter her crew were not paid off for the season, as was usual, but kept on board because of the plague; the cost of keeping sailors on the payroll was a severe drain on resources. Action duly resumed in the early summer of 1666, when the French joined the Dutch against the English for the terrible 'Four Days' Battle, of which Samuel Pepys wrote much, concluding 'I do find reason to think that we are beaten in every respect, and that we are the losers'. The tables turned at the end of July, when the Dutch fleet was convincingly beaten, but *Vanguard* against lost her Captain, John Whitty. The very next year the Dutch were back yet again, capturing Sheerness and sailing up the Medway to set fire to ships in Chatham. In an attempt to blockade the river, various ships were sunk, one of them the *Vanguard*, just below Rochester Bridge, and there she stayed, efforts to raise her having been in vain, even though all the other sunken ships had been successfully recovered. Thieves stripped her of anything remotely valuable. Thus on 13 June 1667 perished the second *Vanguard,* with a proud list of battle honours to her credit.

Lieutenant-Commander Kemp tells us that in 1678 Pepys, by that time Secretary of the Admiralty, visited Portsmouth to check on the building of some of his 'thirty new ships', including the latest *Vanguard*, a second-rate three-decker of 1357 tons, armed with

90 guns and a crew of 640. Unfortunately Pepys himself was one of many innocent Protestants shut up in the Tower on false charges, and while he struggled to collect evidence in his favour the thirty new ships lay unused in harbour. Eventually Pepys was restored to office and James II came to the throne, with greater respect for the Navy than his impoverished predecessor. The third *Vanguard* was among the fleet that put up token resistance to William of Orange, and then as part of an Anglo-Dutch force, successfully tackled the French in the battle of Barfleur in 1692. Not long afterwards she was ordered into Portsmouth for repairs, but sent on to Chatham because she was in such a poor condition. A three-decker of those days was not in any case fit to face the winter gales, but each spring she was brought up to full complement ready for action that did not come. Thus she remained until 1703, when a fearsome storm wreaked havoc throughout southern England. *Vanguard* was driven on to a mudflat. She was recovered, and in 1711 actually refitted and recommissioned, for no more than a few months' guard duty. In 1723 she was renamed *Duke*, and the third *Vanguard* was deleted from the record.

1748 saw the launching of the third-rate *Vanguard*, 1414 tons, built by Philemon Ewer at East Cowes at a cost of £25,175. She carried 70 guns and a crew of 520. She was a two-decker, the three-deck design having proved unwieldy in bad weather. Ewer received £8,009 for building her. She was the largest ship he had ever built, and such was his pride in the achievement that his granddaughter was baptised Mary Vanguard Fenn on the day of the launch, 16 April 1748[68]. This *Vanguard* (the ship, not the child) saw service in the New World during the Seven Years' War, fighting the French in Canada. On one occasion she found herself alone facing a squadron of eighteen French ships, but got away unscathed. After some time spent blockading ports in Nova Scotia she was involved in supporting Wolfe's attack on Quebec, which was not an easy task, because of Wolfe's mercurial temperament. His orders were continually changing. The early 1760's saw her in the Caribbean with Rodney's force at the capture of Martinique. In 1774 *Vanguard* was sold out of the service.

The fifth ship to be named *Vanguard*, at 1662 tons, was completed at Deptford in 1787. Intended as one of the many 'seventy-fours' built at the time, pierced for 74 32-pound guns, she in fact carried 82, a formidable armament, and a crew of 589. She was nevertheless classed as third-rate. This was to be a famous member of the family. The French Revolution made relations with Europe distinctly uncertain, and *Vanguard* was among those commissioned into the Channel fleet when the French declared war in 1793. Returning to Plymouth in 1794, she struck a rock and had to put in for repairs; the rock is apparently still known as 'Vanguard Rock'. She went off to the West Indies for a couple of years, parrying French action there. At the end of 1797 the newly-promoted Rear Admiral Horatio Nelson, recently recovered from the loss of his arm, was eager to get back to sea and have a crack at Napoleon, then at the height of his ambition. For his flagship Nelson chose HMS *Vanguard*, and hoisted his flag on 29 March 1798 at Spithead. In May, after entering the Mediterranean with a small company of ships, *Vanguard* was dismasted by a sudden gale, and repaired in Sardinia. Lt Cmdr Kemp quotes Nelson, writing to his wife, as seeing this to be a judgement on his vanity, from which he intended to learn. Not long thereafter came the battle of the Nile, and resounding victory for Nelson and *Vanguard*. In 1800, Nelson switched to *Foudroyant* as his flagship, taking Captain Hardy with him, and Captain Brown assumed command of *Vanguard*. In the years that followed *Vanguard* saw service in trade protection in the West Indies, and in the Baltic, putting pressure on the Danes to lend us ships. She was paid off in 1811, and spent the remaining ten years of her life as a prison hulk and a powder ship. She was broken up in 1821. There is a neat little model of her in the Malta Maritime Museum in Vittoriosa, commemorating the part she played in ridding the island of the French.

Vanguard the Sixth, a Symonds design, was launched in 1835, of 2609 tons, carrying 80 guns. She spent time patrolling the eastern Mediterranean, and sitting quietly in the Channel Fleet, seeing little or no action. She took no part in the Crimean war. The Navy Records Society's collection of naval ballads includes one about 'The Vanguard', which is reproduced in Annex 2; there is no date, but the commander is named as 'Mickey Walker'. Baldwin Wake Walker served for a short time from 1 September 1836 as Commander aboard the sixth *Vanguard*, under Captain Sir Thomas Fellowes, and the ballad may refer to his regime. If so, it was less than palatable to the men:

> 'But if to sea I go again, I'd sooner swing in a halter,
> Before I'd sail in any ship commanded by Mickey Walker
> Then let us sing the *Vanguard*'s praise, proclaim her valiant name,
> Cruel usage I have met with since I sail'd in the same.'[69]

In 1848 Walker was to succeed Symonds as Surveyor of the Navy, but the ship achieved no such renown. Renamed *Ajax* in 1867, she was broken up in 1875, the last of the wooden *Vanguards*. This re-christening, according to Commander Lamb, was because 'the name *Vanguard* was wanted for one of a class of steam-driven ironclads about to be built'[70].

In 1867 the requirement was for second-rate fighting ships of moderate size, partly because the amount of money spent on giants like *Warrior* was hard to justify, but also because the intention was to use them for service abroad, where the adversary was expected to take the shape of armoured cruisers. To keep pace with develop-ments in other countries, at least four would be needed. Reed's design for a central battery on two levels was accepted in February, at an estimated cost of £220,000, and *Audacious* and *Invincible* were laid down on Clydeside by the end of June. Then came a pause, while the Admiralty pondered. Was this central battery idea going to work? Were twin screws really a good thing, seeing that no other nation had fitted them to heavy warships, and shipbuilders did not like them? Would Reed's other ideas, affecting stability and sailing characteristics, be as seaworthy as he claimed? Was the broadside format really finished (the central battery was after all little more than a broadside with a bulge)? Should turrets be given another try? For the first time, the Admiralty decided to consult the seven leading private shipbuilding firms about whether a different design might meet their requirements better. Seven designs were duly submitted, but none of them appeared as good as Reed's original after all. So the order went out and *Vanguard*'s iron hull was laid down on 21 October 1867 at Birkenhead, where the turret ship *Captain*, later to founder with her designer aboard, was also under construction.

The atmosphere of a shipyard in the great days of iron shipbuilding can hardly be better described than in the words of Charles Dickens in *The Uncommercial Traveller:*

> 'Ding, Clash, Dong, Bang, Boom, Rattle, Clash, Bang, Clink, Bang, Dong, Bang, Clatter, bang bang BANG! What on earth is this! This is, or soon will be, the *Achilles,* iron armour-plated ship. Twelve hundred men are working at her now; twelve hundred men working on stages over her sides, over her bows, over her stern, under her keel, between her decks, down in her hold, within her and without, crawling and creeping into the finest curves of her lines wherever it is possible for men to twist. Twelve hundred hammerers, measurers, caulkers, armourers, forgers, smiths, shipwrights; twelve hundred dingers, clashers, dongers, rattlers, clinkers, bangers bangers bangers!'

Achilles was being built at Chatham four years earlier than *Vanguard*. As a class, the *Audacious* ironclads might have been relatively small in size, but they were as big as the first generation first class French ironclads, and carried heavier armament. Each was 280ft long, with a beam of 54ft and a draught of 22ft (85m x 16m x 7m), and displaced 6000 tons. Up to the level of the main deck the hull was double skinned, an armoured belt 8 inches thick amidships, tapering to 6 inches at the ends, giving protection to the guns. As armament developed, the increasing calibre and weight of guns meant that fewer could be carried. The *Audacious* class was supplied with six 9 inch muzzle-loading rifled guns on the main deck and a further four in the embrasures on the upper deck (the relatively small number of guns led to their outmoded classification as 'second class' ironclads). On the upper deck the battery structure, together with the increased tumble-home (inward slope above the waterline) to give a clear field of fire, meant that deck space was restricted and inconvenient. Inside however there was more space because the guns were concentrated in the centre section. Ballard comments that 'Naturally therefore the *Audacious* class were popular in the service.'[71] The design won plaudits all round: 'Very clever ships – so many good qualities in a small, handy hull'[72], or as Vice Admiral Tarleton put it after inspecting *Vanguard* in August 1875, 'These ships are exceptional.'[73]

The hull itself, despite its thickness of iron and teak, had one potentially serious design flaw. There were tough transverse bulkheads, intended to divide the hull into compartments so that any penetration of the hull would not lead to the loss of the ship, but there were no wing passages, which could have helped contain any inflow of water. This may have been an economy measure, or simply based on the assumption that the hull was not at serious risk of being breached anyway. Before the *Audacious* design appeared on the drawing-board, Nathaniel Barnaby had written[74] that the *Warrior* hull had:

'... an inner water-tight side for additional security, in the event of the ship receiving injury below the armour by the blows of a ram, or by any other means. It has been assumed in the construction of all these ships, that shot cannot be made to penetrate a ship's side more than two or three feet below the surface of the water.'

In the *Audacious* design the omission of wing passages was compounded by the main deck being set lower than usual, so that the top edge of each bulkhead came barely three feet above the waterline. But the hull was never tested under battle conditions, and only when *Vanguard* sank did anyone notice the deficiency. Even then, according to Ballard, nothing significant was done about it.

Each of the four sister ships had two sets of 2-cylinder horizontal return connecting-rod engines, with six rectangular boilers at 30 lbs pressure, producing 4,830 horsepower, and driving twin screws, diameter 16 feet 2 inches (5m), one behind the other, each consisting of four blades mounted in pairs. Having twin screws meant that the draught could be shallow, an advantage for steamers – nevertheless both *Audacious* and *Invincible* managed to acquire damage to the bottom in their early days. Shallow draught was a distinct disadvantage, however, while under sail. They were equipped with a huge spread of sail, greater in proportion to hull dimensions than for any other Royal Navy vessel. With a coal-carrying capacity of only 460 tons, which would last for three days at full power, sail was a necessary back-up rather than a luxury. The loss of *Captain* made the Admiralty more aware of the dangers of instability, and the *Audacious* class masts were shortened, *Vanguard*'s fore- and maintopmasts by as much as ten feet. Reed had put many hours into the design of a gun platform that was well clear of the water but could carry such a spread of sail, with a centre of gravity higher than that of the earlier iron ships, which were notorious for 'rolling their guts out' (as Ballard claims the seaman would put it). He seems to have overdone it, because on first trial *Audacious* rolled not at all, but heeled alarmingly to the wind even with no sail up. The answer was ballast in the form of 360 tons of cement, after the inclusion of which the four became beautifully steady gun platforms. The navigating officer of *Vanguard* said she was 'a most comfortable ship in bad weather'[75].

Under steam, the *Audacious* class were fast and manoeuvrable. All had balanced rudders except *Iron Duke*, which was fitted with a hinged rudder. This meant that while the three could turn, if not on a sixpence, then within a perfectly respectable circle of between 318 and 423 yards (290 to 387 metres), *Iron Duke* needed at least 505 yards (461m). On the other hand the hinged rudder gave better control while under sail. Generally the shallow draught and the drag of the twin screws meant that as a class they were slow sailers, even described as 'unmanageable' under canvas by those giving evidence to the Committee on Designs. In shallow water they yawed all over the place; Ballard says that 'when passing through the Suez Canal they either used a tug ahead or dragged a chain cable'[76].

Vanguard never traversed the Suez Canal. Again in Ballard's phrase, 'she was never sighted from an alien shore'[77]. She was floated out in January 1870 and completed on 28 September of that year. November saw her undertaking an 'Experimental Cruize'[78] from

Plymouth to Lisbon and back, then in the spring of 1871 she had another such cruise and carried out steam trials in company with *Iron Duke*. Some minor modifications resulted, and she was ready for service – not in distant parts, but as a member of the First Reserve Squadron, and Guardship of the Eastern Irish District, based at Kingstown. *Iron Duke* spent three years on the China station and was actually the first capital ship to use the Suez Canal. Early in 1875 she too returned to guardship duty, stationed at Hull.

It seems a dreadful waste of resources to build four warships of advanced design, only to 'put them out to grass' as support to the Coastguard; but the politics of the time required that Britain should not lose her pre-eminence in weaponry, whether or not there might be any real threat to her safety. Perhaps the same 'deterrent' argument still applies in the twenty-first Century, in which the fearsome nuclear submarine HMS *Vanguard* prowls the seas without, one must assume, encountering any enemy vessel – while at the time I write the threat to international peace comes more from fundamentalist terrorist activity than from the armed forces of any nation state.

At this time the heady days of revenue men chasing smugglers laden with casks of contraband brandy were mostly gone, and when the Admiralty transformed the Coastguard service into a reserve for the Royal Navy in 1831, the protection of the Revenue became a minor part of its duties. By 1862, the Chairman of the Board of Customs could report to Parliament that his Board no longer had any control over the service[79]. The duties of the Coastguard now included helping vessels in danger, taking charge of wrecks, and active involvement with the lifeboat service. In Ireland the coast-guards also found themselves helping to put down rebellion and searching out illicit stills in country areas. The service had once been seen as a comfortable backwater for surplus Naval officers. Now it became an important reservoir of manpower, and Naval ships were placed at central points to act as support and provide training in seamanship for a service that had hitherto been entirely land-bound. Coastguard officers and men, known as 'Fleetmen', formed a sporadic part of the complement of their guardships for training purposes. George Goschen, formerly First Lord of the Admiralty, commented on this in his speech in the House of Commons on 28 February 1876:

'The ships … on board which the Coastguard were embarked for sea were iron-clads, and there were various reasons why that class of ship was employed in that service. Those iron-clads were stationed round the coast as administrative centres, and, being stationary for a great part of the year, they had small crews, because it was deemed undesirable to lock up in stationary ships a larger number of men than was absolutely necessary … The ships, besides being administrative centres, took crews of Coastguard men to sea for a month or five weeks, and lastly, while they constituted a very powerful Reserve of iron-clads, available at a moment's notice for going into action, if required, by simply increasing their crews'.[80]

For this task *Vanguard* was commissioned at Devonport on 6 July 1871 for service at Kingstown, south-east of Dublin.

Devonport was the quintessential dockyard town, the first to be developed for that purpose. In December 1690, when the third *Vanguard* was doing her duty in the Channel, negotiations were concluded with the owners of two substantial plots of land on the east bank of the Hamoaze (the name given to the estuary of the river Tamar, dividing Devon from Cornwall). Mr Doidge and Sir Nicholas Morice were prepared to lease, but not sell, a stretch of land that 'was covered with brake and abounded in partridges; no roads or thoroughfares intersected it; and the approaches were merely beaten tracks'[81]; but it was a safe anchorage, well protected from adverse weather or foreign intruders, and thus very suitable for a dockyard. Within a year Plymouth Yard was in production, though it was nearly a decade before Morice and Doidge would allow any houses to be built on their land. Plymouth itself had been a favoured spot for Naval activity for a long time, but now the Yard added a further dimension. In 1695 the Navy Board, asked about the production of 60- to 90-gun ships, reported that 'in His Majesty's Yard at Hamoaze is one dock and in Cattewater one slip, fit for such purposes. From whence it may be gathered that Plymouth is qualified for building four such ships at a time'[82]. Within a century 'Dock', as it was known, had become the largest town in Devon, 'a roaring town of sailors and ships'[83], with a population of 30,000 in 1810, greater than its parent, Plymouth.

The end of the Napoleonic wars however brought recession to Dock. 'Thousands', according to Henry Whitfield, 'were plunged in unutterable misery'[84]. The local authorities managed to pull the community back together, a smart new Town Hall was built, and they summoned up the confidence to petition the King for a new civic name, to show their independence from Plymouth. In 1823 came the news they had been waiting for:

'I am commanded to acquaint you that his Majesty has been graciously pleased to comply with the prayer of the said petition, and to direct that, on and after the 1st day of January next, the town of Plymouth-Dock shall be called and known by the name of DEVONPORT, and a communication has been made to the several Public Departments accordingly.
I am, Gentlemen,
Your most obedient humble Servant,
ROBERT PEEL'[85]

As one versifier put it,

'... 'Tis very strange ...
Why Dock has got another name.
And Devonport, 'tis christened now,
'Tis queer enough, but you'll allow,
'Twixt you and I, and the Dockyard Bell,
I think that Dock sounds quite as well;
But Plymouth's in a mighty bother
To find her whelp desert her mother.'[86]

The gracious gift of a new name from George IV, it seems, gave the town 'a spirit of importance and conscious dignity'. The dockyard itself was not officially called 'Devonport' until after the visit of Queen Victoria and her consort in 1843, but took on the challenge of the new technology of steam and iron with enthusiasm. The basins were not big enough for some of the new designs, and 1844 saw the building of a new steam yard at Keyham, half a mile upstream. In the 1850's the yards were kept busy converting sailing warships to steam, by a method familiar to today's back-street motor trade: 'cutting asunder'. This involved cutting the ship in half and inserting a new centre section. Gradually other yards began to get more orders, and towards the end of the 1860's, Devonport was reduced to repair work and no longer regarded as a first class shipbuilding yard. Many employees were laid off. The Admiralty tried to ease their problems by offering free passage to Canada – but no more than that; they would have to pay for their food and lodging on the voyage, and were left to their own devices once they arrived. Nevertheless this was the home of the fleet, and a town greatly dependent on the Navy.

The rapid growth and fluctuating fortunes of Devonport carried a cost. Every port is full of taverns and a variety of other shore distractions for men who spend long months at sea, but Devonport appears to have undergone some very rough times. At the beginning of the nineteenth century road communications hardly existed, overcrowding was endemic and sanitation worse than primitive. The leat that provided the town's water was already laden with sewage from Dartmoor Prison before it reached the town. Smallpox struck in 1827 and 1872, and cholera in 1831 and 1850, when 900 people died. Around Quarry Lane, families slept, ate, cooked and washed their clothes all within the same small space. The Local Government Board Inspector reported that the 'foetid and sickening smell arising from these abodes of wretchedness baffles all description', that Morice Town was 'the haunt of every vice and misery of which human nature is capable'; every third house was an inn; and children swarmed the lanes in 'absolutely heathen ignorance'[87]. It was in this mixture of civic pride and urban squalor that many of the future *Vanguard* crew and their families lived. Leading Seaman Henry Gaden, my wife's great-grandfather, told the Census enumerator in 1881 that his first two children had been born in Morice Town in the early 1870's.

The station to which *Vanguard* was posted, the Irish port of Kingstown, had many similarities to Devonport. It too had grown up around the Navy and shipping, it too had changed its name by favour of George IV in the early 1820's. In other ways it was very different, and perhaps a more pleasant place to spend a few quiet years. For some time the people of Dublin had felt the need of a better harbour in Dublin Bay than that under the looming bulk of Howth. The approaches to the mouth of the Liffey were hazardous, and many vessels ran aground on sandbanks while waiting, sometimes for days, to enter the river mouth. The clincher came in 1807 when 380 people lost their lives in a November gale. The packet boat *Prince of Wales* and *Rochdale*, a heavily loaded transport, were driven ashore at Seapoint and Blackrock on the south coast of the bay. As a result the decision was taken to build an asylum harbour at the small fishing village of Dunleary. The foundation stone was laid in 1817 by Whitworth, the Lord Lieutenant, and work began immediately on the East Pier, which would eventually be a mile long; the even longer West Pier followed soon after. The pier heads and their lighthouses were finished in the 1840's, and it was not until 1860 that the harbour was declared finished. Meanwhile the fishing village of 70 cottages had mushroomed, 'It is one of the few towns in Ireland to have started from nothing and reached maturity all within seventy-five years of the nineteenth century'[88]. The population had risen to 10,500 by 1851. The King's visit in 1821, and the change of name to Kingstown by royal decree, set the tone for the development, and the start of the Kingstown-Liverpool Mail Packet service in 1826 established it as the principal mail and passenger link with England. On top of this, Kingstown acquired a railway link with Dublin in 1834, making it a desirable place to live.

To begin with living conditions for the men who worked on the harbour construction were dreadful. 'In 1823 there were 1,000 workers, some with their families, living in huts on Dalkey Commons without sanitary facilities or running water ... Outbreaks of typhus and cholera as well as injuries were commonplace, and in the early days of harbour construction no medical treatment was available'[89]. Rapid growth created overcrowding in the town in the 1840's, as it did in Devonport. Charles Halliday, a local humanitarian, 'described Kingstown's tenements which housed large families in one or two-room hovels without toilets, light, or air ... he also deplored the fact that the railway had cut off free access to the sea for bathing for ordinary people, while the rich such as Lord Cloncurry insisted that the railway company build bridges and private baths for their use'[90]. But Kingstown was smaller than Devonport, and the mention of the privileged rich signals a great difference between the two seaports. Unlike industrial Devonport, Kingstown was to become a popular watering-place, with luxury hotels, great houses, yacht clubs, and coffee-houses for those with the time and money to enjoy them. 'In 1830 Kingstown was considered the most expensive place in Ireland for food and lodging'[91]. Samuel Lewis's *Topographical Dictionary of Ireland*, published in 1837, says that Kingstown 'has become an extensive and flourishing place of fashionable resort, and the immediate neighbourhood is thickly studded with elegant villas and handsome residences of the wealthy citizens of Dublin. ... The town consists of one spacious street, about half a mile in length, and of several smaller streets and avenues branching from it in various directions; there are also several ranges of handsome buildings, inhabited chiefly by the opulent citizens of Dublin ... From the purity of the air, the beauty of its situation, and convenience for sea bathing, this place has become a favourite summer residence, and is greatly resorted to by visitors ... Kingstown is the head of a coastguard district, comprising the stations of Dalkey, Bray, Greystones, Five-mile Point, and Wicklow Head, and including a force of five officers and thirty-eight men.'[92] The coastguard district later expanded to cover the whole of the east coast of Ireland.

By the time of *Vanguard*'s arrival in 1871, the town had become even more sophisticated, and so it remains today, a delightful place for a day trip from Dublin, with what the guidebooks describe as a 'continental feel', and many of the proud Victorian terraces intact, though the centre of town has been spoiled by a dull shopping mall. The name has changed, reverting to the properly Irish Dún Laoghaire at independence in

1921, but the spirit of the place has not. For the old salt like Leading Seaman Henry Gaden, hardened by years in the Indian Ocean and the Caribbean, it must have seemed a well-deserved rest cure, while for my wife's other great-grandfather, Ordinary Seaman Francis Norton, younger and with much less service, it could have been hugely frustrating to sit in the harbour for weeks on end, however beautiful it might be. The ship's log for these early years of service appears to be missing, but probably made dull reading. The Navy lived by its traditions, of course, and the daily routines of scrubbing and polishing and training filled in much time, but the attractions available on shore must at times have been overwhelming. It is significant that the local citizens found it necessary to establish a 'Sailors' Reading Room' on the Victoria Wharf. Its schedule of rules and regulations says that 'The object of this Institution, which has been erected by voluntary subscriptions, is to provide for Seamen who put into Kingstown Harbour, including those of Her Majesty's Ships, Pilots, and Crews of Yachts – a well-appointed Reading Room during their visits on shore … all swearing and improper language, so unbecoming the character of a man, and so dishonouring to God, must be entirely avoided … Drunkenness, that disgraceful vice which sinks a man below the level of the very beasts that perish, and which is so contrary to order and decency, the men must judge of themselves, cannot be permitted an entrance here'[93]. Boredom was always a potential problem at sea, and greatly exacerbated in a warship with no decent war to attend.

The *Vanguard*'s log for the period from April 1875 does exist, kept conscientiously by Captain Richard Dawkins, but lacking the emotional power of his personal journals. Between April and June of that year she lay at Keyham, having some work done. Regularly Dawkins found himself disciplining his crew: 'Read warrants sentencing W Danby & J Club Pts RMLI to 10 days Cells … Read warrants sentencing Jno Barny AB to 40 days imprisonment in Bodmin gaol … Read sentence of Court Martial on T Coles RMLI to ship's company'[94]. As time went by it looks as if the pressures built up. On 8 June as many as nine sailors and marines were given various punishments 'for conduct'. This was a bad example for the 'Boys', 11 of whom had joined the ship from HMS *Royal Adelaide* in May, and who were put to seamanship, cutlass drill, and schooling under the Schoolmaster. At last on 21 June *Vanguard* set out for Kingstown, arriving on the evening of Wednesday 23. Now Dawkins could allow himself the pleasure of awarding Long Service and Good Conduct Medals to 'the undermentioned men & non commissioned officers in the presence of the ship's cop'y: Wm Mugford WR Std, Jas Stacey Cap Cox, P Duggan, Jas Webber, [and] Rd George Ldg Stokers, Alex Richard Caulk, Josh Bearden Corporal RMA, Wm Dineford RMLI'. These names, or variants of them, appear in the Ledger for September, and the men would have been aboard for the final voyage. Webber and George were to give evidence at the Court Martial two months later. In these years many of the ship's company will have established their families in the Kingstown area, and several Irish surnames appear in the muster list. Devon had acquired close ties with the Dublin area, and men from Devon established the first Wesleyan Meeting House in Kingstown.

Captain Dawkins, who took command of *Vanguard* in October 1873, seems to have tolerated this period of relative inactivity with his customary acceptance of whatever the Navy required of him. Anything would have been better than the years without any command; he had been idle on half pay for 2½ years. His private journals for this period have not survived, and he may indeed have stopped keeping them, since the half-pay years had seen him getting married, finding a house in South Devon, and delighting in the birth of his first son. He wrote often (perhaps daily) to his wife from Kingstown, and sent affectionate notes to little Richard:

> '4 July Kingstown
> My own darling Richard
> I send you a pretty little Tortoise it looks alive and came all the way from China
> … pick a wild flower for Mummy … but don't send her any Snails or Worms
> you can give those to the Rooks in the front field.'[95]

His officers liked and respected him, as later correspondence shows, and he clearly made an impression on the local people. Among the letters of sympathy he received after the loss of his ship was one from Philip Parker of Youghal, who wrote 'I was told by the Chief Boatman here that he knew you were better liked than either of the last three District Captains'[96]. But this gentle interlude was to come to an end harshly and suddenly, very soon.

It was time for the summer cruise. Lieutenant William Hathorn had joined *Vanguard* at Kingstown on 17 July, in readiness for this exercise. Ten days later he wrote to his parents

> 'We cast anchor here last evening - the Admiral arrived at same time & hoisted his Flag aboard "Warrior" – the Squadron at present comprised of the Flag Ship, "Vanguard", "Penelope", "Hector", and "Favorite" – the "Achilles" & "Iron Duke" & "Defence" are expected to day – the Gun Vessel "Goshawk" will act as tender to the Fleet. Leave has been granted until 8 am tomorrow. We had a very pleasant passage round from Kingstown – the Ship was as steady as a Church – and the <u>Captain</u> who says that "<u>She</u> is not going to catch him with his breeches down" – took good care to make everything <u>particularly</u> snug for the night. Originally the "Vanguard" was rigged with a First Class Frigate's Sail the same as the ill-fated "Captain" – but since that dreadful catastrophy *[sic]* her topmasts have been reduced by nine feet – the Courses have been greatly reduced – she has been transformed into a Barque and her double bottom has been filled with <u>360 tons</u> of <u>concrete ballast</u>. She is a capital steamer & can turn in her own length with the double screws – but with any sail on she is immediately rendered most unwieldy.'[97]

Black and unprepossessing and solid she may have been, but *Vanguard* inspired enthusiasm in those who sailed with her. Hathorn was looking forward to seeing something of Ireland (as soon as the weather improved), but all too soon the excitement was to be overtaken by disaster.

Chapter 5

'There were many a brave fellow'

The Officers and men of the First Reserve Squadron

Richard Dawkins of *Vanguard*, to whom we shall return in the next chapter, was a fair example of the sort of person who served as an officer in the Navy of his day: solid middle-class, with some good social connections, devoted to his Queen and country and the values they represented, conscientious in his faith observance, steeped in the custom and traditions of the service he joined when he had barely entered his teens. At 47 in September 1875 he was one of the older characters in our story, but the right age for that point in his career. Captain Henry Hickley of *Iron Duke* was 48, and William Whyte, Flag-Captain of *Warrior*, was 46. Their superior officer, Vice Admiral Sir John Walter Tarleton, was 63. In the earlier years of the century the average age of those of Admiral rank was 76, and promotion had been into dead men's shoes. The Admiralty did make some efforts to clear the promotion log-jam, but having reached such exalted position one could stay for as long as one's influence lasted.

Aboard *Warrior*

Walter Tarleton was born at Cloverley Hall, Whitchurch, Shropshire in 1811, the second son of Thomas Tarleton of Bolesworth in Cheshire. He joined the Navy at the age of 12 years 4 months. He served in the Caribbean, distinguished himself in the Burma war in the 1850's, and became a Captain in 1852. In the 1860's he spent some time as controller general of the Coast Guard, and at the same time was an ADC to the Queen, becoming Rear Admiral in 1868. He then spent three years as a naval Lord of the Admiralty, was knighted in 1873, and took over as Admiral Superintendent of Naval Reserves in 1874. During the First Reserve Squadron's cruise around Ireland in August 1875, having chosen *Warrior* as his flagship, he was promoted to Vice Admiral. He retired 'by age' on his sixty-fifth birthday in 1876, was automatically promoted to Admiral in 1879, and died in 1880. His was a full and exciting service, and his record is full of commendations. Among them are 'gallantry in storming a stockade' and 'vigour, perseverance, skill and judgement' in Burma when he was 40, 'thanks from the Governor of the Cape' when he was nearing 50, and 'satisfaction expressed at zeal and ability shewn on Committee for revising new regulations' in his early 60's. He was a man of many parts, ready to turn his hand to vigorous action or detailed administration as the occasion demanded, and in the record of evidence at the Court Martial he comes over as straightforward, full of experience and used to command, with sound common sense. It came naturally to him to leave it to his Captains to make their own decisions when the squadron ran into thick fog, while his compeers who made up the Court were hidebound by the Regulations, the need for proper signals and an unvarying chain of command. His letters to Dawkins, preserved in the archives at the National Maritime Museum in Greenwich and in the possession of his great-grandson Captain Tarleton Fagan, show him to be a pleasant and compassionate superior. As soon as the court martial verdict was announced he wrote to Dawkins to convey his obviously genuine sympathy, and his private correspondence with his superiors reveals that he was ready to resign to take the pressure off his Captains. Sir Walter Tarleton was the best kind of senior Naval officer.

Tarleton's Flag-Captain on *Warrior*, William Whyte, had a routine career pattern, becoming a Captain at the age of 42, and taking command of *Warrior* four years later in April 1875. He rose eventually to the rank of Admiral in July 1892 and retired at his own request the following month at the age of 63 and with a pension of £850 a year. He died just before Christmas 1912. Whyte makes little mark on our story. His evidence at the Court Martial is brief and to the point. Of his officers, the only one to make a substantial contribution to events was Lieutenant Edward Stratford Dugdale, just 30 years old. He had begun his service at 14 on the training ship *Britannia*, and had a decent amount of service behind him, but did not reach the rank of Commander until he was 35, the rank he still held when he retired early aged 48 in 1893. He does not appear to have suffered many gaps in his postings, and thus was not held back by the lack of opportunity, so it may be that he was among the less able Lieutenants, though his performance before the Court Martial does not support this. He was responsible for signals aboard *Warrior*, and was certainly alert to everything that was happening. He reported to Tarleton as soon as he heard what sounded like signal guns being fired, and the moment he noticed that *Vanguard* and *Iron Duke* were off station. He knew his signal books, both old and new, intimately, and understood the limitations of communicating with flags, guns and the steam whistle in fog. His evidence is a model of clarity and openness; he knew his job and did it as best he could, without interfering with others. It may therefore be that Dugdale's lack of promotion, and the early end to his naval career, were due to health problems. He lived on into his sixties, and died (according to the death certificate[98]) of '(a) syncope (b) asthma (c) carcinoma of pylorus'. Stomach cancer probably developed in later years, and 'syncope' is the medical term for fainting, but asthma could well have hampered his promotion prospects.

One other person serving aboard *Warrior* was Steward Charles Burridge, who was the same age as Dugdale. Burridge's great-granddaughter Linda Johnson tells me that he was an Exeter man, who married a girl from Gosport just before joining *Warrior* in

July 1875. His first daughter was born in Gosport in 1877, and then the family went to Japan, where he was stationed for several years. He died at Haslar Hospital in 1893[99].

Aboard *Iron Duke*

Those aboard *Iron Duke* were of similar stock. Captain Henry Dennis Hickley's career runs almost in parallel with that of Richard Dawkins. Admiral Ballard describes Hickley as 'a close friend of Dawkins'[100] , but there is little evidence of any great friendship. They were both born in Portsmouth, Dawkins baptised at St Paul's Chapel Portsea in 1828, Hickley at Portsmouth St Thomas in 1827. Dawkins' father described himself as 'Gentleman' and Hickley's as 'Merchant'. Hickley joined almost a year ahead of Dawkins, and the only time they served together on the same ship was during the month of December 1846. Any friendship, other than the general camaraderie among brother officers, must have been forged then. Henry Hickley served on a variety of vessels and was promoted at almost the same times as Richard Dawkins. He had also had a few months commanding *Audacious*, the sister ship of *Vanguard* and *Iron Duke*, before taking command of the latter in July 1875 in time for the summer cruise. A significant difference between his experience and that of Dawkins appears in his obituary: he 'had seen no war service'[101], whereas Dawkins, by 1875, had been involved in various conflicts, and wounded in the process.

Henry Hickley came from a huge and many-branched family, with significant naval connections. His brother Victor Grant Hickley (1823-1888) was an Admiral, as was Victor's son Cecil Spencer Hickley (1865-1941). Henry's son John Dennis Hickley DSO died at sea off South Africa; another son, Captain Spencer Allen Hickley RN, died in action in 1914. For information about the proliferation of Hickleys I am indebted to Admiral Victor Grant Hickley's great-grandson, Guy Hickley, and to Elizabeth Edwards, who is not related to the Hampshire family (there are other Hickley families in Leicestershire and London), but has an encyclopaedic knowledge of their genealogy. Henry Hickley's parents were John Allen Hickley of Portsmouth and Elizabeth Anne, née Victor. John Allen had three sisters and a brother, but only two siblings, Mary and Elizabeth, survived childhood. They were all the children of John Hickley and Ann Allen, who were married in Portsmouth St Thomas in 1771. In Elizabeth Edwards' words, 'On socio-economic terms the John Hickley/Ann Allen family is the "crème de la crème" of Hickley society. The way they use and constantly reiterate the "family names" – North, Grant, Allen, etc., is fascinating and the professional background is a socio-economic cameo of the period.'[102] The mid-century Hickleys were Victorian in their production of as many children as possible, but showed their social status in the high proportion of offspring who survived infancy. In poorer Victorian families as many as half of children born failed to reach their fifth birthday, while in the upper-class environment the infant mortality rate was less than 150 per 1,000 live births (in Britain in the year 2000 the comparable rate was 5.6 per

1,000). Hickleys survived. John Allen Hickley's wife Elizabeth produced nine children, who between them were responsible for at least 36 grandchildren, and so onwards. Today there are Hickleys in South Africa and New Zealand, and probably in many other parts of the world, who have some connection with Henry Dennis. The family had all the right connections: Henry's older brothers Victor Grant and Thomas Allen married sisters called North, descendants of the politician Frederick North. Another brother, John George, became ordained in the Church of England and 'had close connections to the Russian royal family. During the revolution they gave sanctuary to the Tsar's family and it seems odd seeing photos of my family at home with their "guests" in Somerset'[103]. Admiral Victor Grant Hickley's wife (apparently known to the family as 'The Black Aunt' – possibly because she wore widow's weeds for some years) had twelve children, of whom the youngest, Alfred Dennis and Thomas Guy, were twins. Guy told me that 'my grandfather (Thomas Guy) ran away to sea from public school at the age of thirteen leaving his identical twin brother to cover for them both, I gather it was not for some years until the true culprit was discovered!'

Among this crowd of characters Guy Hickley has commented that Henry Dennis 'seems to have been a fairly quiet character whereas some other members of the family have been so colourful they could each warrant a book of their own (and some have)'[104]. Of the two Captains, Dawkins is the more driven personality, with a strong sense of duty and of justice, sometimes obviously fighting to control his emotions and do the right thing. Hickley seems more relaxed, to the extent that the 1881 census enumerator listed him as 'Harry D Hickley', while Dawkins does not appear to have allowed himself to be called anything other than 'Richard'. Despite not being given the opportunity to demonstrate his aptitude in battle, Hickley showed up well in other ways. In 1856, aboard HMS *Argus*, his Commander gave him 'high praise for his zealous and humane conduct during the prevalence of the yellow fever, and his general zeal and ability' [105], and a couple of years later Captain Cracroft of *Diadem* wrote 'reporting a very creditable act of presence of mind and promptitude'. In 1862 he gained more praise for 'seizing an American Confederate vessel'. Not everything went smoothly, however. As Captain of *Tamar* in 1869, navigating the Gulf of St Lawrence on the Canadian coast, he managed to run his ship aground on the Isle of Anticosti, and a Court of Enquiry recorded an official Censure. Ten years earlier, in July 1859, rejoicing in his new status as Commander on HMS *Gladiator*, he married Mary Jane Rundle at Alverstoke, on the edge of Gosport, across the water from his home town of Portsmouth. She was 18, he was 15 years older, and by 1875 seven of his eight children had entered the world, their places of baptism – Alverstoke, Devonport, Hull – showing that the family followed him from posting to posting. The last in this list, Hull, was where *Iron Duke* was stationed as guardship before the 1875 cruise.

Not many of those serving under Captain Hickley on *Iron Duke* play much part in the events of 1 September 1875. Among those who do were four Lieutenants. First, Lieutenant Pierre Gervais Evans, who on that day was just a fortnight short of his twenty sixth birthday. Despite his name, Evans was of Irish stock, belonging to the family that held Carker House, Doneraile, County Cork, the son of a Vice Admiral and JP, Nicholas Evans. Evans descendants still live in Carker House. Like his contemporaries he had joined the Navy at the age of 13, achieved a First Class certificate at HMS *Britannia*, and reached the rank of Lieutenant in 1873. While serving on *Audacious*, he seems to have caught the eye of Captain Henry Hickley, and as described elsewhere followed Hickley to various other ships, ending up on *Iron Duke* in July 1875. He was to be more deeply affected by what was about to happen than anyone, save Captain Richard Dawkins. I have made contact with one relative, and that a distant one: Mrs June Cangey (née Evans), who is descended from Pierre Evans' uncle. Evans does not seem to have left any evidence of his presence in the family.

Navigating Lieutenant Heaver Sugden was a great deal more experienced. Born in Gillingham, Kent, in 1836, he might seem old at 39 to be still a Lieutenant, but his career path had been different from that of his young colleagues. From the beginning he had studied navigation, passing his preliminary examination in 1861, and becoming in due course a Master. The Master, otherwise the sailing-master or pilot, knew more than anyone about the handling of his ship, and was so indispensable that few achieved commissioned rank and rose any higher in the service. Sugden had been a Master or Navigating Lieutenant for some ten years by 1875.

Then there are two young supernumerary officers: the mysterious Van Koughnet and the ebullient Stephen Thompson. Lieutenant Edmund Barker Van Koughnet, 26, 'entered abroad' according to his service record[106], and had been without a ship for eighteen months when he joined *Iron Duke* on temporary attachment in July 1875, in his first appointment as Lieutenant. His presence aboard might have gone unrecorded had he not turned up in a boat alongside *Vanguard* at a critical moment. Where he came from I have not been able to trace, but that he was a man of some talent is witnessed by his later appointment as Aide de Camp and Private Secretary to the redoubtable Lord John Hay, whom we shall meet as President of the Court Martial, while Hay was administrator of Cyprus in 1878. He eventually retired with the rank of Captain and married the Hon Lady Jane Charlotte Elizabeth Alexander, daughter of the 3rd Earl of Caledon. He clearly married well. Jane's likeness is in the National Portrait Gallery, and the family lived in a magnificent house in Hertfordshire, Tyttenhanger Park, on an estate with records going back to the twelfth century. The house still stands. Van Koughnet died in 1905 after nine years of retirement, leaving his wife £7,992.0s.6d gross.

Stephen Henry Thompson was the same age as Evans and Van Koughnet, a Yorkshire lad from 'Biltro' (presumably Bilton), who had emerged from *Britannia* with only a third class certificate, and became Lieutenant in 1873. When the accident occurred it was Thompson who took it upon himself to leave *Iron Duke* without permission and do what he could aboard *Vanguard*, conduct which is of a piece with his later exploits, for which he received many commendations. Stephen Thompson was a man of action and invaluable in a crisis: his evidence to the Court Martial reads like a Hornblower novel.

Among the Engineers who later gave evidence at the Court Martial was James Chater, a 34-year-old who had joined the Navy from private trade in 1863. Of all the engineer officers he was the most successful, retiring in 1895 with the exalted rank of Fleet Engineer (having unsuccessfully applied to be kept on beyond the age of 55). Chater died of pneumonia in 1922.

The Marine contingent included Lieutenant Ringrose Drew Tully RMLI, whose present-day relatives Kaye Tully Steele and John Deering live in the USA and Ireland respectively. Ringrose Tully was 38, the son of John Tully of Killaloe, a retired RN Lieutenant. It appears he was aboard *Iron Duke* just for the ride, since he was not formally accredited to her company. He was at the time on the strength of HMS *Endymion* and had been doing Coastguard service at Queenstown, where the Squadron was heading. Three years later Tully was to be retired 'unfit', and he died at Dublin in February 1880.

Among the crew of *Iron Duke* was Stoker 2nd Class Charles Boynes, born at Ashburton in Devon in 1853. His great-grandson Mike Boynes tells me that Charles lied about his age; the Navy record has him two years older when he joined in 1866. He had been a Cook's Mate before he joined the stokers on *Iron Duke,* moving almost literally from the frying-pan into the fire, and he worked his way through the various levels of Stoker throughout his 25 years of service. His father had been a seaman, and his great-grandson has carried on that tradition. Mike writes 'My Great-Grandfather Charles was a great old chap who died in 1934 in his eighties. His wife Eleanor *[née Gimblett – they married in 1880]* outlived him and was killed in April 1941 in the Portland Square bomb shelter during the Blitz on Plymouth. All the family photographs and mementoes of a lifetime at sea were lost that night as well. My father had the enclosed photograph which is why it survived … This event *[the loss of Vanguard]* … changed Charles' life & thereby ours'[107].

Aboard *Vanguard*

Captain Dawkins' Commander, who had taken up the rank on being posted to *Vanguard* in the same month as Dawkins in 1873, was Dashwood Goldie Tandy, aged 35. Tandy was a member of a distinguished Irish family, and less than a year before the incident had married into another such. His bride was Anna Louisa Margaret, only daughter of the late Thomas De Burgh of Oldtown, Nass, County Kildare. Thus while Dawkins, Evans and Van Koughnet all acquired splendid country houses, Tandy found himself welcome in two such: Oldtown was one of Ireland's first Palladian winged houses, built in 1709 by Thomas Burgh MP, Engineer and Surveyor-General for Ireland, to his own design. Tandy himself settled in another fine eighteenth century house, Johnsbrook, Kells, County Meath. His naval career showed steady progress, with a strong recommendation from the Hydrographer for surveying work that he did in the Straits of Magellan in 1869. In the documents about *Vanguard* Tandy's personality does not stand out, but one is conscious of his dependable presence throughout. In Dawkins' words to the Court Martial: 'I would especially desire to bring under the notice of the Court the good services rendered to me by Commander Tandy on this trying occasion, on which he proved himself to be an officer of very high qualifications, exhibiting as he did the greatest coolness in carrying out my orders, which tended considerably towards the good order and discipline and order which I trust will be found to have existed on board, and which he has at all times been most instrumental in maintaining.'[108] Tandy was the best kind of second in command, unobtrusive but efficient.

There was another Commander on board, Gordon Charles Young of HMS *Achilles*. His ship had left the First Reserve Squadron's cruise to return to Liverpool, but Young had been given the job of escorting one of *Achilles'* marines, George Rayner, to Queenstown where Young would conduct a court martial. Rayner, a Private in the 9th Company, Chatham Divison of the RMLI, was accused of 'using threatening language to his Superior Officer and striking his Superior Officer'[109]. With them travelled Lieutenant Alexander Allen of *Achilles* to act as witness. Those who dislike loose ends will want to know that Rayner's court martial eventually took place on HMS *Royal Adelaide* at Plymouth on 25 September 1875. He was found guilty, and sentenced to 12 months' imprisonment with hard labour in Bodmin Gaol, and to be dismissed the service.

Young's presence was to prove helpful in the emergency, but for him it must have been a delicate situation, since as a passenger he had no authority. He was 29, had done his time on *Britannia* from age 13, and had experience on a variety of ships, unusually with hardly any periods of waiting between postings. After he left *Achilles* at the end of 1876, however, he began to endure the same spells of inactivity as his colleagues. He was posted to the Coast Guard in 1881, but from the summer of 1888 until his voluntary retirement (with the rank of Captain) in 1893, he was on 'half pay'. He died in 1912.

For the 1875 cruise *Vanguard* had three Lieutenants: Edward Noble, Edmund Speck and William Hathorn, all in their mid-20's, all having gone through the prescribed training on *Britannia* (Speck and Hathorn, with Evans and Thompson of *Iron Duke,* were all together on *Britannia* in 1863). Edward Rothwell Wheelock Noble was the Senior Lieutenant, with special responsibility for the operation of the pumps. He and Hathorn had known each other for some time, since Hathorn often referred to him in letters home, though they had not served together. Early in 1865 Hathorn wrote 'HMS *Sutlej* is here *[in Valparaiso Bay]* and I saw Noble who looked just the same as he was in England.'[110] Their paths crossed on a number of subsequent occasions. Noble had obtained a First Class Certificate on *Britannia,* but when he went for training on *Excellent* in 1874 was less successful: 'Having failed to obtain 1000 marks for the *[illegible]* Course to be discharged to shore from *Excellent* from the date of commencement of vacation at College, & his time during his stay at the College will in no respect count as sea service.'[111] A promising career looked as if it was beginning to fall apart, and later events revealed how bad things became for him.

Edmund William Speck was 27, a Londoner, and had entered *Britannia* a year later than Noble, gaining a Third Class certificate. He too was 'rejected' on the gunnery course on *Excellent* in 1872, and his subsequent career also showed signs of being blighted by what happened in 1875.

We are fortunate to know a great deal more about Lieutenant William Crichton Stuart Hathorn, since his family kept his correspondence, and in 1996 his sister's granddaughter, Lady Margaret Turton-Hart, passed the papers for safe keeping into the private collection of a naval historian. In some 200 letters and other documents, Hathorn ('Willie' in his earlier letters to his parents, 'Bill' towards the end of his life, and apparently 'Jerry' to his shipmates – though he most often signed himself as 'WCSH') reveals himself as a vigorous and opinionated correspondent, producing some wonderful descriptions of life on board. The letters are a marvellous record of what it meant to be a cadet officer in the late nineteenth century, and deserve a much fuller treatment than I can give here. What follows is necessary superficial. William, born in Bloomsbury, London in 1849, was the youngest of the three Lieutenants, and the most fortunate. The second son of Admiral George Hathorn, he was just a year behind Speck in entering the Navy, and two years behind his friend Noble. Within a year of signing on, at the age of 13, he was off aboard HMS *Clio,* and had printed a ballad (whether of his own composition or not is uncertain) called *William C S Hathorn's Farewell To The Family Fleet, On Sailing From England In HMS Clio, 1864.* The verses make reference to his parents and his many siblings: he had three brothers (Murray, George and Charles) and six sisters (Flora Elizabeth, Mary Euphemia ['Phemie'], Catherine, Penelope Wilhelmina, Annette Grace, and Gertrude Campbell). To these folk we owe the preservation of a unique collection of letters. *Clio* took him straight to the shores of British Columbia and his first experience of really cold weather; then within three years he had travelled down the west coast of the Americas to Panama, and across the Pacific to Tahiti. The regime did him good: 'I should like to send you my photo as I have yours', he wrote from Panama to his brother George, 'but I think it would be better to send good ones than bad – so I won't have it taken here but wait until I get North - I have grown a good deal – I am now 5 ft 6 in & stout in comparison.'[112] In 1867, before a richly evocative passage on the stench from the guano islands off the Chilean coast, he mentions that their flagship, HMS *Zealous,* was not with them but at Vancouver – at that time *Zealous* was under the Captaincy of Richard Dawkins, carrying the flag of Admiral Hastings. Hathorn did not apparently meet his future Captain.

Hathorn came back to Spithead to get over the next promotion hurdle. This mattered: 'I pass my Examination (provisional) in June & am at present <u>sweating up</u> for the same … When I am a Sub Lieut I will get 5s a day (£90 a year) which will be a great help to me, considering my present little pay.'[113] Only a few months later, having obtained his certificate, he had to tell his parents that he owed £41 for uniform, nearly six months' pay in his new rank. That same year's correspondence reveals his political affiliation – 'I am glad to see the Conservatives still in power'[114] – and the dangers of gun drill – 'Haslar Hospital, Thursd: 19th August 1869. My dear Mamma and Papa – I came to this Hospital on the 9th, having come to grief at Gun Drill, I was struck by the side-tackle when jumping over it to man the fall, after having loaded.' The accident kept him in hospital for a full month. He was just 20 years old. Thereafter he had a lengthy spell chasing slavers in the Indian Ocean on *Columbine*, where he found the climate very much to his liking; he dreaded coming back to the Northern cold. It was on *Columbine* that he first had experience as Officer of the Watch, which proved very useful when *Vanguard* was lost.

His early years did not give rise to any particular comment on the official record, but he made his mark. A correspondent wrote 'Willy seems a great favourite with his ship-mates … he is such a good fellow and the younger ones said he was so good to them.'[115] In the six weeks of his posting to *Vanguard,* his first as a full Lieutenant, he must have learned much, since after 1875 the record contains a number of commendations for his skill, such as 'An excellent boat sailor.'[116]. Captain Dawkins referred to him as 'my able Officer of the Watch'. For William Hathorn what was to happen to *Vanguard* was, like every other stage in his colourful career, a learning experience.

Vanguard's Navigating Lieutenant was James Cambridge Thomas, born in Madras, India, and ten years older than his fellow Lieutenants. His career path was similar to that of Heaver Sugden of *Iron Duke*, and like Sugden he had some twenty years of service in the navigational branch behind him. He also knew more about *Vanguard* than most, having come aboard as early as 1872. He had an Australian wife, Ellen, and a 2-year-old daughter in Kingstown.

The Royal Marine contingent aboard *Vanguard* was headed up by Captain Samuel Travers Collins, Plymouth Division RMLI. An Irishman from Bantry, County Cork, Collins was 37 in 1875, and had twenty years commissioned service behind him. At the age of 19, as a 2nd Lieutenant, he had been in the thick of the Anglo-French assault on Canton, and eighteen months later he was in the attack on the Peiho Forts, during which he was 'severely wounded'[117]. He was awarded a gratuity of six months' pay, but his application for a pension 'for Wound' was not granted. He returned to Woolwich in 1863, then after a spell on HMS *Victoria*, then Flagship Mediterranean, he came back to Woolwich again. When Woolwich Division was abolished in 1869 he transferred to Plymouth Headquarters, where he spent some time in hospital. He came aboard *Vanguard* in May 1875, to take command of 115 Marines, with the help of two Marine Lieutenants: William Miller RMA and William H McCheane RMLI. The men under Collins' command were kept as busy as their Navy counterparts, but the three Marine officers could play no part in the running of the ship. Collins' part in the story, as we shall see, could indicate that he was not at all a well man.

The lower graded officers, all specialists, made varying impacts on the events of September 1875. Those who looked after body and soul are hardly mentioned in contemporary accounts: the Reverend Spencer Musson, Chaplain, and Doctors Constantine Keenan and James Fisher, Staff Surgeons. Musson was 33, and born in Bermuda, the eldest son of the Rev Samuel Paynton Musson of Jamaica. He went to Trinity College, Cambridge in 1862, and before sitting his finals took up a curacy in the nearby village of Stapleford for two years, at the end of which he obtained a First in Theology. Immediately he became a Naval chaplain. Keenan was somewhat older – he had qualified at Edinburgh in 1852. Fisher, like so many Naval doctors, was a graduate of Queen's University, Belfast and qualified in 1867. The ships' accounts were kept by Paymaster Charles T Dawson, as meticulous and objective an administrator as one could wish.

Essential to the safety and effectiveness of *Vanguard,* but never to be regarded as the equal of the fighting officers, was the Chief Engineer, Robert Brown. The classic science fiction series *Star Trek* confirmed once and for all the popular conception that all Chief Engineers came from Scotland, and Brown's name hints as much, but beyond knowing that he was born in March 1831 (and was thus 44 in 1875), I have not been able to determine his birthplace. His service record simply states 'No trace of this officer's service prior to 8 Apr 53 in books of Portsmouth Yard'[118]. His experience on steamships had been hugely varied, and he reached the rank of Chief Engineer 11 years before joining *Vanguard*. That he had a sharp tongue is witnessed by his appearance before a Court Martial in 1872, charged with 'insubordinate language to the Navg Lieutenant'[119]; he was severely reprimanded and sentenced to lose 18 months' seniority – but a year later, for un-stated reasons, his time was restored. Quite possibly the Admiralty had decided his outburst to the Navigating Lieutenant of HMS *Reserve* was justified. Brown as we meet him in the records of the 1875 Court Martial is thoroughly professional, quick to act and a considerable support to his Captain: 'My intelligent and able Chief Engineer' as Dawkins described him in his final statement to the Court[120].

Brown's team of Engineers were men in their 30's, also with good solid experience. Valentine Horne was the oldest at 38, having joined the Navy from private trade in 1859. William George Paige had started his training at the age of 20, and obtained his Passing Certificate eight years later. James Redgrave's dates are almost exactly similar, while William A M Vivyan was a couple of years behind his colleagues.

The last officer to mention is the one most unjustly accused of negligence in the loss of his ship, Carpenter 1st Class David Tiddy. He was among the oldest in Dawkins' crew, having been baptised in the glorious setting of St Just-in-Roseland Church in Cornwall in 1825. He became a Warrant Officer Carpenter in 1856 after seven years as a Seaman and Petty Officer, and was certainly, as Admiral Chamberlain said to him during the Court Martial, 'an old carpenter who must have had considerable experience in the strength of ships and their construction'[121]. Commander Tandy, responding to Captain Dawkins' question 'Is the carpenter, in your opinion, a steady and attentive man?' did not hesitate to answer 'Yes'. Yet he was to be subject to the full weight of high-ranking Naval ineptitude.

According to reports presented to Parliament, the total number of the crew of *Vanguard* on 1 September 1875 was 351, including 27 supernumeraries[122] (171 Coastguard 'fleetmen' had also been aboard during the cruise around Ireland, though at the end of July, because of the coming and going of fleetmen to various stations, there were as many as 288 on board). Their names and ranks are listed in the Annexes. Some will make their appearance as witnesses to the Court Martial, but it is worth writing about others who would have been anonymous were it not for their twenty-first century descendants, who have kindly told me what they know of their stories. These are some of the people whose names appear on the list.

Engine-room artificer John Davies (not to be confused with Signalman John Davis, or Ordinary Seaman John B Davis, who were also aboard) was born in Greenwich in 1844. His father Richard Davies was a steam engine fitter, who had moved from the heart of British engineering, Birmingham, to Greenwich and subsequently moved again to Devonport. John started his career as a blacksmith, and joined the Navy when he married at the age of 27 (one witness to the marriage had the splendid name of Charity Truck – of no relevance to our story, but worth recording nevertheless!). His posting to *Vanguard* followed soon after, in June 1875 when he was 30 years old. When *Vanguard* sank John Davies' wife was pregnant, and W E Davies was born in February 1876. WE became a Chief Petty Officer in the Royal Navy. His daughter Marjorie Penn told me that John unfortunately died aboard *Flying Fish* at Yokohama in 1882, but she has no details of his death.

Leading Seaman Henry James Gaden was born in Topsham, Devon - the family lived in the High Street according to the 1851 Census - on 23 August 1847. His mother Elizabeth registered the birth a month later (he seems to have dropped the 'James' almost immediately; it doesn't appear in any other records). His family name is rare in English records, and I have not been able to trace its origin. The earliest reference to the family is the marriage at Topsham in 1810 of Henry's grandparents, William Gadden (from Henry's generation the second 'd' was dropped) and Anne Harriett Dennis. William's son William Richard Gadden, a mariner, married Elizabeth Westcott, again in Topsham, and produced seven children including a girl with the magnificent Biblical name of Asenath. The oldest child was William James. Henry must have looked up to this eldest brother, who was 12 years older and a seasoned Navy man by the time Henry began to take notice. In any case, Henry followed in his footsteps and signed on as a Boy 2nd Class in HMS *Implacable* on 21st October 1862. The circumstances of his signing-on have been mentioned in Chapter three.

Henry went to sea straight away, aboard HMS *Royalist,* a wooden screw sloop, on her maiden tour of duty in the Caribbean. Their job was essentially police work on behalf of British subjects and British ships affected by the American Civil War, both in respect of the Union Navy's blockade of Confederate ports, and of the remnants of the slave trade. In 1867 Henry transferred to HMS *Daphne*, a similar newly built vessel belonging to the East Indies Squadron, whose task was the control of the slave trade in East Africa. *Daphne*'s log is full of references to chasing the fast and manoeuvrable Arab dhows, removing their cargo of slaves, and setting fire to the boats. *Daphne* eventually came home in March 1870 through the Suez Canal only four months after it had opened to traffic. She dropped anchor at Plymouth at 6.35 pm on 11 May 1870, and Henry Gaden's spell of overseas duty was over. He was 22 years old.

Henry went aboard the gunnery training vessel HMS *Cambridge,* and found time to marry Arabella Sandys of Penryn in Cornwall at St James' Devonport in 1870. Three children were born in Morice Town, a district of Devonport (unfairly transliterated as 'Mouse Town' in the Census record) before Henry went aboard *Vanguard* in February 1875, a seasoned sailor with thirteen years of service behind him.

After the loss of *Vanguard* Henry's first ten-year period of service expired. He signed on for a further ten years, and transferred to the Coastguard service. These were years when the heyday of tea or brandy smuggling was over, and the role of the coastguard was changing. Many seamen opted for what appeared to be the easy life ashore, but by all accounts the life of a coastguardman, living in cramped cottages in isolated situations, exposed to the worst of the British weather, was not so desirable. Henry served in a number of stations on the coast of East and West Sussex, ending up on the Isle of Wight until his retirement at the age of 46 in 1894. During his time at Worthing CG station two further children were born, one of whom, George, became the grandfather of my wife Daphne.

To tell the story of Walter Jewell, Private RMLI, I turn to his granddaughter Shirley Stapley, who wrote:

'Walter was born at West Hatch, Somerset, on 12 June 1849, to Daniel Jewell and his wife Ann (née Vicary). His ancestry has been positively traced back to Edward Jewell, believed to have been born in 1741, and possibly to John Jewell who married in 1602 but the latter cannot be proved for certain. The Jewells all came from Somerset but some of the maternal ancestors originated in Hemyock, on the Devon border, and can be traced back to circa 1600.

'Walter Jewell enlisted in the Marines in November 1869 when he was released from duty in the 1ˢᵗ Somerset Militia. For some reason he gave his age as 18 years instead of 20 years. He was described as being five feet tall with black hair, hazel eyes and a sallow complexion. In September 1870 he was sent to the Plymouth Division of the Royal Marines, and it was soon after this that he met his wife Harriet Cann. They could possibly have met through her father George Cann who was also a Royal Marine at this time. His service records give his character as "very good" or "exemplary" throughout his service except at the beginning when it is "only fair". The reason for this seems to be that he was in jail for one day on 2 May 1871, just a month before his wedding! He obviously never repeated any offences as he was awarded later with several good conduct badges. His career in the Royal Marines spanned 21 years as he had re-engaged in 1877. His service was a mixture of time spent at sea on various ships broken by spells at home in the Royal Marine Barracks at Stonehouse, Plymouth. Towards the end of Walter's service in the Royal Marines, he was in the livery section and after he left the corps in 1890, his occupation was recorded as "Coachman and Domestic Service" in the 1891 Census. Soon after this he set himself up in business as a hansom cab proprietor, but it's a mystery where he obtained enough money to have done this. It is believed that he was in partnership with his older brother William and possibly one other person. By the time his youngest son, Stanley (my father) was born in 1896, the business was thriving and operating from several different areas around the city. The hansom cabs would often meet the big liners docking at Millbay by Plymouth Hoe. Walter is shown in various Plymouth directories as a hansom cab proprietor right up until 1903 but soon after that the business failed. There was a family rumour that one of the partners had run off to Australia and it is also known that Walter drank heavily but there is nothing to substantiate exactly why the once thriving business failed.

'Walter and Harriet had twelve children with Anne Bogdanovic's grandfather being the eldest and my own father 24 years younger! Anne's grandfather (another Walter) was alive by the time of the *Vanguard* collision, but as my father was not born until 21 years later, if there had been a different outcome and no survivors, then I would never have been born. Walter died in 1923 but the tradition of Royal Marines in the family lived on. My own father, Stanley Jewell, joined the Corps in 1911 and served at the battle of Jutland in the first world war. He was given a commission in 1940 and sadly died three years later. However I have been able to trace a long history of Royal Marines in my family back to 1845.'[123]

Able Seaman Philip Lequesne's great-grandson, Philip Lecane, tells me that his ancestor was born in Aughadown, near Skibbereen, County Cork in 1853, the youngest of three children born to Cornelius and Mary (née McCarthy) LeQuesne. Cornelius had been born in Guernsey, Channel Islands, in 1805 (the year of Trafalgar), the son of Philip LeQuesne, a merchant sea captain, and Elizabeth O'Leary, daughter of a County Cork merchant. The family were long established in the Channel Islands, one branch running a shipping company that traded as far away as Brazil.

Following the death of his parents Cornelius was reared by his maternal grandfather in Co Cork. Records for 1828 show him holding land on lease from a local landlord; with 28 acres he was a substantial tenant among others whose holdings were mostly 20 acres or much less. He married Mary in 1850. Their youngest child Philip joined the Royal Navy in Queenstown (Cobh) in 1866, aged 13 years, following his brother Cornelius (junior), who had joined the year before. There appears to have been a strong tradition of RN service in County Cork. There was a saying in those parts that 'Royal Navy ships are all metal on the outside and all Cork on the inside'.

The young Lequesne trained aboard *Implacable* at Dartmouth, then had his first 'proper' posting to HMS *Valiant,* Coastguard guardship at Shannon. Thereafter, like Henry Gaden, he saw service on the North American and West Indies Station, returning to Devonport in 1873. After a few months on CG guardships at Queenstown, in his home area, he joined *Vanguard* the day after his twenty-first birthday in 1874.

Philip's Certificate of Service showed that he bought his way out of the navy in 1876. It notes that he was 'Discharged by purchase from HMS Royal Adelaide *[the flagship at Devonport]* 2nd August 1876. Paid £12-0-0 cash' – which amounted to about a year's wages. Philip's sister Mary was housekeeper to a wealthy man in Cork, whom she ended up marrying. The man died in 1876 (his death certificate would appear to suggest that he was fond of the bottle). Not only did he leave Mary well provided for, but he left her two brothers £250 each. This at a time when Philip's yearly wages were £12 15s 0d. Thus Philip inherited 20 years' wages, which may have been the stimulus for his departure from the Service. He married and bought a public house in Queenstown. His great-grandson adds:

'Like many people who win the lotto, Philip lost his fortune and the pub. He ended up as a fireman. He died in 1916. In 1895 Philip changed the spelling of the surname to "Lecane". As Irish people have problems with "Lecane", God only knows how they would have coped with "LeQuesne"!'[124]

Philip's son Thomas joined the Navy and fought at the battle of Jutland; his grandson, also Philip, served in the Irish Navy during the second World War; and his great-grandson, again Philip, lives near Dún Laoghaire (erstwhile Kingstown) and in 2003 took part in an Irish television documentary about the loss of his great-grandfather's ship.

Ordinary Seaman 2nd Class Francis Norton was born in November 1855, the youngest of this selection from below decks. He came from Liverpool, where his father Matthew was a porter. His mother Ann signed the paper confirming his date of birth, but as we have seen even attested documents need to be approached with caution. How he ended up in the South-West is not known, but he joined the Navy at the advanced age of 15, and had barely four years' experience when he joined *Vanguard* on 1 May 1875 – although much of that experience had been aboard *Achilles*, an ironclad with an enormous spread of sail. Unlike the other seamen so far mentioned, his service record is not uniformly spattered with 'Good' or 'VG' in the 'Conduct' column; he sometimes received only 'Fairly Good' or even 'Fair'. After the *Vanguard* incident there is an enigmatic note in his service record: on 21 December 1875 there is a break in service, annotated 'Run Kingstown', followed by 'Re-enters 7 Jan'. The *Iron Duke*'s Captain recorded in the Log that he gave 'special and privileged leave for 14 days' to most of the crew at that time. Maybe he felt sorry for his crew and the 'extras' he had acquired from *Vanguard*, after what they had been through. Francis lost no seniority on rejoining *Iron Duke*, but it does look as though he may have jumped ship for a while. He was after all only just 20 years old. Thereafter for a number of years he served short postings on a variety of vessels, returning to HMS *Cambridge* for gunnery training in between. During one of these spells, in December 1879, he married Mary Jane Farley, a girl from a North Devon farming family. Early in 1885 he joined HMS *Nelson*, and after 3 years was made up to Petty Officer 2nd Class.

Things presumably went well for another three years, including a couple more spells on *Cambridge*, until he joined the crew of HMS *Rodney* in May 1890. The ship's Log describes uneventful cruising off the coasts of Spain and Portugal and the Western Mediterranean, but at some point Francis managed to mess up his career. His service record for 29 December 1891 shows him reduced to the rank of Leading Seaman, with the note 'Disrated for incompetency'. So he remained for the next four years, spending a few weeks on each of several ships, until he retired at the age of 40 in February 1896. He became a baker in the village of Millbrook, and had died before his daughter Martha's marriage in 1903. What is significant to me about Francis is that although he was eight years younger than Henry Gaden, and came from a different part of the country, he must have struck up an acquaintance with the older man, possibly even while they were thrashing about in *Iron Duke*'s boats. Perhaps as a result, in 1903 Henry's son George married Francis' daughter Martha in the District Church of Millbrook, Cornwall, just across the Tamar estuary from Devonport, and thus both became great-grandfathers to my wife.

Last in our group of ratings is Private Robert Thomas Selley RMLI, whose story is told by Maureen Selley, widow of Robert's great-grandson Brian. Robert was born in July 1848 in the quiet farming community of Silverton, near Exeter in Devon. At the age of 17, Maureen relates, 'Robert Thomas joined the 1st Devon Militia. This force would today resemble the Territorial Army. Recruits were usually assembled for 2-3 weeks' drill in Exeter, followed by an inspection. Men received an annual bounty in addition to enrolment money. During a recruitment drive in the area in 1867, Robert was released from the Militia to join the Royal Marines. During his initial enlistment period of twelve years, he spent two years on HMS *Royal Adelaide*, at that time the Flagship in Devonport, then after five months at RM Barracks, Stonehouse, he joined the Portsmouth based gunnery training ship *Excellent* for three years. On 1st May 1875 he joined *Vanguard*. Soon after the traumatic events of the sinking and the Court Martial, Robert married Pamela Kellond, daughter of a carpenter from Stokenham, at the Register Office in Stoke Damerel (the parish that includes Devonport). Thereafter Robert had a number of postings, including a few years in the Pacific, China and the Far East, but he was home often enough to father three children before his discharge from the Service after 21 years in 1888. He went back to the land as an agricultural labourer, 'living in the countryside of St Budeaux, well away from the highly populated areas of Devonport and Stonehouse, in a district more like the little village of Silverton. Sadly, his retirement was to be short lived. On Wednesday 26 August 1891, in one of the cottages opposite Lower Ernesettle Farm, Robert was taken ill. Mr C Lee, who probably worked with Robert, was with him when he died, and the cause of death was later certified by Dr Doudney as "Cerebral effusion" (what we would now call a stroke). Robert was buried at Higher St Budeaux Church on the following Sunday, close to the church porch. Five months after her husband's death, Pamela married again, to Henry Stone, Private RMLI.'[125]

Chapter 6

A Very Steady and Zealous young Gentleman'

Captain Richard Dawkins RN

Richard Dawkins was born on 17 August 1828, and baptised on 3 October of that year at St Paul's Chapel, Portsea St Mary[126], the son of Richard Dawkins of Hambrook Row, gentleman, and his wife Arabella. Hambrook Row was, according to my informant in Portsmouth City Records Office, a smart part of town, but Richard Dawkins (senior) seems to have left little of himself behind. 'A small book with his name in it and a plain gold tie-pin are the only things of his that I have seen,' wrote his grandson in 1938[127]: 'He died while my father was away at sea on his first voyage.' The tie-pin is now in the possession of a fifth generation. Professor Gianni Lombardi showed it to me in Rome in 2003. Arabella, whom he had married in 1826, was the daughter of the Reverend H G Cobbe, of the same family as Miss Frances Power Cobbe (1822-1904), the Anglo-Irish essayist, travel writer and social reformer, whose radical writings from the 1860's onwards show her to be one of the first prominent advocates of women's suffrage. It was Arabella's second marriage. Her first husband was one Jauncey, by whom she had two sons, Henry and Alexander, both of whom went into the Army and rose no further than the rank of Captain. As part of the extended family they were well known to Richard McGillivray Dawkins, the eldest son of Richard (Junior), whose unpublished draft memoir gives much of the family background. He wrote 'Uncle Alexander only appeared on our horizon after my father's death; there had been some trouble between him and my father over money and they had ceased to communicate.'[128] Arabella herself lived on until 1873.

Richard was, like his father, an only son. It was the custom then for lads who wanted to go to sea to join the Navy as soon as they might. Richard signed on in September 1841, just three weeks after his thirteenth birthday. His first voyage as a Volunteer 1st Class was aboard HMS *Harlequin*. His journals from this period, if any, have not survived. In a note of his career written some thirty years later Dawkins simply recorded 'Entered the Service in 1841. Served in Harlequin brig till paid off in 1845.'[129] According to the obituary published in the *Totnes Times* of 28 March 1896, these three and a quarter years were full of incident. 'His first experience of foreign service was as a volunteer of the first-class in the Harlequin during the operations in the Yangtse-Kiang in 1842; and he also served in the boat attack on pirates at Qualla,

Battoo, and Murdoo in Sumatra, in 1844, receiving the China medal for his services.' He had to learn fast in all areas. His Midshipman's Certificate reads:

'These are to Certify the Lords Commissioners of the Admiralty, that we have examined Mr Richard Dawkins Vol 1 Class, in the course directed by their Lordships Memo of the 14th August 1839, & we find that he has a competent knowledge of Arithmetic, Geometry & Trigonometry; a practical acquaintance with the use of the Quadrant and its adjustments and with the manner of making the required observations and computations for finding the latitude by the Sun, Moon and Stars; of taking and working double altitudes, and keeping a Ship's reckoning by the common rules, usually denominated a day's work & we deem him qualified for the rating of Midshipman.
Given under our hands on board HM Sloop Harlequin at Sea this 14th September 1843
G F Hastings Commander
F Edington Master HM Sloop Harlequin.'[130]

This was a significant time for Dawkins, not merely because it was his first spell at sea, but because it established the relationship between him and the man who was to become Admiral Hastings, and who exercised some influence on his naval career. There is a rather confused suggestion in the autobiographical notes of Richard McGillivray Dawkins that the Hastings family were related to the Dawkins' by marriage, and a hint that George Hastings had been helpful in Dawkins' career. The family relationship is difficult to determine, even though Hastings wrote to Dawkins as 'your affec. Cousin'; it probably lies in the Cobbe connection. Richard Dawkins' mother was the daughter of one Rev. H G Cobbe, and George Hastings' mother was Frances Cobbe (not Frances Power Cobbe), daughter of Charles Cobbe, member of a wealthy land-owning Dublin family. Frances had married Hans Francis Hastings, the 12th Earl of Huntingdon, and George Fowler Hastings was their second son. *The Dictionary of National Biography* maintains that George joined the Navy in 1824 at the age of 9 years and 10 months, which if true would be alarmingly early in life. He had been Commander of *Harlequin* for three months when the young Richard Dawkins came aboard.

In the customary certificate issued when Dawkins left the ship, Hastings wrote that he was 'A vy steady & zealous young Gentleman + can work the whole of the College questions.'[131] The eager young teenager was already showing signs of the conscientious and effective naval officer that he would become, and thanks to his 'affec. Cousin' he had made a good start.

A spell in the West Indies on *Vindictive*, then flagship of Admiral Sir William Austen, completed his cadetship, and he became Acting Mate of *Viper* in September 1847 at the age of nineteen. Very soon, in 1848, he was made up to Acting Lieutenant, and continued to acquit himself well. His time on the North American and West Indies Station ended in October 1857, when he was paid off from *Daring*. The note of his

career referred to above says 'Served under the late Sir Wm Peel in Daring Brig. West
Indies on paying off Capn. Peel by his letter reported to the Admiralty that I was
a Zealous, hard working officer; very attentive in *[illegible]* Watch at sea and always
respectful.'[132] Commander Peel's tribute was significant enough to be noted in his
official record of service[133].

The final months of 1848 were spent at the Royal Naval College in Portsmouth in more
training. A note on his final Certificate reads: 'The following Note is made on the Official
report of the Decr. Examination "Mr Dawkins did not pass in Gunnery until Nov 20th in
consequence of a Wounded Arm, and was therefore unable to pass in Navigation on the
7th of November"'.[134] There is nothing to show where and how he acquired this wound,
but 'The Admiralty were pleased to confirm my Actg Comms if I passed – Obtained 1st
Class firing certificate and my promn was confirmed'.

1849 saw Richard Dawkins joining HMS *Rattler*, a ship with a unique history.
Rattler was a product of the fertile mind of Isambard Kingdom Brunel. Launched
in 1843, she was the world's first screw propeller warship. She was subjected to an
extended series of trials, including the well-known tug-of-war against the paddle
steamer *Alecto,* mentioned in Chapter three. The screw design was modified, and
valuable lessons were learned about hull design and the incompatibility between
screw propulsion and the wooden hull. Andrew Lambert sums up *Rattler's* trium-
phant debut thus: 'Under Brunel's direction, she demonstrated that the screw was an
efficient propeller for auxiliary steamships, introduced the concept into naval service
and provided a fundamental input into the development of efficient (as opposed to
effective) propeller forms.'[135]

By 1849 *Rattler* was fully in service as part of the fleet patrolling the West African
coast in an attempt to suppress the slave trade. At this time Brazil was still very active in
human traffic, but the British ships played a steady and effective policing role. *Rattler*
was capable of pursuing a sailing slaver directly into the wind, which contributed to
the speedier end to the trade. 'Was prize officer on two occasions'[136], wrote Dawkins
in his brief career summary. One of these was on 13 October, when *Rattler* took
the Brazilian brig *Conquestador* off Lagos, with 317 slaves aboard. Among Dawkins'
papers at the National Maritime Museum is a chart, with the legend 'Chart showing the Track of the Brazilian Slave Brig 'Conquistador' from the Bights of Benin to
Sierra Leone Having on board 317 Slaves Prize to Her Majesty's Steam Sloop 'Rattler'
Richd Dawkins Lieut. + Prize Officer.'[137] The voyage took about two months, and
the 21-year old Lieutenant was clearly someone to be trusted with a responsible job.
A paper filed with the chart illustrates the extent of those responsibilities. It reads;

'Morning	½ lb Calavances boiled with Salt and a table spoonful of Palm or Ground Nut Oil
Afternoon	½ lb of Farinha or ¼ lb of Rice with ½ lb Jerked Beef or dried Fish boiled with Salt Water 2 Quarts

The above for a full grown Man ¾ for a Woman ½ for a Child'.[138]

('Calavances', according to *Hobson-Jobson, the Anglo-Indian Dictionary*, was a name given to haricot beans, used in Brazil as a substitute for potatoes.) Thus, presumably, were most of the slaves kept alive for the journey that gave them their freedom. Many would have died on the voyage despite Dawkins' best efforts, but he did give of his best. 'I have formed a very high opinion of yr qualification as an officer and sailor', wrote his Captain when he was paid off from *Rattler* a couple of years later.

The next phase in his career he described in the laconic sentence 'Served 3½ years in Modeste in Mediterranean station'. This proved to be a period of more new experiences, and the first for which his journal has survived. *Modeste* left Sheerness in August 1851 and carried Dawkins to his first encounter with the Mediterranean. The journal has highly coloured descriptions of their ports of call in Italy; he thought little of Pisa, except for the Cathedral and the famous leaning tower. In Corfu, 'Sirocco prevails; no one escaped a cold or fever.'[139] On to Asia Minor, where he delighted in the bazaars and the bargaining, though of Turkish baths his disparaging comment was 'For my part I like the Pipe and Coffee the best part of it'. The journal is alive with lyrical descriptions of landscapes and sunsets; you can feel the excitement with which he met each day. Italy introduced him to the performing arts. In Genoa he acquired a love of opera: 'Tenor had pain in his throat, Bally *[ie the Ballet part of the performance]* was v. good.' In Barcelona he witnessed a bull-fight, and with typical thoroughness wrote page after page on the rules of the contest.

In 1852, during a brief visit to Corfu, Richard Dawkins took the first step to becoming a Freemason. He was 'regularly and duly initiated into the mysteries of Masonry' in the Pythagoras Lodge of Corcyra, No. 654, meeting at Corfu, on 23rd March 1852. The Lodge had been in existence for some 15 years, and at the time membership was completely British and predominantly military or naval[140]. He became a Royal Arch Mason as a member of 'Adam's Chapter', Sheerness, in 1855[141].

The declaration of war with Russia reached *Modeste* in April 1854. Britain had no desire to allow Russia easier access to the Mediterranean, so allied herself with Turkey. Most of the Royal Navy's operations in the Baltic consisted of blockading Russian ports, and Dawkins was awarded the Baltic Medal for his part in this early stage of what became known as the Crimean War. Commander Stewart, like his predecessors, was generous in his comments: 'I cannot give up command of the *Modeste* without expressing to you my sense of your constant attention to your duties as second Lieut, and the ready and able assistance you have at all times given to the general duties of the ship. You have possessed my entire confidence and I shall always take a warm interest in all that concerns your Welfare and advancement in our profession[142].'

Lieutenant Dawkins was in the Baltic at the time of the Charge of the Light Brigade at Balaclava in October 1854, and after a short few weeks in England early the following year came aboard HM Steam Battery *Glatton* in May 1855. This volume of the journal begins with caustic comments:

'Found ship in dry dock in a very unfurnished state respecting her internal arrangements – received a Draft of Ordinaries (I may as well enumerate a few of their trades, Farm Labourers, Stable men + I must not forget to mention one who had served Mr Gaunt the Prize fighter as Pot Boy at the Hen and Chickens. These were a fine set to commence rigging the ship with, and we were told we were lucky getting such a good set).'[143]

Then started a fairly leisurely journey towards the battlefront, with the customary diversions: 'Shot 27 brace wild turkeys', he records around the Straits of Gibraltar. Once past Constantinople, the pace of the journal increases. He complains about the quality of their equipment, and about the conduct of other combatants:

'Oct 30th I left the Ship and landed in Stalitska Bay thus shortening the distance to Sevastopol some three miles. The shot and shell which strewed the ground is beyond all belief in fact you could not move a yard without seeing some missile. We visited the Cemetery (Russian) I had often heard Frenchmen would stick at nothing but I could hardly believe any nation would be guilty of destroying wooden crosses &c erected over graves, but there they were and no mistake breaking them down for firewood, I suppose, in the Church a horrible sight presented itself and that was our Saviour crucified pierced with bullets.'

Here, at the siege of Sebastopol, he experienced the full awfulness of war, and was severely wounded in the hand. In 1960 his youngest son John described the incident thus:

'When my father was in a naval party ordered to blow up a rock which was an obstacle in the way of making an easy landing stage for boats, the mine fuse was faulty and part of it exploded under his hand, demolishing the stone and causing a nasty & painful wound, from which he was lucky to keep his finger. The stone was a diamond (odd perhaps even for those days, but my father had an odd taste in jewellery, e.g. small gold nuggets and operculum shells as studs – doubtless souvenirs of some kind). ... My father was very much "the silent service" always ... I know that he habitually wore the ring, with the hole filled with black and red sealing wax (an object of curiosity to many, I have heard) and in that state I inherited it. Anyhow, modern soft sealing wax was so impossible to restore its appearance that I am now having the stone replaced by a plain piece of lapis lazuli (blue for the Navy!) and Harvey and Gore of Vigo Street promise to make an excellent job of it.'[144]

John's description of his father as 'the silent service' is in great contrast to the vigour and passion of the journal Richard Dawkins wrote in his twenties. This phase of the conflict was drawing to a close. Sebastopol was evacuated on 9 September, and the fleet withdrew. The journal entries return to the minutiae of shipboard life during the cruise home, together with expressions of his frustration.

'Captain does not interest himself about the Ship's holds etc …. Not caring how very annoying it is to a 1st Lieut. who perhaps has been trying for a long time to get the Ship in order, this is certainly a very great fault of our Captain's who in all respects is a first rate fellow; selfish to the extreme – he is and that no one can deny. However as my promotion is all I want I must put up with all and at all costs look pleasant.'

They called at Lisbon, but he did not like the place. 'The Opera is the only thing to be done.' Then home at last. '3rd May 1856 Pay off, no men drunk, parted good friends'. His Commander wrote on his Certificate that he had 'conducted himself much to my satisfaction … a very sober off.' Dawkins himself noted that the Commander he had labelled 'selfish' had written 'he will have much pleasure in bearing witness to the Zeal and ability in the performance of my duties together with the serious injury I recd. from an explosion whilst in service onshore in the Crimea'[145]. He returned to more honours: the Crimean Medal with Sebastopol Clasp and the Turkish Medal. He had reason to be optimistic, noting 'may obtain my Cmr. Rank' after the Commander's words of praise.

But this glowing record did not seem to advance his career at all, as the bitter opening to the next part of his Journal makes clear. Immediately on landing at Plymouth he set off to London, to the Admiralty, and demanded promotion 'as the Admiralty said on my getting the appointment was certain Promotion owing to the dangerous class of vessel, and to back up my claims I got on paying off the "Glatton" one of the highest testimonials from Captain Cumming but as a Liar is looked upon as anything but the way he ought to be, I lost my Promotion and not only that the Admiralty appointed me on the 15th day of May 1856 to HM steam corvette "Esk" Captain Sir Robert McClure (the man who discovered the N.W. Passage). I immediately went to the Admiralty and stated I had not been home neither had I any *[illegible]* ready for a four Years secure … only answer I got you must join immediately … A civilian will hardly believe what I am about to state, the excuse the Admiralty gave for appointing me was that they had no other Lieutenant of standing to appoint … Had it not been for my friends I think I would have pitched to the Devil so unfair a Service and that is that it is a certainty. Moreover I felt sure I must get my Promotion at the end of the Commission and then I would say Adieu to the Service, and retire on my 8/6 per diem, that I have fully made up my mind to do.'[146]

His frustration was understandable. Nearly fifteen years of service, much of it at the sharp end of the British war machine, and the powers who controlled his destiny did not seem to want to give him his due. Nevertheless he swallowed his irritation. 'I paid my Lodging House Keeper (Miss Peacock 12 George Street Manchester Square) and started for Plymouth … arrived at Plymouth Sunday May 18th. Went to Townshend's Hotel had supper and turned in. After breakfast went on board "Esk" found her in dry dock at Keyham and the crew hulked on board the "Agincourt".'

Sir Robert Le Mesurier McClure, his new Captain, was a formidable personality. Born in Wexford in 1807, he was adopted and educated by General Le Mesurier, who sent him to Eton and Sandhurst. He took part in the Arctic expeditions of 1836 and 1848 under James Ross, the latter voyage intended as a relief mission in search of Sir John Franklin, who had disappeared in the Arctic in 1845. He soon established a reputation for being impatient with restrictions. Two years later he set out again in *Investigator* as part of a flotilla commanded by Captain Collinson in *Enterprise*, again searching for Franklin. Having come through the Straits of Magellan, *Enterprise* lost contact with the other ships. McClure pressed on up the western coast of the Americas to the Bering Strait, thence to Banks Island, where he was forced to overwinter. It seemed as if he was within sight of discovering the North West Passage at last; later he was to write, 'Can it be that so humble a creature as I am will be permitted to perform what has baffled the talented and wise for hundreds of years?'. Strictly speaking, the answer should have been 'No', but after another winter in the ice he took sledge to Winter Harbour on Melville Island, the point which had been reached from the opposite (easterly) direction by Edward Parry in 1819. Eventually in 1852 the crew of *Enterprise* were found by Captain Pym from Resolute. The expedition that approached from the East had met up with that from the West, which in England had almost been given up for lost like Franklin. However one might quibble about detail, it was acknowledged that in establishing the final link in the route from the Pacific to the Atlantic along the northern coast of Canada, the stretch of water now known as McClure Strait, he had contributed to the discovery, and in any case had been the first man to make his way from one ocean to the other. For this he received the award of £10,000 from the British Government, and was knighted in 1854.

It is difficult to overestimate the hardship and deprivation that Arctic explorers had to face, and McClure's natural ambition and independence of mind were sharpened up by his experiences. It is perhaps not surprising that on Richard Dawkins, he made a less than favourable impression. 'Sir Robert a curious person, he could not speak for half a minute without coughing in his throat and saying <u>Be</u> <u>Gad</u> but on the whole he had a gentlemanly appearance. I remarked at his lips being thin, a sure sign of a hot temper his eyes were Grey and clear also indicating the same thing.' His misgivings were justified. No sooner had *Esk* weighed anchor and rounded the breakwater than McClure said to Dawkins 'Now we have got them fairly away we will draw the string taught', and he began to bear down on the crew. 'The Captain began to show up in his true colours, never satisfied with anything that anyone did. Not only that you could never do anything right, if you did this thing, he would be certain to say you ought to have done the other'. The Atlantic crossing must have been unpleasant under such a regime. When they arrived at Rio de Janeiro however Admiral Hope Johnston reprimanded McClure for punishing people less than 24 hours after the offence had been committed, as a result of which punishment had been given in 'excitement' and hot blood. All this offended Dawkins' sense of fair play and his great respect for Navy regulations. He himself had to impose penalties, such as 24 lashes for theft, 24 lashes for 'Sculking', and 36 lashes to Dan Phaer 'for taking indecent liberties with Willm Laughton RM', but we may be sure he did all strictly correctly and in accordance with the rules.

Esk travelled southwards along the east coast of South America, through the Straits of Magellan in July 1856, and north again to Panama, where McClure took on board generous amounts of provisions for himself, but would not allow Dawkins to replenish general food stocks. At La Union in El Salvador 'The French Consul and a party of Ladies were invited to come on board they did not leave till near Sunset when the wind began blow with great force, the youngster of the Boat after pulling in vain half the night landed them on the Beach and made tents out of the Boats sails. I never shall forget the Coxswain of the Boat when I said I suppose you thought it good fun, he said just look at my arm them women pinched me black and blue as the danger increased – the youngster's description of what he saw cannot be related by me'. The President of Guatemala paid them a visit in February 1857, Dawkins harpooned a turtle, lightning struck the ship ('Thos Gardener, Quarter Master, was knocked down abaft by the electric fluid') – so far, so relatively humdrum, with small irritations looming large: 'We lost one day by coming this way round the World ... the Admiralty have refused the Sunday's pay.' But by now they were under orders to proceed to China, where on arrival they were immediately in the thick of the blockade of Canton. A few weeks later Dawkins transferred to HMS *Calcutta,* carrying with him his certificate from McClure, which commended his 'sobriety, attention and ability' and added 'and has kept a regular Journal'[148]. It was as well that McClure had obviously not actually read the document.

'On arrival in China was appt. Senior Lieut of Calcutta bearing Flag of Ad Sir M Seymour KCB Cmr. Her boats at the attack in Canton.'[149] Once again he was at the battlefront. The line of blockading ships stretched four miles, and the noise of continuous broadsides of shot and shell was deafening. Dawkins noted with pity 'The floating population of Canton amounting to two Millions pulling + skulling for their lives towards the Hunan shore, evidently putting their trust in us'[150]. He himself took comfort in ordinary things: 'A pipe and a glass of grog ... coffee & bread for breakfast'. The journal narrative gathers pace. He was ordered to form a storming party, which he did with success, then told to carry dispatches, which he accepted willingly. He assembled 40 Marines, but there was no gunboat available for them. He commandeered a sampan, located a gunboat and ordered it to collect the wounded. He himself took the gig and pulled to the Admiral's tender *Coromandel*, where he handed over the documents. 'The French Admiral sent to know the name of the officer who took his Despatches, whether I shall ever hear anything more of it I know not'. In fact he did; he was mentioned in despatches for his bravery and resourcefulness, and in due course received the China Medal with Canton Clasp.

He was to be involved in no more great engagements after Canton. At last, at the end of December 1857, he was promoted to Commander on HMS *Comus* in place of Cmdr Robert Jenkins, who had been transferred to *Actaeon* to replace Capt W J Bate, killed in action. He set off aboard *Comus,* carrying the sick and wounded on the long voyage home. In the pages of his Journal the vigorous man of action becomes once more the word-artist, lyrical about the sunsets in the Indian Ocean.

When he stepped off *Comus* on 7 June 1858, he was two months short of his 30th birthday, and had been at sea almost continuously for sixteen years. Time to draw breath and relax, perhaps? He took rooms at Lanes Hotel just off the Haymarket. In fact there was more studying: 'Joined RN College and qualified for Steam'. A year later he was off to sea again, on *Mars* from Sheerness to the Mediterranean. For this period of 3½ years we have no Journal to fill in the details, but it must have proved his worth, because 'the paying off inspection being most satisfactory and being very highly recommended by my Captain M Strange the Duke of Somerset promoted me to Captain.'[151]

But he was not to take command of a ship for three years. This kind of gap between postings was not unusual, but we have no idea of how he filled in his time. To have reached his goal at last but to be prevented from exercising his new rank must have been intolerable. Then his 'patron' came to the rescue. He received the call to take command of HMS *Zealous*, flagship of Rear Admiral George F Hastings. Padfield comments that 'Admirals ... could select most of their own officers when they hoisted their flag ... naturally enough they chose their own sons and nephews first'[152], and this is what seems to have happened. Richard McGillivray Dawkins wrote 'Of his service in the *Zealous* I have a relic. The ship passed through the Straits of Magellan; a hard place to navigate, and so much so that my father had the event recorded by a sketch, from which a painting was made which hung always in his library. The ship is shown steaming past the snow-covered mountains with a huge glacier falling down sheer into the sea. On the frame my father wrote: H.M.S. Zealous, Capt. R. Dawkins, steaming through Magellan Straits, Patagonia, passing the Glaciers, from a sketch by Mr Bedwell, Paymr. On the back of the canvas he wrote; Given and painted by Captn. R. Brydges Beachey, R.N., Dublin, August 1874, to R. Dawkins, Capt. R.N.'[153] A photograph in the possession of Dawkins' great-grandson, Professor Gianni Lombardi, shows Hastings and Dawkins seated, relaxed but smartly uniformed, with a couple of Lieutenants standing respectfully in the background. On the reverse is the photographer's mark: 'Hermanos Phot. 71 Calle del Palacio Lima (Peru)'.

So once again he had gone around the world. Soon after Dawkins' fortieth birthday, Rear Admiral Hastings wrote in his inspection report 'I feel much pleasure in being able to convey to you the impression of my entire satisfaction at the state in which I have again found that ship. I shall not fail to bring under the notice of the Lords Commissioners of the Admiralty the high opinion I entertain of the efficiency of my Flag Ship.'[154]; and when a year later his time on *Zealous* came to an end, Dawkins was able to note that 'The Admiral wrote me the discipline ... and efficiency which the *Zealous* was in he never saw superior during his Service.' In January 1870 he took passage home aboard *Revenge*. He had good reason for wanting to be home again, because at some point the efficient, conscientious Captain had fallen in love. His bride-to-be was the 30-year-old Mary Louisa Davies (née McGillivray), whom he married at All Souls' Church, Langham Place, London on 30 November 1870.

Like his father before him, Richard Dawkins married fairly late in life a widow several years younger than himself. He was 42, she was just 30. Mary Louisa was the posthumous daughter of Simon McGillivray, a significant figure in Canadian history. Her great-grandson, Professor Lombardi, wrote in an article in the Journal of the Clan Chattan Association:

'Simon was the brother and partner of William McGillivray in the North West Company ... Simon worked with his brother in London and Montreal, moving occasionally to Fort William (named after his brother) for the summer season when furs from the North West of Canada were brought to the Fort by trappers. In 1821 the North West Company merged with the Hudson's Bay Company and a series of economic troubles pursued Simon McGillivray. He recovered, returned to London, went back to Canada and then lived for 6 years in Mexico. In 1835, again in London, with partners he purchased *The Morning Chronicle*, at that time the leading Whig journal. He married late, in 1837, Anne Easthope, the daughter of Sir John Easthope, co-proprietor of the *Chronicle*, but died shortly after, in 1840.'[155]

This necessarily condensed account gives a tantalising glimpse of the colourful life of this enterprising and robust personality. Simon, like his brother William, had a great influence on the Canadian fur trade, but did not always succeed in managing his company's assets effectively. A critic once commented:

'That one made the fortune' generations of children were ceremoniously informed as they looked up at a portrait of William McGillivray, the legendary Lord of the North-West. 'And', the adult speaker gravely would add, pointing to a portrait of William's bespectacled brother Simon, 'that one lost it'.[156]

In 1827 Simon's debts were around £250,000, a huge sum for those days, and he was declared bankrupt. His investigations into mining in Mexico restored his fortunes somewhat. There he climbed Popocatepetl, no mean feat for someone with poor eyesight and one leg lame since childhood. In the end it was the support of his long-standing friend John Easthope that forced him into some stability. At the *Morning Chronicle* he earned the reputation of being 'a warm-hearted and impetuous Highlander', and the paper carried regular contributions from Thackeray, Hazlitt and Dickens. Having for some time asserted that a man had no business to marry if he spent his life travelling, he found romance in his early 50's with his friend's daughter. His sudden death at the age of 55 was a loss not only to the newspaper world but also to Freemasonry. He had been a Mason for many years, and was on good terms with the Duke of Sussex, Grand Master of the English Lodge. The Duke established him as Provincial Grand Master for Upper Canada in 1822, and with characteristic vigour he built up and regularised the craft in that country. He held the same office until his death.

The Easthope connection remained significant for Mary Louisa. Her mother's sister Louisa Easthope married Andrew Doyle, who later became proprietor of the *Morning*

Chronicle, and gave much support in the months after the loss of HMS *Vanguard*. Mary had previously married one Richard Bell Davies, who died within a year leaving no children. R McG Dawkins describes him as 'a very handsome man, but flighty and ill to do with. He dispersed no small amount of my mother's money'[157]. Davies's nephew, another Richard Bell Davies, was a Squadron Commander in the Royal Naval Air Service in the First World War, and was awarded the Victoria Cross for bravery during an air attack in Bulgaria in 1915, as well as gathering the CB, DSO, AFC, Croix de Guerre avec Palme and Légion d'Honneur.

Richard Dawkins' new wife was lively, intelligent, and cultured, with much of her father's passion and strength of character, and his life changed radically. Within a year a son, Richard McGillivray Dawkins, was born (prematurely, according to him), and the family acquired a splendid eighteenth century mansion known as 'Maisonette' just outside the village of Stoke Gabriel in Devon, 'situated on an eminence near the bank, and surrounded by trees'[158]. In 1873 Dawkins' mother Arabella died at the age of 82, and a stone in Stoke Gabriel churchyard was raised in her memory. Just a month later a daughter, Annie Theodora, was baptised in the same church, as was her sister Mary Katherine in January 1875.

Again Richard was to be subjected to an infuriating period of idleness. For three years following his marriage the Admiralty did not offer him a command. It was at this time that he wrote the note referred to earlier, as the basis of his case to the Admiralty, which ended:

'In conclusion I beg to state that my sincere wish is to continue in a service I am much attached to, and would not now have appealed but seeing … my being on half pay now over 3 years many of my previous appt. to 1st class ships I trust your Lordships will think I have only done my duty in making this appln hoping that I may receive an early appt.'[159]

Then at last on 14th October 1873 came the summons;

'By Command of the Commissioners for Executing the Office of Lord High Admiral of the United Kingdom of Great Britain and Ireland, &c.
To Captain Richard Dawkins hereby appointed Captain of Her Majesty's Ship *Vanguard*.
The Lords Commissioners of the Admiralty having appointed you Captain of Her Majesty's Ship *Vanguard* their Lordships hereby direct you to repair on board that ship at Carrickfergus, and to report to me the day on which you shall have joined her.
You are further desired to acknowledge the receipt of this communication *forthwith*, addressing your letter thus:
The Secretary of the Admiralty, Whitehall, London S.W.'[160]

The very next day the Commander in Chief at the Nore wrote thus:

'Admiralty House, Sheerness

15 Oct 1873

My dear Richard,

I was rejoiced to read in the Papers & to receive your letter confirming that you had been appointed to '*Vanguard*'. My mind is *[illegible]* relieved as I felt great injustice had been done you in not appointing you as Flag Captain here but this placement will suit you better & thus complete your time for flag. I hear '*Vanguard*' is at Belfast.

My fondest wishes to Mary & wishing all of you every happiness

Ever your affec. Cousin

George F Hastings'[161]

The Vice Admiral had clearly done what he could to advance his cousin's career, but even he had not been able to secure for him a Naval life without long gaps in it. This was to be his last good word on Dawkins' behalf. The Hon. George Fowler Hastings CB died suddenly at the age of 61 in March 1876, the events that ruined his protégé's career fresh in his mind.

The Admiral had himself been Inspecting Commander of the Coastguard at Waterford early in his career, and should have known that *Vanguard* was of course not based at Belfast but at Kingstown, occupied with the same prosaic business of supporting the Coastguard service in the north of Ireland. There was no prospect of the exotic locations and exciting engagements Richard Dawkins had been used to. But he was by now 45 years old, with an adored wife and three children, and perhaps it was time for a more sedate existence.

Chapter 7

'Exercise and Evolutions'

The Summer Cruise and its calamitous end

On Thursday, 29 July 1875, the First Reserve Squadron weighed anchor and left Plymouth for a cruise around the island of Ireland. It was an imposing sight; seven full-rigged ironclads, in the menacing black livery that gave the mid-Victorian naval force the nickname 'Black Battlefleet'. Leading the pack was HMS *Warrior*, still bulking huge enough to deter any enemy, but now entirely obsolete despite a 3½ year refit. At 15 years old *Warrior* was seen as a 'gobby ship', a soft option for older sailors, but at least for the duration of this cruise, she proudly bore the flag of Vice-Admiral Sir (John) Walter Tarleton, the Admiral Superintendent of Naval Reserves (*Penelope* had been his flagship hitherto. He hoisted his flag on *Warrior* on 26 July, and struck it again on 8 September before returning to *Penelope*). Then, in order of age, came *Defence, Hector, Achilles, Penelope, Vanguard* and *Iron Duke*. *Achilles* was of similar dimensions to *Warrior*, and carried the biggest spread of canvas ever seen in a warship, even after her original four masts had been reduced to three. *Defence* and *Hector* were much smaller – displacing around 6,000 tons to *Warrior's* 9,000. *Penelope* was the first twin-screw ironclad to qualify for the battle-fleet, and smaller still at 4,400 tons. The two sister ships, *Vanguard* and *Iron Duke*, 6,000 tons, were the newest and fastest, but development in ship design in the five years since they were commissioned had been so fast that they too were on the edge of obsolescence.

The primary reason for the First Reserve Squadron's summer cruise was the need to give the Coast Guard men a refresher course in seamanship. Admiral Tarleton's Sailing Orders told him 'to proceed ... to cruise for the purpose of exercise and evolutions, both under steam and sail, and also with a view of testing the state of efficiency of their crews in regard to seamanship as well as gunnery.'[162] In the acrimonious debate in the House of Commons on 28 February 1876, the First Lord of the Admiralty (George Ward Hunt) commented that the training element of the cruise was not merely for the benefit of the fleetmen, but also for the regular complement of officers and men, 'and it was as essential to them as it was to the Coastguard that they should be practised in naval evolutions and seamanship'.[163]

Besides this however Hunt, in reply to sharp criticism from his predecessor George Goschen, went on to say that the visit to Cork (the final port of call) was justified in order 'that the people of Cork might have an opportunity of seeing the Squadron ...

The people of Queenstown and Cork had not for several years seen a squadron of our ironclads, and on general grounds it was desirable that the natural and patriotic wishes of the people of Cork should be satisfied'. In these phrases Hunt may have given a glimpse of a hidden agenda. The 'natural and patriotic wishes' of the people of southern Ireland were far more likely to have been quite otherwise. The Irish had largely recovered from the disastrous effects of the potato famine a quarter of a century earlier, and were beginning to regain confidence and a sense of national identity, bolstered by the support of the tens of thousands who had emigrated to America and elsewhere during that time. Isaac Butt had founded what became the Home Rule League a few years previously, but had not been particularly effective. In April 1875 a more formidable personality had been returned to Parliament in a by-election at Meath: the intense and passionate Charles Stewart Parnell, under whose leadership the Home Rule movement rapidly gathered momentum. Gladstone, who had committed himself to the task of addressing what he saw as the legitimate grievances of the Irish people, was now in opposition, and Benjamin Disraeli's Tory government could be perceived by the Irish as less sympathetic. The visit of seven black battleships might well have been intended as a reminder to any potential rebels that Britain still had considerable force at her command. K C Barnaby[164] suggests that besides 'showing the flag', the trip might encourage recruitment, but in view of the political atmosphere a flock of eager recruits seems a less likely outcome.

For those aboard the business of honing skills was taken seriously. Lieutenant William Hathorn of *Vanguard* described the routine in a letter to his sister Flora thus:

'Altho' we were kept constantly employed at different Drills with the Sails, great Guns, Torpedoes, Rifles, Swords and Revolvers, not to speak of what we call <u>Steam Tactics</u> i.e. the evolutions which a Squadron would perform with an end to <u>ram</u> and therefore sink an enemy fleet, still <u>all hands</u> are enjoying the trip in spite of the mimic warfare (without any glory) which we are involved in – I must tell you that we are the <u>Reserve Iron Clad Squadron</u>, we are manned by CoastGuardsmen (those fellows you used to see at Dover) who have to go for a months or six weeks cruise every other year – the total number of Souls in our Squadron including Officers is 4029.'[165]

Three days' cruising saw the Squadron at Bear Haven, in the far southwest of Ireland. A couple of days there, and they continued up the west coast, calling next at Tarbert, in the mouth of the Shannon. As they lay there, on Friday 6 August Admiral Tarleton made an inspection visit to *Vanguard*, and Captain Dawkins took pleasure in demonstrating the effectiveness of the crew's frequent practice at closing the watertight doors. 'He expressed his approval of all my arrangements in this most important matter, the doors having been closed, and so reported by me to the Admiral within five minutes of the sounding of the bugle'[166] In his daily letter to Mary, Richard Dawkins wrote:

'You will be glad to know that he paid us a very great compliment both in the cleanliness of the ship and the smartness of the men ... between ourselves nothing could have gone off better.'[167]

The next day they left for a stop at Galway, from where Lt Hathorn reported that

'About the coasts the chief attraction appears to be 'whisky & milk' – the <u>natives</u> are quite uncivillized compared to the Hindoos - & they (the majority) do not understand a word of our language – the lower classes require great persuasion to come up the Ship's side and when they get inboard they give expression to great wonder, muttering (praises or curses) to themselves all the while. They walk about with great stealth like wild animals, in this particular they remind me of the N.W. American Indians.'[168]

So much for impressing the local population! On they went to Blacksod Bay, from where they sailed northwards to Lough Swilly and Belfast Lough, and on 28 August the Squadron dropped anchor off Kingstown, the port of Dublin. It was a gentle journey, with plenty of time to enjoy the stopping places, or perhaps to satisfy the thirst of the inhabitants for a sight of the Union Jack – though the west of Ireland had lost more than one-third of its younger generation by emigration in recent years, and Galway was a shadow of the city it had been. During the Commons debate mentioned earlier, George Goschen pointed out that the seaborne training element of the cruise could hardly have been great:

'The ships were not very much at sea; indeed they were scarcely at sea at all; they left one place at night and arrived at the next place on the following morning ... The fact was, that they had only been at sea four entire days, and that out of those four days they spent three between Portland and Berehaven ... If the Squadron had been a party of Cook's tourists, who had attempted to go round Ireland without being at sea more than was necessary, they could not have followed a course much different from that which had been taken by the Squadron'.

Moreover, he described an itinerary, which would not have disgraced a Cook's tour:

At Galway ... there was a ball. ... At Belfast there was a lunch, a ball, a dinner, and a series of special entertainments. At Dublin there was a dance, but they declined to attend a ball, because they were "behind time".'

Captain Dawkins did indeed write to his wife from Carrickfergus on 28 August: 'All yesterday I was at Belfast being entertained at the Royal Horticultural Gardens ... no end of a turn out and fireworks – I am now on my way up to the Mayor of Belfast banquet.'[169] But the ships' log books give little indication of such goings-on. There is one mention of a ball, but most entries record mundane housekeeping activities such as the loss overboard of minor items of equipment, taking on board fresh meat and vegetables, training the Boys in seamanship, cutlass drill and the like, maintaining discipline, scrubbing the decks and so on. The Admiral's Journal is scarcely more exciting, recording various staff problems, which often seem too trivial to be referred so far up the line of command. On 7 August, for instance, HMS *Vanguard* reported that her Chaplain, the Rev Spencer Musson, 'had failed to return from leave before the ship sailed from Berehaven'. What could have kept the good clergyman from his duties? The Admiral soberly ordered that he 'be cautioned to be more careful in future'.[170] On 30 August, as they sat quietly in Dublin Bay, it was the Chaplain of the *Penelope* who was causing trouble. He complained of 'inattention by Men during Divine Service'. Vice-Admiral Tarleton resisted the temptation to suggest that it might be the Reverend Morton's own fault that people didn't pay any attention to him; instead he responded sharply that 'the Admiral Supt. considers it was not necessary for him to write a letter to his Captain complaining … unless he had previously made a verbal representation without effect & that the Chaplain should have spoken to the Commander who was present at the Service if there was any reason to complain of the conduct of the Men.' Of such weighty matters did the Admiral's day consist. *Vanguard*'s log is equally devoid of incident, with the sad exception of a death recorded on 24 August, when she was in Belfast Lough. Ignatius Nolan, Ordinary Seaman, was 'killed by a fall from aloft while on duty. Character: Good.' The Admiral's journal says on 27 August that the jury returned a verdict of accidental death, and *Vanguard*'s ledger records the award of £10 to his father 'as compensation for effects'[171]. Nolan is buried in Carrickbrennan.

Gradually, the Squadron reduced in numbers. *Defence* landed her complement of fleetmen at Blacksod Bay and returned to her station at Lough Swilly, and *Penelope* had to depart for Sheerness for urgent repairs. Over several days most of the Coast Guard men based in Ireland were disembarked to go back to their shore stations, leaving fewer men to handle the ships. *Vanguard*, for instance, put ashore 171 fleetmen before setting out on the final leg of the cruise with only 351 men instead of the full complement of 450. *Iron Duke*, however, kept her fleetmen, who were to be returned to their stations in the northeast of England. The original plan was for the cruise to end at Kingstown, where *Vanguard* would resume her guardship duties while *Iron Duke* returned to Portland with *Warrior*. The extra leg was added at the last minute, when Vice Admiral Tarleton received a letter from Sir Alexander Milne which read: 'There is a strong letter from Cork asking that the ships should visit Queenstown as 7 years have elapsed since any of our squadrons have been there I wish you could manage to call in there for three or four days.'[172] Later questions were raised about why *Vanguard* should have needed to proceed on the final leg, since she had disembarked all her fleetmen and could have stayed at Kingstown.

Dublin had been as hospitable as Belfast, and the presence of the Squadron had aroused much interest. The press reported that 'well-laden steamers and hundreds of pleasure yachts went out to make the circuit of the ships daily'[173]. But the junketing was coming to an end. The sun rose just before 6 am on Wednesday, 1 September 1875, with the promise of a warm, languid late summer day. The squadron had been active early, taking soundings and recording weather data. By 8 am the barometer stood at 30.13, and the temperature was already 67° F (20° C). The sky was overcast, and there was no wind. Signals passed between the ships[174]: 5.45am, *Hector* to Flagship: 'Request permission to hoist in steam pinnace'. 6am, Flagship to general: 'Send vouchers for fresh beef and vegetables by 8 am'. 6.30am, Flagship to general: 'Blue working dress for boat's crews, blue and white hats'. 8.00am, Flagship to general: 'Cross Royal yards. Get up steam'. 8.51am, *Vanguard* to Flagship (semaphore): 'Capt to Capt: shall have "Victoria's" boat alongside until Anchor is aweigh. If you have any letters to send, I will send them in her'. Flagship to *Vanguard*: 'Capt to Capt: Much obliged'. Gradually the bustle increased as they prepared for the final leg of their Irish coastal cruise, 170 miles southwards to Queenstown (Cobh), the port serving Cork. Only a few more days, and they would be home again, with the family. They were adequately provisioned; only the day before *Iron Duke* had taken on board 461 lbs of beef and 72 lbs of vegetables. In the tension while they waited for the signal to weigh anchor, a careless Marine dropped his bayonet in the sea, and it was entered in *Vanguard's* log: 'Lost overboard by accident Bayonets pat.53 one'[175] Then at last came the order, and at 10.30 in the morning the remaining five ships of the Squadron began their stately progress out of Kingstown harbour, under steam.

It was a perfect day for the trip. The Royal Engineers' Observatory at Phoenix Park in Dublin described 1 September in their records as 'Fine & Pleasant'[176], but of all the people who were called to give evidence at the Court-Martial, only Private George Leatherbarrow RMLI had enough poetry in his soul to tell the assembled Admirals and Captains that it was 'a beautiful day'.[177] He was posted on watch on the lifebuoy, at the stern of *Vanguard*, and the sun shone throughout his time on duty. The ships were in close order, in line astern: *Warrior, Hector, Vanguard, Iron Duke,* and *Achilles.* To begin with their course took them roughly north-east, around the Kish Light Vessel which marks the northern end of the Kish Bank, a long series of sandbanks some 10 km off the Irish coast. The Kish Light is a well-known feature of the seascape. James Joyce mentions it in *Ulysses:* 'Far on Kish bank the anchored lightship twinkled, winked at Mr Bloom'. The first all-electric light vessel replaced it in 1954. Then in 1965, after various ingenious designs had been submitted to cope with the sands of the Kish Bank and the winds that had scotched earlier projects, a lighthouse was erected on the spot. Today its light can be increased from two million to three million candlepower in fog.

A sixth vessel had set out with the Squadron, the little *Hawk*, described by the Press as 'the Admiral's yacht', but actually one of the *Warrior's* tenders, was despatched to Queenstown by the shorter route, inside the Kish Bank.

Having rounded the light, *Achilles* parted company, off to Liverpool, and the four remaining ironclads headed almost due south. They were in no great hurry. The Admiral aimed to arrive at Queenstown with the ebb tide on the Friday morning, and the speed was set at 7 knots. Soon after midday the Admiral gave the order 'Form columns of divisions, line ahead'. This meant that instead of the four vessels sailing in a single column, they should form two columns (of two ships each), in parallel, four cables (about 750 metres) apart. There were two ways of achieving the desired formation, for each of which there was a different signal. One method involved the whole squadron making a 90° turn, then each pair of ships turning back to the original course, with a short interval between their manoeuvres. That way, the second pair (or Division) would have little distance to make up. Apparently the accepted way to perform this move was to turn to starboard, which could have brought the squadron dangerously close to the Kish Bank; perhaps for this reason the signal which Admiral Tarleton ordered was for *Vanguard* and *Iron Duke* each to make an eight-point (90°) turn to port, then when they had reached the required distance, to turn back to the original course. This meant that the second Division was well behind *Warrior* and *Hector*, and had to speed up in order to come parallel with them. Accordingly, *Vanguard* and *Iron Duke* increased speed to 8 and 8½ knots respectively. The sun shone. From *Vanguard,* the flagship, with *Hector* obediently following, was clearly visible on the starboard bow; and *Iron Duke* 2½ cables astern, keeping her station exactly.

Not a lot was happening on board. Navigating Lieutenant James C Thomas pricked off the ship's position on the chart at about 12.10, and checked that not only was she clear of the Kish Bank, but taking a course (S½E) which took her progressively further away from it; then he went below, probably with a sigh of relief. The team at the wheel were pursuing their task conscientiously: Petty Officer 1st Class Thomas Martin, normally Coxswain of the launch, was doing duty as Quartermaster of the Watch (in naval terminology, the Quartermaster is the senior helmsman), alternately at the wheel or 'at the conn' (directing the steering), taking turns with Quartermaster James Ahern. The seaman 'at the conn' stood by the standard compass on the bridge, looking straight ahead. Later Thomas Martin was to comment that *Vanguard* had not been steering so easily that day as she usually did; she yawed about half a point each way.

Robert Martins, Yeoman of Signals, was also on deck but handed over the watch at noon to Signalman John Davis. Keeping lookout were Pte George Leatherbarrow on the lifebuoy, where he relieved Pte George Sparks, and, on the fore-topmasthead, Ordinary Seaman George Cooper. At about 12.10, George reported seeking a bark, some 7 or 8 miles away, on the port bow, but that was the sum total of excitement. The crew settled into a comfortable routine.

At 12.30 the watch changed again. Lieutenant William Hathorn came on deck to take over as Officer of the Watch, and noted that they were still some 3 cables astern of their proper position in relation to the First Division. Chief Gunner Alfred Smith, as Mate of the Watch, took his station by the after bridge engine-room telegraph.

Signalman Thomas Porter relieved John Davis on the battery-deck. George Sparks swapped places again with George Leatherbarrow at the stern. Down below, Engineer Valentine Horne had conveyed a message from the Captain to Chief Engineer Robert Brown to the effect that he should keep a good command of steam. Horne also asked whether a boiler that had previously been ordered to be burnt down should be kept going. 'Yes', said Brown; and a little before 12.30 he went to the engine-room to check that the orders had got through. There he found that the second senior Engineer, William Paige, had just taken charge of the watch. There were in the engine-room a Petty Officer and two men oiling the machinery, and an engine-room artificer was on duty in the stoke-hole. All routine, no problems anticipated. Captain Dawkins, who had been on deck since the early morning, satisfied himself that all was in order under the control of Lieutenant Hathorn, and at 12.35 at last climbed down the companionway for a break.

Then came the fog. Suddenly, without warning, a solid bank of fog rolled towards the Squadron. Hathorn watched as the flagship disappeared into the murk, then two minutes later, at 12.40, *Vanguard* was enveloped. Visibility shrank to almost nothing. One lookout said he could barely see his own ship's taffrail. Immediately Hathorn sent Alfred Smith to call the Captain, and ordered four Ordinary Seamen to take up extra lookout positions. Thomas Pengelly and John May went respectively to the port and starboard sides of the upper battery – Pengelly remembered being told several times to keep a good lookout – and William Hill and Michael Murphy to the port and starboard catheads (projections near the bow to which the hoisted anchor was secured), with instructions to keep a good lookout ahead. George Sparks, lookout on the lifebuoy, clambered up on to the grating to see better; he knew *Iron Duke* was close behind, but could no longer see her. Captain Dawkins hurried up on deck once more, and immediately ordered a reduction in speed to 6 knots, then to 5. To William Paige in the engine room a disembodied voice through the speaking tube said 'reduce speed to 25 revolutions', and three minutes later to 18.

Somehow they had to tell the rest of the Squadron that they were slowing down, especially *Iron Duke*, right astern. The rule was, according to the Night Fog Signal Book, that 'During a fog the speed of a fleet … should not exceed 3 to 4 knots per hour', but so slow a speed could make the Squadron liable to be carried by the tide on to the shoals. At the same time, Article 2 stated that 'During a fog the fleet is to maintain the same order and steer the same course as it may have been doing before the fog came on'[178], with any reduction in speed depending on instructions from the flagship. Whistling had been heard from the general direction of *Warrior*, but not a discernible signal. In fact Admiral Tarleton had ordered his signal guns to be fired every half hour from 12.35 until 3.30 to indicate his ship's position, 'sounding continuously the steam trumpet', but the Second Division had not yet caught up with *Warrior* and *Hector*, and the fog smothered the sound of the Admiral's signals.

As it happened, Tarleton had decided that a flurry of signals could be a distraction to his Captains, and they were best left to decide for themselves what to do.

Without orders from the flagship, Richard Dawkins had done just that; but what signal to send? The steam whistle was already blasting away, sounding the 'pennants', followed by a full-throated blast with the cowl open. Several witnesses remarked that *Vanguard* and *Iron Duke* both had the loudest whistles they had ever heard – so why was there no response from *Iron Duke*? Dawkins called a hurried conference on deck. To Lieutenant Hathorn and Robert Martins, Yeoman of Signals, he said 'What is the proper signal to make? Will continuously blowing on the steam whistle show that we are reducing speed?' Both responded that they knew of no other appropriate signal. One difficulty was the time involved. To make a signal, first a 'preparatory' had to be sent and a reply awaited, to be sure that the other party was listening; then the signal to reduce speed actually involved three separate figures, taking around two minutes to complete.[179] To use the signal guns meant they had to be loaded first, all of which took time. Making a deafening din with the whistle seemed the best bet. Martins was just about to go below to fetch the signal book, when Michael Murphy, on the starboard cathead, saw the other ship.

Questions were asked at the Court-Martial about Ordinary Seaman Michael Murphy's abilities as a lookout. On 16 September he explained to the assembled dignitaries that 'I have been taught rifle firing with a ball, and have found that my sight was good, but not on all occasions. I have been treated by a medical officer for defective eyesight on two or three occasions. The last time was when I was serving on board the Barossa, and at the naval sick quarters at Yokohama. ... I last tried at a mark in February last. The sight of my left eye is a good deal stronger than that of my right.'[180] (later in the Court Martial it was reported that Murphy had been examined by two medical men, who said that he had fair average sight, and could see distinctly objects from 300 to 500 yards distant). But the harder the formidable group of senior officers pressed him, the more firmly Murphy insisted that he had indeed seen a ship crossing *Vanguard*'s bows. He saw 'the appearance of a hull and the loom upwards', though he could not say whether she was a steamer or not. She appeared to be crossing the bows from port to starboard. He called out 'Ship right ahead'.

Nobody else saw the apparition, but the other seamen on lookout forward heard Murphy shout. It was less than five minutes after the fog had come on, and the buzz of activity immediately became more frantic. Captain Dawkins ran forward to the forecastle, crying out 'Stop her!' William Paige in the engine room was checking the timing on the engines, ensuring the reduction to 18 revolutions, when he received the order over the engine-room telegraph, and shut off the steam to both engines. Dawkins said to Murphy 'Where is she?' Murphy pointed. 'I can't see her', said the Captain. Meanwhile Lieutenant Hathorn had ordered the helm to be put to starboard. In a matter of seconds, Dawkins had just managed to make out the shape of a ship, and decided that the danger had passed; he ordered 'Full speed ahead', and the engine-room telegraph sounded again. Paige had barely finished shutting the engines down. He grasped the wheel on the starboard engine with both hands and began laboriously to turn it to full steam. Then he reached for the wheel to do the same with the port engine, but before he could do so there was a dreadful crash. The *Iron Duke* had run into *Vanguard*, and the waters of Dublin Bay began to rush in.

★ ★ ★ ★ ★ ★ ★ ★ ★

Aboard *Iron Duke*, the day had hitherto been equally uneventful. After *Achilles* had peeled off to return to England, *Iron Duke* found herself at the rear of the column. Then came the order to 'form columns of divisions', and Captain Henry Hickley stayed on deck to make sure the manoeuvre (or 'evolution' as the Navy called it) was carried out properly. At the time *Vanguard* seemed to be making better speed than *Iron Duke*, and the tail-ender was lagging behind. To Hickley, as to his fellow Captains, it was important to do things correctly in accordance with the rule-book; but he had a good team on deck who could be relied on to carry out orders to the letter, or to use their initiative if necessary. Lieutenant Stephen Thompson had been Officer of the forenoon Watch, 'a good signal officer, and who always looked after the signals in evolutions' according to his Captain[181]. Thompson comes across as a lively and positive personality, eager to do his job, and meticulous in signals procedure. He it was who first noted that the ship was dropping behind. This was his description of what happened following the signal to form columns of divisions: 'On the signal being hauled down the leader of the second division [ie *Vanguard*] went off to port about eight points, the *Iron Duke* following the motion of the *Vanguard*; the speed of the ships being about seven knots, the revolution flag of the *Vanguard* showing 42, and the revolution flag of the *Iron Duke* being at 50. The *Vanguard* hoisted the preparative when nearly four cables from first division, and then hauled down almost immediately afterwards. Both ships ported their helms to resume their original course – S½E. This evolution, through being performed rectangularly instead of on line in line of bearing, and in consequence of the flagship not reducing speed we became very much astern. Immediately on seeing this I called the Captain's attention to the fact.'[182] What had happened, as we have seen, was that as a result of the particular way in which the ships were ordered to form two parallel columns, *Vanguard* and *Iron Duke* had to speed up in order to get into the correct position, and *Iron Duke* had to keep an eye on her distance from *Vanguard*. The whole business is complicated for the non-nautical reader by the use of two different measures of speed: the rate in knots, and the revolutions of the steam engines. All this mattered because of the later argument over which ship was going at what speed after the fog came down, and why.

At 12.15, satisfied that all was as it should be, Captain Hickley at last went below, 'it being my impression that a fog was not coming on, I left the deck, having been there all the forenoon, in charge of the officer of the watch. ... I gave orders for the *Iron Duke* not to get astern of her station, the *Vanguard* and the *Iron Duke* being at this time three cables apart.'[183] (Their station was supposed to be two cables behind the leader. A cable equated to about 600 feet.) It was almost exactly the same moment that Captain Dawkins had left the deck of *Vanguard* for a brief respite.

Lieutenant Thompson was relieved at 12.30 by Lieutenant Pierre Gervais Evans. Thompson handed over the Watch with the instruction 'steer south, half east, close order, columns of divisions in line ahead, on no account get astern; look-out men are on the top-gallant forecastle, although there is no fog, but I perceive banks ahead, which will in all probability be on the ships in less than half an hour.'[184] 50 revolutions, he warned, would not be enough to make up their position. Thompson, apparently the only man to spot the oncoming fog, did not actually go below, but stayed to give the signalman a hand.

All seemed placid. The men on watch kept their eyes and ears open. Signalman Nehemiah Bale was posted on the starboard side of the battery, watching for any signals from the flagship. He could see *Vanguard* in line ahead, flying No. 4 signal flag denoting 45 or 46 revolutions. Way up forward, perched on the jibboom end, was Boatman James Watson, one of the Coastguard contingent. On the forecastle was Ordinary Seaman Henry Wilson; on the topmasthead, Ordinary Seaman Walter Woolcott, precariously poised on the starboard side of the masthead, on the fore part of the after cross-trees. He too saw *Vanguard* before the fog came on: 'She was then a little off the starboard bow, and about 300 yards distant. He did not know the meaning of a cable, but he should think she was under two cables.'[185] Woolcott said he had been 'brought up in a training-ship', but that hardly excused his lack of the basic skill of judging distances at sea. Also on watch on the topgallant forecastle was William Mains, Chief Officer of the Coastguard, normally based at Cleethorpes. When he came on watch at 12.25 all was clear; he could see Walter Woolcott up above. Mains was an over-meticulous witness at the Court Martial; at one point the President said peremptorily that 'The Court do not require so much detail in answering'[186]. At the helm was Able Seaman James Caven, under orders from Quartermaster Thomas Price Rose who was 'at the conn'.

Lieutenant Evans kept gently increasing speed, to get back on station with *Vanguard*, which appeared to have put on a spurt. Down in the engine room James Chater was duty Engineer from 12.30, when they were making 52 revolutions. At around 12.35 the order for full speed came through, and the engine-room replied 'If we had the other half-boiler turned on we should be going 58'. Chater said that in theory it would take him about seven minutes to reach 60 revolutions, which ought to have produced 10½ knots in calm weather. Evans reckoned that the ship did not actually exceed 8.2 knots.

The lookout men were in place, following Thompson's orders. Thompson himself was poised with his hand to his ear, listening for the flagship's signal guns. Evans was standing on deck, sextant in hand, when the fog rolled in, and at 12.40 he lost sight of the flagship. Straight away he told Henry Latters, Chief Officer of Coastguard, to go and tell the Captain. In the moments Latters was below *Vanguard* disappeared from sight. Then Evans took a decision that came to haunt him for the rest of his short life. *The Times* reported his evidence to the Court Martial thus: 'On losing sight of her, knowing the speed the *Iron Duke* was going at, and not wishing to follow in the exact wake of his leader, for fear she might have to stop, he gave the order to starboard. Her head went off one point to S by E½E, and he gave the order to keep her course S½E. The Captain was close to witness [ie, Evans] by that time, and he told him that he had given the vessel a slight sheer, as he did not like to follow exactly right astern of his leader.'[187] This sounds like common sense. *Iron Duke* was going flat out to catch up with *Vanguard*, which was dead ahead, and moving more slowly. The fog was sudden and thick, and it takes a while to put the brakes on a 6,000-ton iron ship. The risk of collision must have seemed huge and imminent.

A few weeks later Evans stoutly defended his decision to sheer out of line without getting permission from his Captain. 'I have been in the combined squadrons, and know their custom in a fog. ... I have never steamed at full speed in squadron in any ship I have been in in a dense fog.'[188] He knew the rule-book, and his Captain, well enough to be confident of making his own decisions.

But Captain Hickley thought otherwise. As soon as he came on deck, he went to the starboard side of the battery and asked Evans what he was doing. Evans told him. Hickley retorted 'That will not do; get into line again' and ordered the helm a-port. James Caven, at the wheel, received a volley of orders in quick succession from Quartermaster Thomas Rose: starboard, hard a-starboard, then half a turn to port. Out of the fog, for a few seconds, came the harsh sound of *Vanguard's* steam whistle, and Captain Hickley was eventually satisfied that his ship was back on station. 'That will do; bring her to her course again', which Rose translated to Caven as 'steady starboard', a quarter turn. Rose later said that the ship was steering easily that day, yawing no more than one-quarter point each way. Hickley ordered the man standing by the steam whistle to answer *Vanguard's* signal, but their whistle would not respond. The steam had not been turned on to it. The Mate of the Watch was told to remedy this. He ran down the after ladder and met Engineer Richard Rundle, who hurried to turn on the tap and then raced back to the whistle.

It was 12.45. Signalman 2nd Class Samuel Martins had just brought the foghorns to William Mains, kneeling at his lookout station on the topgallant forecastle, when out of the wall of fog there appeared a shape. Mains jumped to his feet and yelled 'Go astern, Sir, the *Vanguard* is close under our bows,' and ran to the ladder leading to the upper battery. At the same time Hickley saw *Vanguard* across *Iron Duke's* bows. He stopped the port screw in an attempt to swing his ship round, but saw it would not work in time, so ordered full speed astern with both engines. The order had barely reached the engine room when the shock of the collision ran through the ship. Richard Rundle had his hand on the steam whistle ready to signal. Walter Woolcott was thrown off the topmasthead on to the after part of the crosstrees. James Watson just had time to clamber from the end of the jibboom to the bowsprit when he was thrown on to his face on the deck. *Iron Duke* began to back off, but the fatal damage had been done.

Chapter 8

'My God, here is a ship right into us!'
Saving all hands from the sinking ship

Dr James Fisher, ship's surgeon, was sitting in the *Vanguard's* wardroom reading the newspaper when a fellow officer came in and remarked on the sudden thick fog. Fisher went to look out of one of the ports, and cried out, 'My God, here is a ship right into us!' The two rushed on deck just as the collision occurred. Spars and blocks from *Iron Duke's* jibboom and bowsprit were flying everywhere. Orders too flew in all directions: 'Screw down the watertight compartments', 'Fire the minute guns' and 'Blow the steam whistle' in quick succession from Captain Dawkins on the forecastle, 'Boats' crews away' from Lieutenant Hathorn, 'Close up everything below' and 'Pipe "hand out boats"' from Commander Tandy, who with most of the other officers had also hurried on deck as soon as they heard the crash. The crew got down to well-rehearsed drill on closing the watertight doors at 29 different places, engineer officers and stokers supplementing the members of the watch whose duty this was. Carpenter 1st Class David Tiddy and his small team were ordered by Lieutenant Hathorn to see that all ports and scuttles were closed.

Down below, there must have been confusion. Chief Engineer Robert Brown raced down the engine room ladder, only to see what Engineer William Paige described thus: 'The water rushed over the engine-room flat and down through the gratings on to the engines, forming a sort of cascade over the engines. I also heard a rush of water behind the port engines. I tried to ascertain exactly where this was coming from, but I could not. I looked down towards the injections, as I thought probably I might put on the bilge injections. They were covered with water and could not be got at ... the water was about a couple of feet above the plates, and the injection sluices are a foot below the plates. The water was rushing rapidly over them.'[189] While Paige struggled, Brown went to the main deck (the next deck below the upper deck), saw some of the engineers, and ordered them to get on with closing the watertight doors, and to pass the word along to make sure everything was closed up. Then on to the upper deck, to report to the Captain that the ship had sustained a serious injury on the port side of the engine-room, and that she was sinking. His report made, he returned to the main deck to help screw down the watertight doors. Meanwhile James Borlace, Engine-room Artificer, was trying to start the main drain donkey-engine to pump the water out, but the bar needed to start the engine had been thrown somewhere by the shock of the collision. Within two minutes the water was half-way up his thighs. He thrashed about under the water in a vain attempt to find the bar; by now the water was up to his hips. The pressure in the boilers was rising alarmingly. Borlace set the spindle valves to blow off the steam. The water was 'dashing into the ashpits, bringing out the ashes and smoke, lapping the flame from under the bars back into the stokehole.'[190] In a few minutes more the water began to put the fires out.

Henry Rose, another of the Engine-room Artificers, was stationed at the steam fire engine, but reported to Brown that he could not get it to pump, and the water in the stokehole was up to his waist. He said that all the fires were out except the two foremost on each side. At about the same time Borlace ran along the deck towards the engine-room and up the ladder to the battery, pausing only to fix a couple of catches on a door that Engineer James Redgrave was closing. Borlace found William Paige and told him breathlessly that 'My fires are all out'. 'Yes,' said Paige 'I have reported it to the chief engineer, and I am getting pumps rigged. Now go and make yourself useful in closing the watertight doors.'[191]

The two tasks of closing the watertight doors and trying to get the pumps working occupied most of the crew in the minutes immediately following the collision. Of the Engineers, William Paige had been on watch in the engine-room; his colleagues Valentine Horne, James Redgrave, Angus Leitch and William Vivyan were working flat out on door closing. This could be a cumbersome procedure. Some doors were closed by a remote mechanism which involved getting a metal cap plate off and turning a screw on the main deck. There was a shortage of spanners – or at least, the spanners that existed were considered sufficient for normal happenings, but clearly their number made the process of getting the doors shut even slower. Later there would be caustic questioning about spanners at the Court Martial. Redgrave, whose specific responsibility was the watertight doors, gave evidence that he started on the cap plate for the port shaft alley door mechanism, asked Brown for a spanner, got the cap off, gave the spanner to Leading Stoker Richard George for him to carry on there, then went to the lower battery to close the tunnel doors. He shut the port door, then opened and closed the starboard door again, because Horne had told him it was not properly shut. Then to the provision-room flat (flat: a lobby giving access to one or more compartments) to help close the doors before and abaft the engine-room flat, in 85 and 99 bulkheads. This had taken some ten minutes.

Lieutenant Edward Noble was responsible for all the pumping operations. The steam pumps, of course, would not work if there were no steam in the boilers. James Borlace had set it to release gently, and the fires were out. At about 1 o'clock Captain Dawkins gave the order to man the hand (Downton) pumps. The pumps were rigged and began to do their job; men pumped furiously for about fifteen minutes. Among the hands rigging the pumps was an extra pair, belonging to the vigorous Lieutenant Stephen Thompson of *Iron Duke*. Having given the order on his own ship 'Away all boats' crews', Thompson jumped into the starboard cutter and made his way to *Vanguard*, which he boarded without specific orders, and then set about giving help wherever he could.

It may have been Thompson's boat to which Captain Dawkins gave the message 'Ask Captain Hickley if he will take us in tow'. Commander Tandy, on deck, heard it, but the existence of this simple query – to which no answer was ever received – was the subject of some doubt at the Court Martial. It is difficult to see how a tow could have been set up in the fog and in the time available. Meanwhile Valentine Horne, checking the watertight doors, first saw the problem with the door in 99 bulkhead. The catches were not properly fastened, and water was coming through from the bottom. 'I got a heavy hammer from the pump close at hand and tightened up all the catches except the two bottom ones of the centre part of each door. I tried to fasten those, but could not move them. One of the other catches on the starboard doors seemed slack, that I could do nothing with.'[192] He went quickly to tell Brown, who came to see for himself. He saw that the closure was wrongly positioned, but that nothing could be done because of the level of the water on the other side. The water had risen as far as the engine-room flat. Horne suggested that something 'might be stuffed in round the corners'. Brown 'directed Mr Horne, the senior engineer, to take the rug off my bed and try if he could do anything towards stopping it'[193]. 'I returned with the rug' Horne later told the Court Martial 'and tore two or three strips, and told the carpenter, who was standing by, to try and see if he could press the strips under the door into the aperture where the water was coming out, as he had a chisel in his hand. This had little or no effect.'

By this time – around a quarter past one – *Iron Duke* had come alongside, and her boats had already taken off a number of *Vanguard*'s crew. First to go were the sick and the prisoners (presumably including the unfortunate George Rayner, the accused from *Achilles*). Of *Vanguard*'s own boats, two cutters on the port side had been smashed in the collision. Commander Tandy saw that the one sound cutter and the gigs were lowered and started taking on passengers. In the process Leading Seaman John Marshall (unofficially promoted to Petty Officer by the Press) crushed two fingers between boats; amazingly, he was the only casualty in the whole operation. Tandy then gave the order for the pinnace's derrick to be hoisted. Commander Young went to give a hand. When they tried to lower it, the mechanism failed. As they tried to ease its progress, boat and derrick together slipped and fell; the pinnace was stove in. Young went to the bridge and asked Tandy if he could be of any use to him. Captain Dawkins asked him to 'mark the ship's side, and let me know if she was settling down.'[194] Young enlisted the help of Lieutenant William McCheane RMLI, and Lieutenant Van Koughnet, who had presumably arrived in one of *Iron Duke*'s cutters. Young asked Van Koughnet, who was alongside, 'to place a mark on the ship's side to show how fast the ship was going down. In an interval of about three minutes she had sunk about 4 inches.'[195]

One officer, not identified, kept a very cool head, and was able to write about it not long afterwards. His letter was widely quoted in the press. He wrote: 'I now went below, and superintended the transfer of the public records, books, &c, into the boats. After doing this I again went on deck, the water having reached 25 feet above the bilge. The order was now given for the men to get into the boats, and shortly afterwards I got over the stern into the boat with the books. I then came alongside, and took as many men into the boat as she could carry, and went on board the *Iron Duke*.'[196]

Just at this moment Captain Samuel Collins, the most senior Marine officer on *Vanguard*, came to Dawkins with a strange request. He asked permission to transfer to *Iron Duke*, even though most of the men under his command were still aboard *Vanguard*, and would be there for another twenty minutes or so. Dawkins was outraged. He thought Collins' conduct thoroughly reprehensible, and said so to the Court Martial in due course. It is difficult to understand what prompted Collins, unless he was unwell. He had been severely wounded in the Far East some years earlier, and the stress of the accident might have told on him.

Captain Dawkins called a conference with his senior officers, Commander Tandy, Navigating Lieutenant James Thomas, and Commander Young. The time was 1.20 pm, half an hour after the collision. The water was pouring in, and the Downton pumps had no hope of keeping up. From all three Dawkins had the same advice: 'We don't think you can save the ship, and we ought to save the lives of the crew'. He gave the order 'Come up from below'. The remaining crew abandoned the pumps, and marshalled on deck ready to get into the boats. Robert Brown, following the men up, noticed that the water in the engine room seemed to be rising less rapidly, so he ran to tell the Captain that if they could keep the provision room flat and the hold clear of water, they might have a chance. Dawkins ordered the men back to the pumps, but almost immediately Brown reappeared saying 'I have made a mistake, Sir; pumping is useless, and nothing can be done to save the ship.' The pumps were abandoned once again.

The intrepid Lieutenant Thompson was below, attending to some pumps. When he heard the order he 'sang out "Stay, I will go and see by whose orders"'. Captain Dawkins confirmed: 'Yes, they must come up, as the pumps are of no further use, and the ship is sinking.' Thompson went below again, and passed the order on to Lieutenant Noble. Then he was off, padding about in his stockinged feet with a lantern, checking closed doors and observing the rising water. At 99 bulkhead he 'was attracted by a hissing noise and a slight fall of water which was coming through the crevices each side of and above these bulkhead doors. I drew Lieutenant Noble's attention, and said 'Look how useless the water-tight compartments are, if water comes between the crevices like that'. Some areas were still almost dry; in the provision-room flat the water 'only wet my socks a little. I had no boots on.'[197] Valentine Horne was also still below. As he paid a last visit to the stokehole, he heard a voice call out in triumph 'I have opened them'. It was Leading Stoker Peter Kid, who had been labouring all this time to open the auxiliary valves. All for nothing. Horne told him 'It was no use doing that, and that he had better go on deck, because all the men had been called away to leave the ship.'[198] The water brimmed over the engine-room coaming. The ship settled gradually. At last, some fifty minutes after his ship had been given her 'fatal stab', Richard Dawkins ordered Tandy and Thomas into his galley, and himself was the last to leave the stricken *Vanguard*. The guns, the shouted orders, the scream of the whistle, the blast of escaping steam, had gone. The Captain's galley carried its passengers to safety aboard *Iron Duke* in the damp silence of the fog.

There they stood and watched the last minutes of *Vanguard*. Mrs Saxby's story makes the most of this moment: 'The *Vanguard* heeled over and sank, righting herself, however, as she went down, "and groaning," the men said, "as if she knew that her time was come," while the water rushing in and over her made a noise like the convulsive sobs of a dying giant!'[199] She was writing in 1891, and seems to have been familiar with the only generally available eye-witness account, that of the mysterious officer who saved the ship's books, and who wrote to his friend in Maidstone: 'The fog had now cleared off, and we all stood on the deck of the *Iron Duke* watching for the finale of the catastrophe. A little before 2 o'clock she heeled gradually over until the whole of her enormous side, to the keel, was above water. Then she gradually sank, righting herself as she went down, stern first, the water being blown from hawse holes in huge spouts by the force of the wind rushing out of the ship as her bows sank. She then disappeared from view. Our fellows were much saddened to see their home go down, carrying everything they possessed. We had been paid that morning, and most of the officers lost that in addition. Fortunately I had my pay and also my watch in my pocket.'[200] That last sentence exemplifies the breezy tone of the letter. Clearly he was an officer with his wits about him, and able to make the best of the situation. Lieutenant Hathorn wrote similarly to his parents: 'Exactly at 2 pm the Ship foundered. Such a sad sight were her last struggles that all Hands were heartsick. After the collision we commenced to get boats out to clear away wreck &c but the water gained on us so fast that we were obliged to employ everyone at the Pumps – but they proved to be of no avail – in the mean time the boats of '*Iron Duke*' came to our rescue & with heavy hearts we left the magnificent Ship. I did not save a single thing but what I at present stand in – nor did anyone else that I am aware of except those whose duty it was to save the Public Money &c ... mind that everything is strictly private.' (In fact he did save something, as he had already written: 'I very fortunately saved the greater part of my Cash that I had that day received from the Paymaster – so that I do not need money – in this respect (having £10 about me) I was much more fortunate than others'.[201] The Captain was older, and felt the loss even more keenly. The *Times* reporter at the Court Martial was touched by the fact that 'Throughout the whole of the proceedings Captain Dawkins was much affected at the mention of the loss of the ship'[202].

One thing in particular might have saddened Dawkins. It was widely reported in the Press that 'It was remembered by someone that the Captain's favourite dog had been left behind. There were many a brave fellow ready to risk his life to endeavour to save the animal, but the order was given for no-one to attempt it, and the poor dog was the only living thing known to have perished on board.'[203] *The Times* on 3 September was more laconic: 'A favourite dog belonging to the Captain also went down with her' - but the *Daily Telegraph* said it was Commander Tandy's dog. If the poor beast existed at all, it does not seem to have been the Captain's cherished companion, since there is no mention at all of a dog in the stack of correspondence between Dawkins and his family and friends after the incident. The case for the truth of this sad little tale is not proved.

During all this excitement the flagship and *Hector* were plodding on towards Queenstown, quite oblivious of what was happening a short distance behind them. Vice Admiral Walter Tarleton had set a speed of 7 knots for the Squadron after they had rounded the Kish Light (achieved by a rate of 33 revolutions of *Warrior's* engines). That would, he calculated, get them to Queenstown on the ebb tide on Friday morning. When the fog came on, he knew that the rule book said ships should proceed at no more than three or four knots, but was also aware that the tide was setting them towards the shoals on the Irish coast to their right, so any slowing down could prove hazardous. At the same time he knew that the Second Division to their left (*Vanguard* and *Iron Duke*) would have to sprint to catch up, since the fog had come on so soon after their manoeuvre to 'form columns of divisions'. Tarleton comes across as a sensible, level-headed man, who knew and trusted his officers. He told the phalanx of top brass at the Court Martial that he 'considered it safer in the fog so suddenly coming on to leave the handling of the ship to the individual discretion of the officer in command in whom I had every confidence … The Captains had the instructions for fog to govern them, and were at liberty by those instructions to reduce speed should they deem it necessary. I considered I should distract their attention by doing more than indicating the position of the flagship which I did by firing guns every half-hour, and by sounding continuously the steam trumpet.'[204]

Indeed as soon as the fog began to show itself Flag-Lieutenant Edward Stratford Dugdale asked Flag-Captain William Whyte for the fog signal book and pointed out the relevant sections on speeds and signals, then went and told the Admiral. Whyte ordered guns to be fired, to show the Squadron that the flagship was maintaining speed. The first signal gun to be fired was a 12-pounder, which would not carry far; from then on they switched to a 7-inch gun with a 19lb charge, which might be heard 5 or 6 cables (around 1 kilometre) away. The guns were sounded every 30 minutes from 12.30 to 3 in the afternoon. The Second Division does not appear to have heard them. Signalman John Davis on *Vanguard* was listening out for signals from the flagship, and heard her whistle at about 12.40 but no guns – but at the time the *Vanguard*'s own steam whistle, acknowledged to be one of the most powerful in the fleet, was blasting away behind him. On *Iron Duke* Signalman Nehemiah Bale was also on watch for signals from the leader, but heard nothing. He did confess to the Court Martial that he was deaf in one ear. Various people reported having heard a distant whistle, but where it came from or what it signified nobody seemed to know.

Warrior kept up a whistled dialogue with *Hector* in the fog, and the two ships maintained their speed and station, assuming that all was well with the Second Division. A little after 1pm the fog lifted enough for the flagship to signal to *Hector* to reduce speed slightly. This helped, because to issue such an order by steam whistle would have taken far too long (each ship in the Squadron in succession would have needed to repeat, first the preparatory, then the signal itself). *Vanguard* and *Iron Duke* were still not visible. Dugdale said that 'The port column not being in sight when the fog lifted, he did not deem it necessary to inform the Vice Admiral on that point. The ships in the other column would probably proceed at seven knots, but being so far out of station he considered that the Leader of the port column would regulate his ships'[205]. The *Vanguard*'s signal gun was heard on *Warrior* some time after 12.30, but nobody considered it significant. At about two o'clock the fog cleared enough for Captain Whyte to take his spyglass and look towards the Second Division. He could see both *Vanguard* and *Iron Duke*, apparently still steaming in line, although 'it was somewhat foggy and the ships were indistinct. He could, however, see the upper part of the hull'[206]. This must have been a few moments before *Vanguard* finally sank, and is a good illustration of how deceptive mist and fog can be.

At 9 am on Friday 3 September *Warrior* and *Hector* steamed gently into Queenstown harbour, to be met by the tender *Amelia* with the astonishing news of *Vanguard's* end. Several telegrams from the Admiralty addressed to Admiral Tarleton had been received at Cork on the Thursday evening, but there was no way of getting in touch with him. According to the press, 'The excitement on board when the news was read from the *Amelia* tender was intense. The crews shouted for joy when informed that no lives were lost.'[207] By three o'clock that afternoon they had weighed anchor again and were on their way back to Kingstown, carrying carpenters, divers and artificers from the guardship HMS *Revenge*.

The news had reached land at about 3 am on Thursday morning, when *Iron Duke*, carrying all the officers and crew of *Vanguard*, arrived at Kingstown (not the most comfortable of journeys, with the 350 *Vanguard* people crammed in with the 405 crew and 210 fleetmen of *Iron Duke*). One report says that Commander Joseph McCullen of the revenue cruiser *Victoria* was the first to be told, and 'In Kingstown on Friday the greatest consternation prevailed, as the *Vanguard*, being stationed here, the majority of the married men's wives reside in the town, and the first news which arrived was that all hands had gone down with her.'[208] According to the anonymous author of the 'letter to a friend in Maidstone':

'At 11 o'clock I was sent on shore in Dublin Bay, with despatches and telegrams. I drove eight miles to Dublin, and after two hours in bed, broke the news to some of the officers' wives, and reported the disaster to the Lord Lieutenant. So you see I carried with me to Dublin the news which next day put Great Britain into excitement and consternation.'[209]

The officers found what space they could to pen telegrams home. William Hathorn's read 'Twenty miles from Kingstown collided with *Iron Duke Vanguard* foundered all Hands saved with nothing but what we stand in', and Richard Dawkins wrote 'All safe at Kingstown *Vanguard* foundered after collision with *Iron Duke* thank God all saved will write immediately'. Then they proceeded to prepare their official reports on what happened.

During those awful hours the two Captains must have rehearsed again and again what had happened, or appeared to have happened, and if there were blame, who should bear it. There is hardly a hint of this in the documents which survive. Captain Dawkins spoke more than once during the Court Martial about the 'skilful and masterly' handling of the *Iron Duke* during the incident, and Captain Hickley said at one point that 'Captain Dawkins and I conversed constantly on our terrible misfortune'[210], but none of Dawkins' many letters or notes refer to what passed between them. What we do know is that Dawkins found a corner of the crowded ship that night and wrote, as he had done every day, to his wife Mary in Stoke Gabriel[211]:

'*Iron Duke*, Kingstown, Sept 1ˢᵗ

My own darling Mary,

Just after leaving Kingstown we got a dense fog and from some unknown reason or other the *Iron Duke* ran straight into us and we sank in one hour, thank
God I saved every body and was the last to leave the old ship, Captain Hickley
behaved very bravely but think his Career is ended as he was going nearly 9
knots in a fog, I had taken every precaution and no one can see any blame is
attached to *Vanguard* of course there will be a Court Martial. It is a sad thing
Mary but I thank God as I say to the best of my belief and God grant all was
done by us, Tandy and all the officers think the same I managed to save a few
of my things but of course have lost a lot, but don't worry yourself my darling
it is just one of those things that we are all subject to, our men behaved very
well. Kiss me darling, I cannot write more but really I feel I did well to avoid it
and so every one says and if a man will be so unfortunate to run you down you
cannot help it.

Your loving husband

Richard

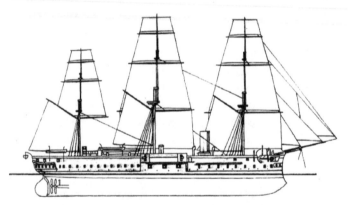

Outline drawing
of the *Audacious*
class of central
battery ironclads
(*Audacious,
Invincible, Vanguard*
and *Iron Duke*)
(length 280')

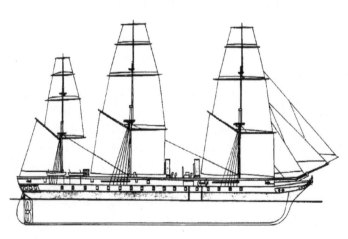

Outline drawing
of HMS *Warrior*
(length 380').
Presumed to
be by Ray
Woodward,
from E H H
Archibald: *The
Metal Fighting
Ship in the Royal
Navy 1860-1970*.
Attempts to trace
the copyright
holder have been
unsuccessful.

Chapter 9

'This sentence was most unjust'
The *Vanguard* Court Martial

The consternation that prevailed in Kingstown on Friday 3 September 1875 was as nothing to the storm that broke out in the newspapers and in naval circles that same day. Telegraph messages had been sent to Queenstown and to the Admiralty as soon as *Iron Duke*'s message reached Kingstown early on the Thursday morning, but it was not until Friday that the press published the shocking news. *The Times* carried this sober announcement:

> We have received the following lamentable intelligence from the Admiralty:-
> 'The Lords of the Admiralty much regret that news has been received that Her Majesty's ship *Iron Duke* came into collision with Her Majesty's ship *Vanguard* during a dense fog this morning, at 12 50, off Wicklow. All lives were saved. Her Majesty's ship *Vanguard* has, unfortunately, sunk in 19 fathoms water.
> Admiralty, Sept.2'

The Daily Telegraph and other papers printed the same communication, under a more prosaic heading (simply 'Admiralty Report'), and all carried colourful reports of what happened, with varying degrees of accuracy. Both broadsheets managed to get the list of officers aboard *Vanguard* and *Iron Duke* wrong. As usually happens in military mishaps, a security blanket was imposed. *The Times* said that 'The strictest reserve is kept on board the *Iron Duke*, and access to reliable sources of information is closed with jealous vigilance. Persons seeking admission, unless in an official capacity, are sternly warned off, and various devices have been resorted to in order to learn all the particulars of the occurrence. The public is manifesting an eager desire to get a full and authentic narrative. Facts, however, are of necessity comparatively few, the accident being unattended with any of the calamitous consequences which have invested other collisions on the deep with tragic interest.'[212]

Facts being few, the Press grasped any rumour going, thereby causing those in the know much frustration. William Hathorn wrote 'The <u>story</u> that Mams quotes about the gallantry displayed by a man who saved all hands by turning off the steam – is one of the numerous delusions which have appeared in the newspapers.'[213] The inaccuracy and inequity of the Press was to become a familiar theme in the young Lieutenant's letters as the weeks passed.

The first press reports had however said good things about the two Captains. Dawkins 'remained at his post until the last moment … manifesting the utmost self-possession and courage throughout the trying scene', and Hickley 'is an officer of great experience', said *The Times*. The *Telegraph's* report[214] allowed Dawkins 'great intrepidity and courage', but its leader column gave a hint of what was to come. It began 'A deplorable occurrence – which must by no means be styled an accident until inquiry has proved whether negligence had anything to do with the matter – has sent to the bottom one of the finest men-o'-war in Her Majesty's service', and went on to talk about 'a melancholy example of blundering and bad seamanship … too shocking, ridiculous, and ruinous … a lubberly spectacle … our ships are wasting away by rust and blunders faster than we are building them'. Even the Wicklow herring-boats managed to find their way about in a fog (though they also reported that the Holyhead boat had been delayed by the fog, and the mail had not been delivered). The *Telegraph* did pick up on one positive element, 'the awful efficiency of the ram as an engine of war'. There would be a lot more of this to come.

Iron Duke was sitting in Kingstown harbour, missing her bowsprit, jibboom, and all her head gear, including the scroll figurehead, but still seaworthy enough to ferry officials out to the wreck. *Warrior* and *Hector* left Queenstown for the site of the wreck at 3 pm on Friday, carrying workmen from Haulbowline to give what help might be needed. On arrival they found *Vanguard's* masts projecting out of the water, already marked as a hazard to shipping by buoys and lights. Vice Admiral Tarleton wrote to Sir Alexander Milne: 'I went on board I.Duke before she left, + approved the conduct of *Vanguards* crew which was beyond praise. + I had an opportunity of telling them that the Queen had sent a Telegram expressing her deep regret at the accident, + of her thankfulness that there had been no loss of life. The discipline observed aboard *Vanguard*, + Hickley's presence of mind + promptitude in hoisting out his boats + coming to the rescue after the ships had separated prevented most lamentable consequences – I have *[illeg]* Ponsonby a précis of the Capt's letters, as he desired information for Her Maj. – From what I can make out the collision was owing to Hickley's error in judgement in porting his helm without knowing.'[215]

At 5 o'clock on Friday afternoon the Admiralty steam tender *Vivid* (the 'swiftest vessel in port', according to the *Telegraph*) left Devonport with a couple of divers and 'appliances', under the direction of Staff Captain Batt, Master Attendant at Devonport Dockyard. Robert Barrie Batt was to find himself at the centre of things for a while. He was 53 and had the sea in his blood. For the benefit of the 1881 Census he said he had been born 'aboard HM Ship, at Sea'. He had entered the navigating branch of the service – the sailing masters or pilots - through Master Assistant and 2nd Master, passing his Master's certificate in 1844. The Master's was a highly professional task. He knew his ship and its capabilities intimately, and thus most Masters tended to stay longer on one vessel than the fighting officers. Batt however moved from ship to ship quite frequently, building up a good variety of experience. Becoming a Master did not lead automatically to promotion, as did the main career ladder, but changes in the structure of ranks meant that he had been promoted to Staff Commander aboard *Indus* in 1864, then to Assistant Master Attendant at Keyham dockyard in 1868. In 1869, at the age of 47, he married Charlotte Augusta Reed, and four years later took over as Master Attendant at Devonport. In dockyard parlance, the Commissioner was in charge of the yards, and the Master Attendant in charge of the ships afloat. There was considerable interchange between dockyard officers and those who went to sea, and it was not uncommon for the senior posts at a yard to be occupied by retired sea officers. For his task at the wreck of *Vanguard* he was regraded Staff Captain. It was now his job to decide what on earth was to be done about this massive chunk of metal obstructing the sea lanes, and he began shuttling between his home, Dublin Bay, and London.

Batt arrived at the wreck aboard *Vivid* at 7 o'clock in the evening of Saturday 4 September, and returned the next day to report to Sir Alexander Milne, the First Sea Lord. By Monday he was back in Plymouth, and sailed again for the wreck on Tuesday 7 with 50 men in the steam tug *Carron*. Meanwhile his divers had got to work, and already discovered that even in half-decent weather the strength of the current made operations difficult. The gunboat *Orwell* was now stationed at the site, and *Vanguard's* tender *Amelia* was ferrying technicians and officials to and from Kingstown. She might have made some money by plying for hire; apparently boatloads of sightseers came the sixteen miles from Dublin and Kingstown to see for themselves: 'A party of excursionists on a steam-tug, with much fiddling and merrymaking on board, came out from Dublin. In honour of the commander of the Orwell, the musicians played *Rule Britannia*, but with the grim humour which distinguishes the sons of the Emerald Isle, on passing the wreck the tune was changed to the *Bay of Biscay*.'[216]

The early news reports mentioned the watertight compartments, and one went so far as to allege that 'no-one thought of' shutting the watertight door in the after bulkhead. Edward Reed, the principal designer of the *Audacious* class of central battery ironclads, was quick to write in defence of his design, and had a long letter published in *The Times* on 4 September. The leading article that day said that 'the gist of his letter is that the principal object of building a ship of war in this way is safety during action'[217]. That did less than justice to a carefully argued statement of the problem of balancing sufficient watertight compartments against the convenience of those who had to move around the ship, and a frank admission that 'in my estimation the system of division into water-tight compartments does not provide for the security of the ship under all possible circumstances of ramming, nor do I think that it can be made effectual in this respect under all circumstances with the engine and boiler compartments so large as they necessarily are'[218]. What must have happened, he surmised, was that *Iron Duke's* ram had caught *Vanguard* just where a bulkhead was, thus flooding two compartments at once. On the Monday there appeared another Reed letter: 'In my desire to keep my letter of yesterday's date short … I appear to have said less than was desirable respecting the water-tight compartments of ironclads.'[219] He wanted to emphasise that what happened as the result of an accident during manoeuvres was not the same as what might be expected in the course of battle, and that the closing of the watertight doors was a crucial and well-practised part of safety procedures. 'That they have proved in a considerable degree efficient ... is shown by the fact that a ship which, without them, would have sunk in about three minutes ... kept afloat for nearly an hour'. Reed was quite rightly defensive of his design.

Meanwhile others had taken up their pens and started what became a small flood of ideas, comments and suggestions. 'A Naval Officer' disdainfully commented that ships should not sail in such close order. 'Gunner' said it wouldn't have happened if only the powers that be had taken notice of his simple suggestions about signalling with steam whistles (actually it would, because *Vanguard* did signal, but nobody who heard the whistle understood its meaning correctly). Thomas Brassey made 'with diffidence' a similar point about signalling with guns. 'Naval Architect' asked ten apparently pertinent questions about the position and weight of the wreck, the nature of the sea bottom, and so on. 'J.A.P., Rear-Admiral' defended the 'stringent, precise and carefully worded' Admiralty rules on navigation, and went on to give his sensible opinion that any ship would fall back on dead reckoning in so thick a fog: 'The fogs in the Irish Sea, from my own knowledge, rise far above a ship's masthead, and, once surrounded, it simply becomes 'dead reckoning' until the fog lifts. ... The Squadron was close to the Wicklow banks; the tides were at their strongest (springs), and the set runs wildly on the Wicklow and Arklow shoals; the flood tide brought up the fog, which, hour by hour, grew denser, and, as the sun went down, the darkness of a new-moon night added to the dangers of navigation in those narrow seas.'[220] (In fact of course the incident was all over by early afternoon.) To these suggestions were added a plethora of ideas for raising the wreck, to which we shall return in Chapter 13. The Admiralty must have found it all too much, because it was announced on 7 September that no attempt would be made to raise the wreck until after the winter.

One element missing from the newspaper reports is any eyewitness account from *Vanguard* of what happened. It had been reported that officers and crew were under strict instructions to say nothing to anybody ('Mind that everything is strictly private' – William Hathorn to his parents). One exception is the document referred to earlier that was printed in the national and regional broadsheets on 8 September, purporting to be a letter from an officer on board *Vanguard* to 'a friend in Maidstone'. In full, it read as follows: 'We arrived with the Reserve Squadron in Dublin Bay on Saturday morning, and I went on leave that afternoon to stay with some friends in Dublin. I came back on Tuesday, on which day there was a dance on board the flagship and a banquet on shore, with fireworks, &c, in honour of the fleet. Wednesday was a lovely day, and at 11.30 a.m. we sailed for Queenstown. At 12, luncheon, and then a smoke. I finished my pipe about 20 minutes to 1, went into the wardroom, and said to Dr Fisher, who was reading the newspaper, 'What a thick fog has suddenly come on!' Fisher went to look out of one of the ports, and cried out, 'My God, here is a ship right into us!' We rushed on deck, and that moment the *Iron Duke* struck us with fearful force, spars and blocks falling about and causing great danger to us on deck. The *Iron Duke* then dropped astern, and was lost sight of in the fog. The water came into the engine-room in tons, stopping the engines, putting the fires out and nearly drowning the engineers and stokers. Amid all the danger one man connected with the engine-room had the presence of mind to let the steam off, otherwise the enormous boilers would have burst. What the effect would have been God alone knows. The ship was now reported sinking fast, although all the watertight compartments had been closed. But in consequence of the shock some of the watertight doors leaked fearfully, letting water into the other parts of the ship. Minute guns were being fired and the boats were got out. Unfortunately two boats were destroyed by the *Iron Duke*. None of the boom boats – that is, the big boats – could be got out, as the stays, &c, had been carried away by the collision. At this moment the *Iron Duke* again appeared, lowering her boats and sending them as fast as possible. The sight of her cheered us up, as we had been frightened she would not find us in the fog in spite of the guns. The scene on deck can only be realized by those who have witnessed a similar calamity. The booming of the minute guns, the noise of the immense volume of steam rushing out of the escape funnel, and the orders of the captain, were strangely mingled, while a voice from a boat reported how fast the ship was sinking. And fast she was sinking too – six inches in 15 minutes. A ship of such great size going down six inches in every quarter of an hour is fearful; and the fact of her being an iron ship, with enormous guns, made it worse. I now went below, and superintended the transfer of the public records, books, &c, into the boats. After doing this I again went on deck, the water having reached 25 feet above the bilge. The order was now given for the men to get into the boats, and shortly afterwards I got over the stern into the boat with the books. I then came alongside, and took as many men into the boat as she could carry, and went on board the *Iron Duke*. All hands were out of the ship by 1.35, about 40 minutes after the collision. The fog had now cleared off, and we all stood on the deck of the *Iron Duke* watching for the finale of the catastrophe. A little before 2 o'clock she heeled gradually over until the whole of her enormous side, to the keel, was above water. Then she gradually sank, righting herself as she went down, stern first, the water being blown from hawse holes in huge spouts by the force of the wind rushing out of the ship as her bows sank. She then disappeared from view. Our fellows were much saddened to see their home go down, carrying everything they possessed. We had been paid that morning, and most of the officers lost that in addition. Fortunately I had my pay and also my watch in my pocket. At 11 o'clock I was sent on shore in Dublin Bay, with despatches and telegrams. I drove eight miles to Dublin, and after two hours in bed, broke the news to some of the officers' wives, and reported the disaster to the Lord Lieutenant. So you see I carried with me to Dublin the news which next day put Great Britain into excitement and consternation.'

The letter has enough detail to appear authentic, and is probably from one of the young Lieutenants; not, it would seem, from Hathorn, because in his correspondence he never mentions a mission to Kingstown. This letter certainly conveys better than any other source the feeling of rush and confusion. The 'friend in Maidstone' obviously recognised its value.

Far less widely reported was a letter from 'a sailor who was on board the *Iron Duke* at the time of the collision'. An unidentified press cutting among the Hathorn papers, dated 4 September, is the only evidence I have of the existence of this letter. It read: 'I do not know if you have heard anything respecting the collision with our ship and the *Vanguard*. You see we weighed anchor yesterday morning to proceed to Queenstown, and we had not been out many hours when it came over very foggy indeed. In fact, when I went on deck I could not even see the water over the ship's side, and about five minutes to one we had the sad misfortune to run into our sister ship, the *Vanguard*. And a few minutes after we heard signal guns of distress. We got our boats out, and, thank God, the fog cleared away and just allowed us time to save her ship's company and see her go down, which was one hour an a quarter from the time we struck her. Thank God, not one life was lost, but I reckon that 600,000*l* will as much as ever pay for her and the damage done to us. We are now laying at Kingstown. We got back here about eleven o'clock last night. We have about one thousand souls on board, and we are awaiting orders from the Admiralty what to do, but I expect we shall have to go to Plymouth to have defects made good.'

The incident occupied several column inches in the press, but there were other matters that were as noteworthy to readers. Less than a month had passed since Captain Webb had triumphantly swum from Dover to Calais for the first time, and he was making a sort of royal progress round the country. August had also witnessed another sinking, that of the royal yacht *Alberta*, described in the next chapter. The Coroner's inquest was going on at the time of the *Vanguard* incident, and naturally such reports held more public interest than wrangling between naval architects and salvage 'experts'. Later on there were lurid reports of a spectacular murder in Whitechapel to fill the pages. That the loss of *Vanguard* remained headline news as long as it did was due to the reports of the Court Martial, the timing of which was at last announced on 8th September.

For Dawkins and his colleagues this was a dreadful time, waiting for the Court Martial to get started. Of course there had to be a Court Martial. If a ship had been lost, the first task was to establish who was to blame, but the effect on those involved would have been to exacerbate the intense stress of what happened from the moment the fog rolled over the ship to the point when Dawkins himself was last to leave her. Dawkins' many friends rallied round, and wrote encouraging letters, showing real sadness and sympathy – one went so far as to write 'PS I shall address this to the *Vanguard* tho' she lies 15 Fms deep'[221]. The ship was to his friends what she had been to Dawkins, a living organism. Many of the letters were on black-edged paper, in mourning for the loss. Perhaps it was less helpful to receive, as the Captain did from J Allen Windle of the Mariner's Church, Kingstown, a pamphlet entitled *The Way of Salvation*, by the Reverend J D Waddington – but in its way that too was a friendly gesture. Any such would have been welcome, especially since despite confident expectation expressed in the newspapers, there had been no official hint that Captain Hickley and the officers of *Iron Duke* were going to suffer a Court Martial too. Was *Vanguard*'s crew to take all the blame for her loss?

William Hathorn felt fairly secure. On 2 September he had written to his parents: 'I was Officer of the Watch at time of collision & every precaution was taken to ensure our safety – so that no blame is likely to be attached to me.' Two days later he added 'The result of the Court-Martial about to be held is very doubtful indeed - & therefore it is likely to work great good, for it will compel the Authorities to define their Instructions more clearly – at present they are very confusing to say the least.'[222] This was to prove a false hope.

The waiting came to an end fairly soon. At 10 in the morning on Friday 10 September 1875, the Court Martial assembled aboard HMS *Royal Adelaide*, flagship of Port-Admiral the Hon. Sir Henry Keppel, moored in the Hamoazé at Devonport. Presiding was Rear Admiral Lord John Hay KCB, second in command of the Channel Squadron. The members of the Court included Rear Admiral William C Chamberlain, Superintendent of Devonport Dockyard, and various Captains of ships then in port: Captain Charles W Hope of *Resistance*, Captain Radulphus Bryce Oldfield of *Indus*, Captain Thomas B Lethbridge of *Black Prince* (sister ship to *Warrior*), Captain the Hon William J Ward, of the gunnery training vessel *Cambridge*, Captain William H Edye of *Impregnable*, Captain George H Parkin of *Triumph*, and Captain A C F Heneage of *Royal Adelaide*. The Legal Assessor was William Eastlake, Deputy Judge Advocate of the Fleet.

The President, Lord John Hay, was an imperious figure. The fourth son of the Marquis of Tweeddale, he had entered the Navy at the age of 12 and seen service similar to that of Richard Dawkins, in the China War and at Sebastopol. He entered Parliament in 1857 and served intermittently for seven years as an MP, becoming a Lord of the Admiralty in 1866 and from 1868 to 1871 and again during the 1880's. He went on to command the Channel Squadron in 1877, 'took possession of and administered Cyprus, 1878'[223], and was made Admiral of the Fleet in 1888. He died during World War I at the age of 88. In September 1875 he had just celebrated his forty-eighth birthday. The tone of his questioning during the days that followed illuminates a comment in a letter from Eardley Wilmot to Richard Dawkins a few weeks later: 'You know my opinion of Lord John Hay!'[224]. K C Barnaby points out[225] that of these nine gallant officers, only three were from ironclads (*Black Prince* and *Resistance* were broadside ironclads), the rest having experience only of wooden ships, and this background is betrayed in many of their questions.

Of the other members one of the Captains was certainly an original: Algernon Charles Fieschi Heneage (later Sir Algernon) was 41, and had also served in the Crimea. He was to become Commander-in-Chief on the Pacific Station and at the Nore before his retirement with the rank of Admiral. It was Heneage's personality rather than his naval prowess which impressed. Padfield tells the story of how 'One superb sailing officer, Captain Heneage, celebrated for his exquisite elegance and shining dark curls, refused to heed the names of any of his Chief Engineers, but referred to them all by the name of the first 'Chief' he had sailed with'[226]. Later in his career, according to Richard Hill, 'Admiral "Pompo" Heneage wore white gloves for inspections, replaced as necessary from a spare stock carried on a salver by his coxswain … A legend in his lifetime, … Heneage terrified officers and ratings with his zero-tolerance of dirt, slovenly dress and incorrect ceremonial.'[227] Geoffrey Regan adds that 'His affectation was such that he could not bear to think of a common sailor washing his clothes and so he took 20 dozen shirts to sea and sent the dirty ones home on every available ship bound for England. … On one notorious occasion a seaman took a step forward and steadied Pompo as he was climbing up a gangplank, which had the effect of turning him puce with rage. "Dat man!" shrieked Pompo. "He touched me!"'[228] From a Court composed of such people, the outcome of the hearing might already have been guessed.

The *Illustrated London News* carried a series of sketches, which can be taken to have the accuracy of photographs. The illustration of the Court Martial, drawn during the evidence of Admiral Tarleton, conveys the atmosphere aboard the old *Royal Adelaide*. A cramped, low-ceilinged room, almost filled by a table around which sit the members of the Court, grave-faced and proudly bewhiskered, supervised by a bust of the Queen. In a corner is another small table, at which Captain Dawkins and his assistant James W Lishman sit, and chairs are provided for the other 'Prisoners', Lieutenants Hathorn and Thomas. Beyond the large table the space is divided by a rail, behind which stand the newspaper reporters and the sailors and marines in attendance. It seems strange that Richard Dawkins had 'no advocate, counsel or solicitor for his legal defender'[229] - Lishman was no more than a Royal Navy Paymaster, who 'appeared also as the Friend and on behalf of the other officers & the ship's company of HMS *Vanguard* '[230] – but it appears to have been the right choice. Lishman wrote 'to Dawkins after the Court Martial saying that 'Everbody at the Admiralty thought it was wise of you to have my assistance rather than that of a Lawyer for Lord John Hay would have sat upon the Legal man at every turn and made it most unpleasant for you and him.'[231] In the event it is difficult to imagine how much more unpleasant the whole experience could have been for Dawkins.

So the process began. According to the record, the whole of the ship's company was present, though that would have created an intolerable crush. Punctiliously, the absence on leave of Captain Hickley was noted, as was the fact that James Morgan and William Warrell, Ordinary Seamen, were absent without leave. Six *Vanguard* crewmen were reported as sick in hospital, to wit Patrick Duggan, Caulker; John Marshall, the Leading Seaman whose fingers had been crushed during the sinking; Henry Richards, James C Green, and William Norman, Ordinary Seamen; and Private William G Golby RMLI. Then Dawkins, Hathorn and Thomas were brought into court. The charges under Sections 91 and 92 of the Naval Discipline Acts 1866 were read out, followed by a reading of reports written to the Secretary of the Admiralty by Dawkins and Brown, and to Dawkins by Hathorn and Alfred Smith, all dated 1 September. Further reports written by Hickley, Lieutenant Thompson, and Admiral Tarleton were laid before the Court – and these formalities completed, the mass of the ship's company were allowed to go, leaving Richard Dawkins, his lieutenants and James Lishman tucked into their corner of the room to face their prolonged ordeal.

An ordeal it must surely have been. The Court sat for seventeen days, Monday to Saturday over almost three weeks, from 10am to about 4.30pm each day, asking question after question (1,517 in all), going over the same ground again and again, picking at small points, poring over charts and plans. The bound copy of the proceedings held at the Public Record Office in Kew is 4¾ inches (12 cm) thick, dwarfing all other court martial files in the 1870's. The investigation was thorough, but sadly flawed. It started well enough. Captain Dawkins was asked if he had any complaint to make against any of his officers, and responded 'I have to disapprove of the conduct of one of the officers, namely, Captain Collins RMLI'[232]. Then he made a lengthy statement to the court of what had happened to his ship, referring to charts that the court studied. After a lunch break, Navigating Lieutenant Heaver Sugden of *Iron Duke* produced more charts of the Wicklow coast, and the members of the court began their plodding examination of the detail of Richard Dawkins' statement. Where were *Vanguard*'s signal logs? (At the bottom of the Irish Sea.) What boilers were alight? What orders were there about firing muskets as a signal from the stern when the engines stopped? What was known about the mysterious vessel that was supposed to have crossed *Vanguard*'s bows and precipitated everything? How far off could *Vanguard*'s whistle be heard? (In fact all agreed that she had a very powerful blast, 'one of the most powerful steam cowls he had ever heard.')

Saturday brought more of the same. Captain Dawkins was quizzed about his speed in the fog, and why he had thought fit to slow down when he had received no signal from the Admiral to do anything of the kind. He tried – the first of many attempts – to make the court understand how little time had elapsed between the moment the squadron were enveloped in fog to the sudden unexpected impact from *Iron Duke*, but met with no comprehension. He was given the chance to amplify his complaint about the Marine officer: 'I have to complain to the Court that Captain Collins, RMLI, asked leave and obtained it from Commander Tandy, to leave the *Vanguard* and go to the *Iron Duke*. To the best of my belief this was about 20 minutes before the last of the detachment left the ship. There was no reason to my mind for this officer to leave the *Vanguard*, and I considered his conduct was most reprehensible, and I informed him, in the presence of the Commander, that I should leave the Court to deal with it. It is a standing order on board the *Vanguard* that no heads of departments leave the ship without the Captain's permission when he is on board, and as I never left the bridge from the time of the collision to the final leaving of the ship my permission should certainly have been asked.' What seems to have annoyed Dawkins was not so much Collins' disregard for the ships' rules, as the fact that he wanted to be off before all the men under his command had been disembarked. In any case, Lord John Hay said that 'the Court will not go into the matter at this present time', and the complaint was passed to the Admiralty. When this was announced a few days later, Dawkins stressed that he 'hoped the Court would understand that he did not wish to cast any reflection whatever on the gallantry of Captain Collins'. But the legal process had been set in motion, and a month later Admiralty Board General Minutes recorded: 'Captain S T Collins RMLI '*Iron Duke*' to be severely reprimanded for asking permission to leave '*Vanguard*' while his Detachment were still on board'[233]. Collins was 37, ten years younger than Dawkins. Like Dawkins, he had been present at the capture of Canton in 1857, and a couple of years later in the attack on the Peiho Forts in June 1859 had been severely wounded, to the extent that he applied unsuccessfully to be invalided out of the Service. He had suffered enough stress already, and who knows what effect the imminence of sinking might have had on him.

Hathorn and Thomas were called to give their stories, and the second day came to an end. Monday 13 September was given over to Admiral Tarleton and the officers of his flagship *Warrior*, with much discussion of signal gun procedure, and a statement from the Admiral that when the fog had come down he expected his Captains to use their discretion as to what speed they adopted. More about signals on Tuesday, including the questioning of signalmen from *Vanguard*, and then on Wednesday 15 the ship's lookout men were put through their paces, including the unfortunate 24-year-old Michael Murphy, whose possibly defective eyesight was probed. He of course was the man who had first seen the sailing ship crossing *Vanguard*'s bows, and it was clear that the court had some doubt about whether the ship had existed at all. Happily on the following Monday a telegram arrived, forwarded by Admiral Henry Keppel, which read: 'The following has been received from Commr. Tuke, Coast Guard, Malahide, Co. Down:

'The Norwegian Timber Vessel which is reported to have caused *Vanguard* to deviate from course is now discharging Northwall, Dublin.'

The next day it was the turn of more lookout men and those who had been at the wheel, and the court made a start on the engineers, beginning with William Paige. Again they seemed to have little understanding of the time pressure under which everybody on *Vanguard* had been working; Paige was expected to have made superhuman efforts to stop both engines and restart them. He explained the normal manning of the engine room, and went on 'he could not start both engines at the same time, because there were two wheels in connexion with the throttle valves, one on either side and one on each engine. These would have to be opened one at a time, the reason being that they were rather hard, and he had to use both hands on one wheel. Two people could start both engines at the same time, but one could not.' Despite this admirably clear statement, Lord John Hay pressed him: 'You received an order for both engines to go ahead at full speed; why did you not obey it by starting both engines at once?' Paige, presumably with some restraint, said 'I did obey it, but, as I said before, I could only open one valve at a time. Between one engine starting and the other also starting there would only elapse a few seconds of time. In going in and out of harbour there are two engineers stationed in the engine room, but when running with the fleet one is considered sufficient'. This exchange illustrates well the harsh and often arbitrary nature of the court's questioning of witnesses. An order was an order; physical obstacles to carrying out that order were to be ignored, and the court appeared to presuppose idleness and inefficiency in everybody from *Vanguard* whom they questioned.

The court next turned to the *Iron Duke* officers, and Lieutenant Pierre Evans made a stout defence of his decision to sheer off course a little, in case *Iron Duke* should run into *Vanguard,* a decision he thought himself justified in making in the absence of Captain Hickley, who had gone below. The President's view was evident in his questioning: 'Have you any explanation to offer for having intentionally and deliberately forsaken your station and sheered the *Iron Duke* out of line?' Again no account seemed to be taken of the circumstances or the application of common sense to a sudden change in the weather. What mattered was who had given what orders, or, if none had been given, why anybody had done anything at all to avoid possible disaster.

On day 10 of the hearing, Tuesday 21 September, the President announced that they had concluded the first part of the enquiry, and would go on to look at the measures taken for saving the ship and her crew (notably, in that order). The day ended with a farcical session with Commander Young, the officer from HMS *Achilles* who had been a passenger aboard *Vanguard* on his way to Queenstown to conduct a Court Martial. Obviously he had no authority or formal position on *Vanguard,* but the court harried him about why he had not taken the lead in ensuring that the watertight doors were all shut. 'Did you volunteer to attend personally to this subject of vital importance, knowing that the presence of an officer of your rank and experience would have urged everyone under you to be most rapid and correct in the execution of those duties?' asked Admiral Chamberlain. Young sensibly answered that he wouldn't have been much use, since he didn't know the geography of the ship.

Chamberlain, the old wooden-walls man, also put to Commander Young the first of a series of questions that were to make the court a laughing-stock among the new breed of ironclad sailors: 'Question 1098: Did it not occur to you towards the early part of the collision, if not later, that the whole of the spare sails of the ship roughly but sufficiently weighted might if thrown overboard in large bulk properly attached to the ship from forward and above, been jammed into the hole by the great rush of water?' Young courteously said there hadn't been time. When a wooden sailing ship had been holed below the water line, it was common practice to plug the hole with a wad of sails, leaving water pressure and the ship's natural buoyancy to do the rest. It was a responsibility of the Carpenter's team to patrol the wing passages on the lookout for shot-holes to plug. It made no sense at all to adopt this procedure in an iron ship, but the court kept coming back to it. Thus, Lord John Hay to Captain Dawkins on day 13 of the enquiry: 'Question 1238: Can you give any explanation of no attempt having been made to stop or check the leak, either by sails outside, or by materials inside, shored up against the site of the leak?' Dawkins answered: 'The shoring up of the fracture from inside I should consider not practical at all. – At the time I felt the *Vanguard* to be sinking, – there was no time then to get sails prepared to go over the side. The suggestion of sails was never made to me, nor do I conscientiously believe, when I first knew the *Vanguard* was going, that I could have got them up, or that they would have been ready for service.' Nevertheless they tried again with the

Carpenter, David Tiddy, Chamberlain sternly calling him 'an old carpenter who must have had considerable experience in the strength of ships and their construction'. Tiddy certainly knew *Vanguard* better than anyone else, having been aboard since she was commissioned, and at 50 was older than any of the other witnesses, but the members of this court did not readily abandon their preconceptions.

Another point on which Dawkins was pressed, and other witnesses were repeatedly asked, was whether any request had been made to *Iron Duke* to tow *Vanguard* into shallower water. Dawkins remembered having asked for such assistance, and other witnesses supported him, but there had been no response from Captain Hickley, and the assumption was that everybody thought the ship would go down much faster than she did.

Over the next few days much time was spent on the deployment of pumps, and the shutting of the watertight doors. The court simply could not understand why the Captain had not immediately ordered all pumps to be activated, so that the ship stayed afloat. Edward Noble, the senior Lieutenant, was asked why he had not considered it his duty to run about all over the ship making sure that pumps were going full blast, but sensibly replied that knowing other Lieutenants were stationed in other parts of the ship, he thought it his duty to look after the fore part, where he had been told to be. *Vanguard* was well supplied with pumps, but one immediate problem for Dawkins and Brown, his Chief Engineer, was that the stokehole flooded rapidly, putting the boiler fires out within some six minutes of the collision, thus extinguishing any steam power for the most effective pumps. Brown was asked whether he had ordered the bilge injection to be turned on, and he patiently explained that there was no bilge injection; instead there was a procedure involving the condensers, which would have taken up to half an hour for all four engines. The engine room would be flooded well before that could have been accomplished. There were of course hand pumps, two 9 inch and three 7 inch Downtons, which if fully operating (explained John Trickett, Chief Engineer and Inspector of Machinery at Keyham Dockyard) ought to have shifted some about a ton of water a minute – whereas Barnaby calculates[234] that the sea was coming in at a rate of between 800 and 900 tons an hour.

The watertight doors presented a similar problem. Some of them did not fit as well as they should, and water ran over the sills, but this could have been caused by the force of the impact. Besides this, Robert Brown told the court that ventilation holes had been cut in Nos. 85 and 67 bulkheads on both sides of the ship, admittedly only 6inches x 4inches (15cm x 10cm), and high up under the deck above, but through which water would certainly flow. The Dockyard had cut these holes the previous June, but for some reason Captain Dawkins knew nothing about them. It would have made little difference if he had, because the *Iron Duke's* ram had penetrated *Vanguard's* skin close to bulkhead 85, breaching two adjacent watertight compartments. Such an impact on a wooden hull would have simply made a big hole. On iron construction, besides a hole 9foot 6inches (2.9m) high and 3foot (0.9m) wide, there would have also been 'a multitude of rivet holes and other small openings in the sixteen ft wake of the driven in armour plate and possibly some damaged pipes etc'[235]. It is significant that only Captain Lethbridge of the ironclad *Black Prince* showed any understanding of this, asking Alexander Moore, Chief Constructor at Devonport: 'Are you not of the opinion that the inner skin in the neighbourhood of the blow, owing to its being stayed by the athwart-ship bulkhead in the double side, has materially shaken the inner skin of the ship and thereby caused heavy leakage?' Moore seems relieved to reply 'I think it extremely probable that a considerable portion of the ship in the neighbourhood of the fracture has been disturbed and received considerable injury, especially in regard to the starting of rivets'.

It became increasingly evident from quite early on in the proceedings that the members of the court were mostly still living in the age of wood and sail, and in a service dominated by concepts of proper procedure and budgetary constraints. They appeared much more concerned about why more had not been done to save the ship than about commending the Captain and crew for a disciplined and well-ordered evacuation with no casualties apart from John Marshall's fingers. Of course, as the newspapers were eager to point out, the cost of what now lay on the seabed was about half a million pounds sterling, which would roughly equate to £23 million in 2001. Captain Dawkins said that about £1000 and the ship's papers had been saved (except apparently the signal log), but much else had gone, including a large amount of stores. Among them were 26,000 biscuits, nearly 5,000 candles and 470 lbs (213kg) of mustard. Charles Dawson, *Vanguard*'s Paymaster, produced an inventory for the benefit of the court, and was promptly told to go away and 'make the statement more clear'. His amended version can be found at Annex 3. The only items to which any significant value appears to have been attached were the officers' plate and wine, reckoned to be worth £560.

Above all, the overall attitude of the court gave the impression that they assumed nobody other than *Vanguard*'s crew could be held responsible for what had happened. Sir Walter Tarleton, Captain Hickley and others from *Warrior* and *Iron Duke* were questioned, but (apart from Lieutenant Evans who had been Officer of the Watch on *Iron Duke*) less rigorously than 'the prisoners' and their colleagues. Tarleton was asked to explain himself when he spoke of leaving things to his Captains' discretion after the fog came down, but the court did not press him too hard. Richard Dawkins and his men were on trial, and the verdict could clearly be seen coming.

Dawkins had his final chance to avert disaster on 28 September at 2 o'clock, when he spoke for over 20 minutes, summing up his position in words that were both precise and passionate, touching on all the arguments that had been put forward. He paid tribute to the courage, discipline and devotion of his officers and crew, singling out for special praise some who might be especially liable to censure, such as Hathorn and Brown. He stressed his own responsibility for his decisions: 'We were now in the fog. I at once, owing to long-standing and strong feelings on the subject, was dissatisfied to rush through the water in a dense fog at a speed of eight knots, and prepared, as leader of my column, and in the absence of any instructions from the Admiral by signal or preconcert, to act according to my own judgment, which, as I shall presently show, was precisely what I was relied on to do.' It was a powerful and persuasive statement, peppered with phrases that recall the lively entries in his journal twenty years earlier. In his words, the collision was 'her fatal stab from the *Iron Duke*'; the sudden weather change prompted 'one enters a fog as though through an opaque wall, that all before him is shrouded in a darkness that may be felt'. 'In conclusion', he said, 'It is due to myself, my officers, and ship's company to state that on my ordering the crew a second time to the pumps on the suggestion of the Chief Engineer, I was acting entirely against the advice of the principal officers except the Chief Engineer ....We all felt it was our duty to go down with the *Vanguard* rather than the smallest shadow of a reflection should ever be thrown on our conduct or efforts to save our noble ship. We now leave the case in the hands of the honourable Court, with complete confidence that we shall be held to have acted judiciously before the accident and becomingly afterwards.' Brave words, misplaced confidence, and futile effort.

The Court Martial convened for the seventeenth day on Wednesday 29 September at 10.15 am, and immediately went into closed session for four hours. They reassembled at 2 o'clock, all the witnesses were ordered back into court, and the Judge-Advocate, William Eastlake, read out the sentence: 'Having heard the evidence which has been adduced on this inquiry and trial, the Court is of opinion that the loss of Her Majesty's ship *Vanguard* by Her Majesty's ship *Iron Duke* coming into collision with her off the Kish Bank, in the Irish Channel, about 50 minutes past noon, on the 1st of September last, from the effects of which she foundered; that such collision was caused:

'Firstly, by the high rate of speed at which the squadron of which the vessels formed part was proceeding while in a fog:

Secondly, by Captain Dawkins, when leader of his division, leaving the deck of his ship before the evolution which was being performed was completed, as there were indications of foggy weather at the time:

Thirdly, by the unnecessary reduction of speed of Her Majesty's ship *Vanguard* without a signal from the Vice-Admiral in command of the squadron, and without Her Majesty's ship *Vanguard* making the proper signal to Her Majesty's ship *Iron Duke*:

Fourthly, by the increase of speed of Her Majesty's ship *Iron Duke* during a dense fog, the speed being already high:

Fifthly, by Her Majesty's ship *Iron Duke* improperly sheering out of line:

Sixthly, by the want of any fog signal on the part of Her Majesty's ship *Iron Duke*.

The Court is further of opinion that the cause of the loss of Her Majesty's ship *Vanguard* by foundering was a breach being made in her side by the prow of Her Majesty's ship *Iron Duke* in the immediate neighbourhood of the most important transverse bulkhead – namely, that between the engine and boiler rooms, causing a great rush of water into the engine-room, shaft alleys, and stokehole, extinguishing the fires. In a few minutes the water eventually finding its way into the provision-room flat and provision-rooms, through imperfectly fastened water-tight doors, and owing to leakage near 99 bulkhead. The Court is of opinion that the foundering of Her Majesty's ship *Vanguard* might have been delayed, if not averted, by Captain Dawkins giving orders for immediate action being taken to get all available pumps worked, instead of employing his crew in hoisting out boats; and if Captain Dawkins, Commander Tandy, Navigating Lieutenant Thomas, and Mr David Tiddy, the carpenter, had shown more resource of energy in endeavouring to stop the breach from the outside with the means at their command, such as hammocks and sails; and the Court is of opinion that Captain Dawkins should have ordered Captain Hickley, of Her Majesty's ship *Iron Duke*, to tow Her Majesty's ship *Vanguard* into shallow water.

The Court is of opinion that blame is imputable to Captain Dawkins for exhibiting want of judgment and for want of duty in handling his ship; and that he showed a want of resource, promptitude, and decision in the means he adopted for saving Her Majesty's ship *Vanguard* after the collision.

The Court is further of opinion that blame is imputable to Navigating-Lieutenant Thomas for neglect of duty in not pointing out to his Captain that there was shoaler water within a short distance, and in not having offered any suggestion as to the mode of stopping the leak on the outside.

The Court is further of opinion that Commander Tandy showed a great want of energy as second in command under the circumstances.

The Court is further of opinion that Mr Brown, the chief engineer, showed want of promptitude in not applying the means at his command to relieve the ship of water.

The Court is further of opinion that Mr David Tiddy, carpenter of Her Majesty's ship *Vanguard*, is open to blame for not offering any suggestions to his Captain as to the most efficient mode of stopping the leak, and for not taking immediate steps for sounding the compartments and reporting from time to time the progress of the water.

The Court adjudges Captain Richard Dawkins to be severely reprimanded, and to be dismissed from Her Majesty's ship *Vanguard*, and he is hereby severely reprimanded and so sentenced accordingly.

The Court adjudges Commander Dashwood Goldie Tandy and Navigating Lieutenant James Cambridge Thomas to be severely reprimanded, and they are hereby severely reprimanded accordingly.

The Court adjudges Mr Robert Brown, chief engineer, and Mr David Tiddy, carpenter, to be reprimanded accordingly.

The Court imputes no blame to the other officers and ship's company of Her Majesty's ship *Vanguard* in reference to the loss of the ship, and they are acquitted accordingly.'

Chapter 10

'Le bon temps reviendra'?

The immediate aftermath

The Court's verdict must have stunned all the accused. Seventeen days of exhaustive questioning, and the members of the Court seemed to have made up their minds that Captain Richard Dawkins and his officers were guilty, regardless of what they might have heard in reply. A silent and bewildered group left *Royal Adelaide* as evening drew in, and within hours the letters of sympathy began to be delivered to Dawkins. Lieutenant Noble was one of the first, writing from his cabin on the hulk *Canopus*, where all of *Vanguard*'s crew were temporarily housed. He wanted 'to say how truly and correctly we, the three Lieutenants, feel the injustice meted out by the Court this day. We have experienced during our service in the late '*Vanguard*' your kindness, and consideration and friendly assistance when carrying out duties under your direction … thoroughly sympathise … 'le bon temps reviendra' – <u>we</u> shall never forget your conduct towards us, and the kindness and <u>tact</u> which made your reign so pleasant.'[236] Significantly, Vice Admiral Tarleton, who had travelled back to his base at the Naval Reserves in Spring Gardens, London that day, took the trouble to write before going to his bed to express 'sincere sympathy with you in the distress you must feel at the conclusion the Court has come to. No one can regret more than I do the disastrous termination of our previously successful Cruize, and the pain you feel is shared by yours very sincerely, J W Tarleton'. When the Court's verdict was published in the next day's *Times*, Admiral George Hathorn wrote 'As a father I most gratefully thank you for your generous consideration & kindness to my son'. (Dawkins' reply is among the Hathorn papers, and well illustrates his mood; after saying nice things about Hathorn Junior he launches into a defence of his position – 'I have been made a victim'.[237]) Among those who knew Dawkins the shock was great, as was concern for his state of mind: as early as 7 September Alex Crowder Crookshank had written from the Vice-Regal Lodge at Dublin Castle to Dawkins' cousin Jauncey that 'There are painful rumours here that his mind has been affected by the loss of his ship'[238]. As the days passed their anger mounted.

It was not so, or at least not immediately, with the official organs of public opinion. On 30 September, the day the verdict was published, *The Times* carried a rather pompous leader that must have pleased Lord John Hay and his colleagues. 'The sentence is by no means light', it read, 'To Captain Dawkins, indeed, it involves nothing less than professional ruin. But it is hard to see how any other conclusion could have been reached.

The loss of the *Vanguard* has been felt by the entire nation to be not only a disaster, but a disgrace, and it would have been difficult to acquiesce in any verdict which found no one guilty for such an event. ... When such an event does happen, we demand, at least, that it shall be shown to have been quite unavoidable; that proof shall be given that all due precaution was employed before the accident, and every possible means devised and put in practice for mitigating the disaster afterwards. In the case of the *Vanguard* none of these positions can be thought to have been made out. There were neglect and careless-ness beforehand, and there was even more remarkably an almost total want of resource subsequently, when the fatal blow had been struck. It appears clearly to have been the opinion of the naval officers who have had the unpleasant duty of sitting in judgment upon their fellows that the loss of the *Vanguard* has been occasioned by a series of gross blunders ... We are sorry for those who have been thus singled out for disgrace, but we feel at the same time that they could have expected nothing less, and that the public opinion of the country will approve, however reluctantly, the sentence which has been pronounced.' The leader went on to repeat the Court Martial's strictures about noth-ing being done to plug the hole made by *Iron Duke*'s ram, about Dawkins' apparent concentration on saving his men rather than his ship, about the pumps not being started immediately, about no attempt to tow the ship to safer water. It was as if the esteemed journalist had not read his own paper's reports of the evidence. The next day a well-wisher wrote from Ealing to Mary Dawkins in Stoke Gabriel: 'I shall call on the Editor of The Times tomorrow Morn^g + endeavour to bring him to reason – but of course he is a big man and may regard me as a Very Small one – my one hope is that Mr Delaney is spoken of as a very amiable <u>gentleman</u>.'[239] Mary's postbag contained several other indignant notes from family and friends, calling the verdict 'totally unjust' and a 'cruel sentence' - this from Mrs Tandy, presumably the Commander's wife. Tandy himself was thoroughly disillusioned, writing to Dawkins 'I don't feel the slightest interest in going on in the Service.' Charlotte Gillespy wrote to Mary 'Do you not think there will be a great reaction in the public mind against such a decision? I feel so indignant and angry.'

William Hathorn probably spoke for his colleagues when he wrote with barely disguised irritation to his parents, while at the same time putting his finger on a basic weakness in Captain Dawkins' defence, his honesty:

'You must excuse my criticizing the late verdict beyond saying that I consider it a very just one allowing that the same standard is meted out to Adml. Tarleton, Capt Hickley & others of "*Iron Duke*". The <u>public</u> will never arrive at the real truth of who is the proper person to blame – it is most wonderful how deceiv-ing the evidence is to a person who was not present to witness the real state of affairs – hence the <u>opinions</u> which one hears expressed by people who simply trust to the newspapers for their information – are painfully absurd. I am very sorry indeed for Capt. Dawkins – but at the same time you must remember that he made a fatal blunder in his defence by acknowledging that he had made a mistake. Good night. All is for the best – it is not worthy of yr. pens to confute any wild statements that you will read in the newspapers – With best love, yr. affect. Son '[240]

The editorial team at *The Times* took a while to sense the general surge of anger. On 1 October the leader went over the circumstances of the incident again, picking out other aspects, such as Dawkins' absence from the bridge when the fog came down – ignoring of course the fact that he had been at that station for several hours without a break. It speculated 'If the *Vanguard* had not reduced speed, or the *Iron Duke* had not increased speed, or both ships had kept in line, or both Captains had kept on deck, or both ships had known what signal to give and had been prepared to give it … the disaster would in all probability have been avoided.' *Punch* revelled in the confusions and contradictions of the Court:

'NAVAL AND MILITARY INTELLIGENCE
Vanguard Court Martial
By the Court. Captain D, why did you slacken speed when you got into a fog?
Captain D. If you please, Sir, I thought –
By the Court. What the devil business had you to think? Up to the mast-head immediately, Sir!

★ ★ ★ ★ ★

By the Court. Captain H, why did you *not* reduce speed when you got into a fog?
Captain H. If you please, Sir, I did not think –
By the Court. What the devil business had you not to think? Up to the mast-head immediately, Sir!'[241]

Gradually doubts began to be expressed. 'Engineer', writing in *The Times* on 2 October, firstly made the one positive point that the authorities were to sieze on: 'The collision …. proved, if it proved anything at all, the irresistible power of the ram as a weapon of attack.' He however doubted this, and went on in detail to describe how 'we may fairly suppose that the *Vanguard* was placed in about as dangerous a condition as she could be placed in, in calm weather, by a vessel of the *Iron Duke* class running into her at about seven knots speed.' In his view *Iron Duke*'s ram made enough of a hole for some 70 tons of water a minute to flow through, and that despite the main pumps being useless because the engine room was flooded, the circulating bilge pumps ought to have been able to shift half of what was coming in. Later commentators did the sums differently. Admiral Ballard wrote that 'they never attempted to find out how fast the water was coming in, or they would have discovered it was at a rate of about 50 tons a minute, since the ship's displacement increased by quite 3500 tons in the seventy minutes between the collision and the foundering'[242]. KC Barnaby however calculated[243] the inflow as much less, at 800 to 900 tons of water per hour, but even this he said the auxiliary pumps could not have coped with. In any case the two flooded compartments made up more than half of the length of the ship at that level. The crucial factor in the impact, which 'Engineer' missed, was that the inner skin of *Vanguard's* double bottom was not penetrated. If it had, says Barnaby, 'this would have started a torrent of water direct into the engine room and foundering might well have been a matter of ten minutes as expected by Commander Young, and not the actual hour and ten minutes.'

On that day, Saturday 2 October, the Lords of the Admiralty began their official inspection of the dockyards at Devonport. They were a glittering group, led by the Rt Hon George Ward Hunt MP, First Lord of the Admiralty, whose later handling of the incident laid him open to scathing attacks in the House of Commons and in *Punch*. Hunt was 50 and had been in Parliament 18 years. In Benjamin Disraeli's first admin-istration, he had been Chancellor of the Exchequer, and established his reputation by arriving to make his Budget speech in 1869, only to find on opening the famous red box that he had left his speech at home. He is on record as Britain's largest Chancellor, at 21 stone. It is said that Disraeli had to reassure Queen Victoria that 'he has the sagacity of the elephant as well as its form' – a judgement that was not to be borne out by events. He was appointed First Lord when the Conservative government was returned to power in February 1874, but according to the Dictionary of National Biography he was better versed in agriculture than naval matters, and 'his adminis-tration of the Admiralty was signalised by a melancholy series of disasters'. Perhaps because of these stresses he was to die only two years later, of gout, in Homburg. I have not yet discovered whether Ward Hunt Island, the point from which expedi-tions to the North Pole are launched, or the similarly named cape and strait in New Guinea, are named after this family, but the Rt Hon George seems the least likely person to inspire such immortality.

Ward Hunt was accompanied by his fellow Lords, Admiral Sir Alexander Milne GCB, Captain the Rt Hon Lord Gilford RN, and Sir Massey Lopes MP, together with Rear Admiral Sir William Houston Stewart CB, Controller of the Admiralty, the Hon A F Egerton MP, the First Secretary, Culme Seymour RN, private secre-tary to the First Lord, and Colonel Charles Pasley RE, Director of Engineering and Architectural works. This was clearly a very serious inspection. After looking at vari-ous parts of the yard and partaking of lunch, the party descended on *Iron Duke*, which had been sitting in dry dock for the best part of a month, with people poking around her bows. The inspecting party proceeded to do the same. 'A staging had been erected around the prow of the vessel, and their Lordships closely inspected the ram which sent the *Vanguard* to the bottom off Wicklow Head, on the 1st of September. Looking at the prow from the top of the dock no injury was apparent, but on a closer exami-nation it was seen that across the centre and upper part of the ram a slight ridge had been furrowed, while on its port side an indentation had been made just sufficient to start the joint or seam of the iron plates.'[244] Their Lordships had a good look at a plan of *Vanguard* drawn 'on the side of the *Iron Duke*', which showed the 9 foot (3m) long hole, 2ft 6in (750mm) at its widest, made by the ram. Then they went on board, to meet Lord John Hay and Admiral Chamberlain of the Court Martial team, and to be shown round by Commander Tandy and Engine Room Artificers James Borlace and Henry Rose, who had been dragged in to face their tormentors again and demonstrate the exact procedure for closing watertight doors, getting pumps started, and so on. 'The watertight doors leading from the engine-room into the stokehole were closed and reopened several times' – not the most comfortable experience for a dozen important people in a confined space. But at least, according to *The Times* reporter, they saw for themselves how hard it was to know for certain that a watertight door was actually properly shut, and how impossible it was to get at the suction valve in the boiler room quickly if the rivet were broken (as it had been on *Vanguard*) and water was coming in fast. 'Their Lordships then left the *Iron Duke*'. If only they had made such a visit before the Court Martial hearing.

On the following Monday *Iron Duke* was the setting for a more personal gathering. *Vanguard*'s officers came together to entertain their Captain to dinner. 'On leaving the *Iron Duke*, the whole of his late ship's company voluntarily turned up to testify their respect to Captain Dawkins, whom they would have heartily cheered but for the express wish of the gallant officer that no such demonstration of their feeling should be manifested.'[245]

Support for Dawkins was growing quickly, and fingers were being pointed in another direction. On 2 October the *Illustrated London News* had confidently predicted that 'there will be another Court Martial, on the captain and officers of the *Iron Duke*'. Dawkins' friends had written in similar vein. Lishman, who supported Dawkins and his fellow-accused at the hearing, wrote that he was thoroughly disappointed with *The Times* and that 'the common opinion in London appears to be that Captain Hickley will be <u>completely</u> ruined'[246]; and Flag-Captain Whyte of *Warrior*, after saying that he was very grieved by the verdict, added 'I suppose that old Hickley will be the next'. But the first salvo in what was to become a barrage of discontent was the front-page article in the *Naval and Military Gazette* published on 6 October 1875. The anonymous writer made no attempt to conceal his disgust at the treatment Dawkins had received at the hands of the Court Martial.

'Nothing can be more discouraging to a naval or military officer, than the feeling that he will certainly be sacrificed to that unholy idol, public opinion – whenever such a sacrifice may appear the easiest way of escaping from any difficulty .... A butcher's cart dashes round a corner into a gentleman's carriage, and a horse worth a hundred and fifty guineas is reduced in three minutes to a value of ten shillings for the kennel, but no gentleman would on that account dismiss in disgrace and without a character the coachman who for thirty years had been his efficient and faithful servant .... Because Captain Dawkins has lost his ship by a very simple and apparently quite unavoidable accident, he is treated worse than the equally innocent coachman ... he is punished in pocket and in naval and social position, and what makes the punishment still more severe than it could have been ... he is wounded in his professional honour and reputation.'

The writer went on in similar vein, emphasising that Dawkins' superior officer or others involved were better targets for 'the high officials of the Admiralty chafing for an object for personal blame'. He avoided comment on the detail of the Court Martial proceedings, but ended: 'Dozens of men might have done something, and something might have been useful – first, to avoid collision, and secondly, to mitigate its results, but that in no degree affects the shame to the country of an innocent man being ruined in his reputation, of a distinguished officer being degraded before the world because somebody did not do something which nobody thought of, and in such an unparalleled occurrence could scarcely be expected to think of.' The general opinion among the Captain's fellow officers was clearly much the same. Hugh Barnaby wrote to Dawkins that he had met an Admiral (whose name is illegible), 'an old Trafalgar hand', who said 'Why I think he ought not only to have been honourably acquitted but highly commended. If any of the members had been there they would not have done half so well. Sails and hammocks. Old women'.

At last *The Times* picked up on the prevailing mood. On 12 October a leading article appeared that ventured to say:

> 'We believe that in Naval society strong dissatisfaction now exists as to the conduct of the Admiralty in reference to the loss of the *Vanguard* .... Every one has been waiting for some expression of opinion from the Admiralty *[on the Court Martial verdict]*. It was understood that a Court-Martial would be held on the officers of the *Iron Duke*, but that the Board of Admiralty could not make up their minds to the painful task of directing an inquiry into the conduct of their recent colleague, now the Superintendent of Naval Reserves, who was in command of the squadron when the collision occurred .... It seemed to the public, who followed the evidence, that of the three officers found mainly responsible for the catastrophe, Vice-Admiral Sir William *[sic]* Tarleton, Captain Dawkins, and Captain Hickley, Captain Dawkins was at any rate the least to blame. Yet he, so far, is treated as solely responsible for the calamity, and a disagreeable impression is current that the Admiralty shrink from the duty imposed on them.'

The barrage of criticism affected the senior naval staff more severely than the public could know. Lord Halifax wrote to Sir Alexander Milne, the First Naval Lord, that 'I feel for you most sincerely for it must be most painful to you to find so much disapprobation in the public press of the line taken by the Adm'y .... If the *Vanguard* disappears before the winter is over it will save you all trouble.'[247] Vice Admiral Sir Walter Tarleton had carried on a correspondence with Captain Dawkins in which he had given Dawkins much support and encouragement, without ever committing himself to agreeing or disagreeing with the verdict of the Court Martial. Now he felt so much under pressure that he was moved to offer his resignation. He wrote:

'Private   Oct 4th 1875
+ Confidential   58 Warwick Square SW
My dear Sir Alexander,

I cannot shut my ears to the cry that has been raised by the Press, in consequence of the finding of the CM on Captain Dawkins, that one of the causes of the loss of the '*Vanguard*' was the high rate of speed at which the Squadron under my command was proceeding in a fog. At present there is a lull, in anticipation of the proceedings to be taken with regard to Capt Hickley, but when those shall have terminated, it may be expected that the cry will be renewed louder than before, and probably calling for censure on me. Looking these facts in the face, I have been turning over in my mind what it becomes me to do under the circumstances, and I write to you as an old friend on whom I can rely for counsel in the first place; and in the second, confidentially to you as the First Naval Lord, to inform you of what I propose to do unless you see objections to it.

I propose to write an official letter to the Board, now or later, stating that I have observed in the finding of the CM on the loss of the '*Vanguard*' that one of the causes assigned was the high rate of speed at which the squadron was proceeding in a fog, that I had explained in my evidence before the Court my reasons for not immediately decreasing speed in the Flag Ship, and also that as the ships were not in station when the fog so suddenly shut them from view that I deemed it safer to leave the regulation of speed to the leader of the Port Column; that I deferred to the judgement of their Lordships, + that if in their opinion I was wrong in this view, that I would request permission to haul down my Flag. It seems to me that by my thus taking the initiative I should relieve the Adm^{ty} from any embarrassment they might feel in dealing with me, would satisfy the press which is clamouring for more than the Captain's condemnation, and by accepting my full measure of blame would relieve the Captains from some of its weight, and enable a future Adm^{ty} to make use of their services if they thought fit.

Please give me a line (in strict confidence) to say what you think of my proposition
Believe me sincerely yours
JW Tarleton
If you think proper to show this to Mr Hunt you can do so.'[248]

Ward Hunt's response was prompt and unambiguous: 'I am very much against your proposal to send in your resignation.'[249] The offer was repeated a few months later, but again rejected. It was a generous gesture, but not politically acceptable. There is some suggestion that Tarleton supported the Tory administration, while Dawkins later on campaigned actively for the Liberals, and certainly Dawkins believed he was the victim of political intrigue. Some six months after the accident he was to write to Tarleton:

'That my professional character was ruined by some malicious person behind my back I am fully convinced of from what I heard at the Admiralty before joining *Vanguard* and this no doubt is brought to bear against me.'[250]

Early in 1876 however it seemed much more a case of the Admiralty against everybody else. Milne wrote to Tarleton that the question had arisen of why *Vanguard* should have needed to go on the extra final leg of the cruise. He went on

'It is as well that this should be cleared up for I hear that even the party in office will go against our Minute namely Hay, Price + others and Mr Hunt will not have a single naval man to support him, all this is very awkward with the strong feeling in the House against us.'[251]

In the end nothing was going to move their Lordships. On 12 October, the day the aggressive *Times* leader appeared, the Admiralty issued their eagerly awaited Minute, that quelled no suspicions at all. Instead it made things worse. It began smugly: 'The evidence adduced at the trial was, as regards the conduct of all persons concerned, so complete and exhaustive that their Lordships deem it unnecessary to order any further inquiry with a view to fix responsibility upon anybody for the loss of the ship.'[252] It went on to state their Lordships' view that

'The high rate of speed of the squadron as a whole in fog did not in any way contribute to the disaster.'

Vice Admiral Tarleton had been justified in keeping up speed initially; but was wrong to say that his Captains could act on their own initiative in fog. 'The opinion expressed by the Vice-Admiral … is one which their Lordships cannot approve'.

Tarleton had given the less effective of two possible orders to 'form columns of divisions'.

The loss of *Vanguard* was in their view ascribable to two things: her reduction in speed, and the fact that Lieutenant Evans took *Iron Duke* off course briefly.

'Their Lordships attach no blame to Captain Hickley'.

In sum not only were their Lordships 'pleased to approve' the sentences passed by the Court Martial, despite their first point being a flat contradiction of the Court's verdict, but without warning or supporting evidence they added one of their own: 'and they order Lieutenant Evans to be dismissed from Her Majesty's Ship *Iron Duke*'.

So nobody else was going to be put on trial, no more evidence would be sought, blame had been squarely allocated, all was done and dusted. *The Times* leader on that day welcomed this apparent decisiveness, but humbly suggested that there were questions still to be answered. Phrases like 'the Vice-Admiral must certainly be congratulated on his good fortune' give the tone of the argument. As to the addition of a sentence on Evans, the writer commented 'If this sentence be just, it requires a clearer explanation than we can discover in the Admiralty Minute why Captain Hickley ... should be acquitted of all blame.' The next day's leading article was yet more direct: 'The reputation of the present Board of Admiralty ... will not be raised by their Minute on the loss of the *Vanguard*.' On Tarleton's escaping censure, it read 'This seems to be a grave miscarriage of justice, the mischief of which it is difficult to measure,' and drew the conclusion that the Board could not condemn Hickley if Tarleton were to go free. The article ended thus: 'The moral of the Minute for naval commanders is – do as little as you can, leave everything to your subordinates, and then, if anything goes wrong, throw the blame on the inferior officer. But this, we venture to submit, is not the wholesome old tradition of the British Navy. It is a new sea-doctrine, a 'fond thing vainly invented' by the present Board, repugnant to earlier notions of Naval responsibility, and which the Admiralty four years ago would have scouted as decidedly we do now.' No wonder that the lawyer Andrew Doyle, uncle by marriage of Mary Louisa Dawkins, wrote to her about 'that iniquitous Minute of the Admiralty'[253]. William Hathorn, similarly, wrote to his parents

'I see that you are still interested in what the newspapers say of the late Admiralty minute – which I am rather sorry for – considering that it has not been the good fortune of anyone here to have read one single true article on the subject. The press have been kept in a most wonderful state of ignorance in this matter & it has called forth the supreme contempt of the Navy.'[254]

The public mood was joyously summed up in the most natural way, in the form of a popular ballad, still the way in which many illiterate ordinary people kept pace with the news. Just after the accident the usual sort of song had emerged, starting with 'Come listen to my story/Of the dangers of the sea', and castigating the 'gentlemen/ Who lose their ships at sea' while praising 'our gallant-hearted sailors' (see Annex 2 for this and other verses). After the Court Martial however a different ballad was sung on the streets, in which the blame was shifted squarely on to 'The Lords of the Admiraltee'. The verses are full of barbed and accurate comment, and must have been acutely uncomfortable for their Lordships, had they the misfortune to hear them being sung.

After a while the national newspapers began to lose interest in the case. It had after all had a decent run, with the Court Martial proceedings maintaining interest. Now other things came to the fore. Rather longer-lived in the public interest was the incident in the Solent a month earlier, when the royal yacht *Alberta* – strictly speaking a tender to the Queen's favourite yacht *Victoria and Albert* – ran into a small craft, the *Mistletoe,* which ran across her bows unexpectedly in clear, bright windless weather. *Mistletoe* sank immediately, with the loss of three lives. Her Majesty was aboard *Alberta*, intending to enjoy a pleasure cruise around the Isle of Wight, along with some members of her family and her personal secretary. The sailing master was

Commander Welch RN, but on that day *Alberta* was under the command of the Queen's nephew, His Serene Highness Prince Leiningen, who normally captained *Victoria and Albert*. At the time the Queen (in virtual purdah after the death of Prince Albert) and her entourage were not generally popular with the British people. Welch and Leiningen were subjected to verbal and physical abuse as they left the courthouse in Winchester after a judgement that while admitting there should have been a better lookout kept aboard *Alberta*, no blame need be attached to the senior officers. A satirical ditty about how easily Prince Leiningen got off is among Richard Dawkins' papers at the National Maritime Museum in Greenwich[255] (see Annex 2), but it is not clear whether he wrote it. That this was going on at the same time as the *Vanguard* proceedings led to some speculation; thus Andrew Doyle, writing to Mary Dawkins on 4 October 1875, reported that 'at the Club – one of them observing "Dawkins has been sacrificed to Prince Leiningen"'[256] *Punch* of course made a good meal of it. One item describes a dialogue between Mr Punch and the Naval Lords, who are unusually merry, and chatter, among other things, about 'Well – I was talking to these fellows about that affair on the Solent. One of our ships ran down a yacht, don't you know, caused a couple of inquests, and then we said that the matter wasn't of sufficient importance to call for any official investigation! Wasn't *that* good? Ha! Ha! Ha!' Then, later in the exchange, the same Lord explains 'A squadron of Ironclads went into a fog, by order of the Admiral in command, at full speed! Funny notion, wasn't it? Ha! Ha! Ha! Well, one of the ships, having no fog signal, ran into another ship and – Ha! Ha! Ha! – ship No. Two went to the bottom! Wasn't that a joke? … of course there was a Court Martial … and what do you think we did? You will never guess!' Mr Punch was bemused. 'Why, sir, we did – nothing! Now, wasn't *that* a joke?'[257]

The Queen naturally found the whole thing dreadful. She is reported to have written to the Princess Royal 'I assure you I wish I cld. avoid ever going on the Sea again wh. as we happen to be an Island and Osborne is on one, is quite impossible'[258]. With delightful understatement, the Rev Francis Kilvert wrote in his diary 'This is the first accident that has ever happened to the Queen in travelling and she is terribly distressed. It is an awkward thing for the Sovereign to destroy her own subjects.'[259]

Naturally the *Alberta* case held readers' attention for longer. Besides, there were the preparations for the state visit to India of the Prince of Wales, the first time such a thing had happened. Moreover, the press carried all the details of a gory murder in Whitechapel (not the famous 'Whitechapel murders'; Jack the Ripper came later), so the sufferings of Dawkins and his men faded from the public consciousness – except perhaps for the readers of *Punch*, who continued to be subjected to variations on the same jokes about naval incompetence for another six months.

Some time in November the First Lord of the Admiralty, Ward Hunt, managed to provide perfect material for the satirists. In a speech to a gathering of civic dignitaries he appeared to make light of the loss of *Vanguard*. His political opponent George Goschen said in the House of Commons some while later 'all [*the House*] knew of what the right hon. Gentleman had thought upon the subject was derived from a gay and festive speech he had made at a civic feast, in which he spoke with enthusiasm of the ramming powers of the *Iron Duke*.'[260] *Punch* doubtless overdid the sarcasm in its version:

> 'In returning thanks for the Navy, Mr Ward Hunt said …"The *Blunderer* and the *Incapable* came, as you well know, into collision the other day. I am very sorry that both sank, and that six hundred men were drowned. But does no gleam of hope shine out from that accident? I am certain there does. It proves that we possess magnificent vessels. What is a ram for, if it is not to run down a ship? (Cheers)".'[261]

In the days after the verdict and the Minute Captain Hickley wrote to Vice Admiral Tarleton that 'Poor Captain Dawkins has gone to his home on the Dart sadly upset poor fellow, and one can only hope that the cloud that is on him now will lift in time.'[262] At first Dawkins did indeed have some hope of restitution. Lieutenant Hathorn wrote 'You will be glad to hear that Capt Dawkins writes to the Ship in the best of spirits & hints that he is likely to be sent to Hong Kong as Commodore.'[263] Meanwhile he had some expected routines to follow, such as submitting his claim for compensation. The Admiralty was not a soft touch. Their Board Minutes record that all claims from officers for the loss of effects were paid, *except* those from officers who had been reprimanded. Claims for wines and mess stock were not paid.[264] Hathorn, who had received no censure, was able to tell his parents early in November that 'The compensation for *Vanguard* losses has been paid – I received £90 – the officers who were reprimanded have forfeited every cent of compensation. Unfortunately we had a large stock on board – valued altogether at about £300 – my share as an individual of the Mess will be about £20.'[265] Eighteen months later it was reported in the Commons that the Government recognised compensation levels had been inadequate[266], but for those who had received no compensation at all life was pretty bleak. Navigating Lieutenant Thomas wrote to Dawkins in January 1876: 'By their decision I am discharged to half pay with only the clothes in which I stood … I am getting tired of having nothing to do from one weeks end to another.'[267]

Dawkins himself was busy, working obsessively on trying to clear his name. His notes cover every detail of the case against him as it had emerged at the Court Martial[268]. 'It is of importance to bear in mind', he began, 'that the Admiralty ordered not only a Court Martial but also an enquiry to be held by the same Court into all the circumstances connected with the loss of the ship and I did not consider it an honourable course for me to pursue to point out the shortcomings of others which the Court had every means of discovering; but it is clearly a duty I now owe to myself to make known some of the most important points that apparently escaped the notice of the Court Martial together with my own remarks on the proceedings.'

He went on to fill what were to him obvious gaps in the Court's understanding. On the matter of the ship's speed, he wrote 'My first words to the Officer of the

Watch was you are going at such a high rate of speed when you can hardly see your own ships length ahead that no act of Parliament will clear us if an accident happens. I said both to him and the Yeoman of Signals What is the Signal for reduction of speed – Make our Pendants by the Steam Whistle and blow a continuous blast on the whistle. I said do it and reduce speed.' On the accusation that he had failed to ask for a tow to shallower water:'I did send to Captain Hickley to ask him if he could take me in tow by one of his officers who came to our assistance. And I had no idea that Captain Hickley would have forgotten the message as the first words I said on going on board *Iron Duke* was, did not you get my message asking if you could tow me He said "Yes. But I consulted my officers as we did not think it safe to go near you as we thought you were sinking".' Then about the vexed question of stopping the hole:'I cannot conceive any sailor imagining that a hole 9½ feet in length 2½ in width with ragged edges could possibly be stopped by any means in my power and I think my opinion is borne out when I say that at Devonport Dockyard a trial was made by Admiralty order for a mat specially fitted to stop the aperture in a caisson about 2 feet square and 12 feet under water. It failed …' (In a later document he wrote 'It was said by a very able Admiral in our service it was a pity Dawkins did not throw some old sail over, not that it would have been the slightest use but it would have satisfied the Public.') What had also emerged was the ventilation holes in 85 and 67 bulkheads that Dockyard staff had cut without the Captain's knowledge, giving the water an easier passage from the engine room to the boiler room. Ventilation was important, but the *Western Morning News* pointed out the dangers in an item headed 'A dangerous method of ventilating ironclads' in November 1876. Apparently even the dockyard's Chief Constructor had not known this was going on.[269] Chief Engineer Robert Brown, Commander Tandy and Navigating Lieutenant Thomas wrote constantly, confirming points of detail, trying to help. Thomas for instance clearly remembered his Captain ordering someone in a boat alongside to 'ask Captain Hickley if he can take me in tow'[270]. As the weeks went by and hope of his reinstatement faded, Dawkins worried away at the detail, trying to find any loophole. He consulted everyone he could think of, even trying to track down Ordinary Seaman Murphy, the lookout whose eyesight was said to be defective. H W Markham wrote that 'the man Michael Murphy was drafted from the *Royal Adelaide* to the *Liberty* on Nov 15/75 for Sea Service, and I presume is now serving in her'. In fact Murphy was not on the high seas. Two weeks after he joined *Liberty* he was invalided out and spent some time at Stonehouse Hospital, and the record seems to show that he did not go to sea again. Dawkins wrote letters to the Admiralty, but back came the discouraging replies:'Their Lordships are not prepared to interfere with the sentence of the Court Martial held to enquire into the loss of the ship'[271].

Politically, matters came to a head on 28 February 1876, in a monumental debate in the House of Commons. The Prime Minister, Benjamin Disraeli, cleared the way by ordering 'that the Orders of the Day be postponed until after the Notice of Motion relating to the loss of H.M.S. *Vanguard*'[272]. Mr Goschen then rose – the Rt Hon

George Joachim Goschen, aged 44, Member of Parliament for the City of London, a prominent Liberal who had been Gladstone's First Lord of the Admiralty for four years until the Liberals were voted out of office. He knew his subject, and it became clear that in many ways he was better briefed than Ward Hunt, the current First Lord. Goschen wanted to know what Hunt really thought about the *Vanguard* incident, since all the House had heard were flippant remarks (see above). He cited the 'celebrated' Admiralty Minute, and the adverse reaction to it: 'How deeply the country had been stirred on this question was well known'. He described the incident in detail, and the reasons why the First Reserve Squadron were there in the first place. Goschen's speech had delightfully vicious passages such as 'What was done then in the way of exercises and evolutions in the course of that cruise? During the whole of that cruise, if he might say so without being thought flippant, the only signals given were the waving of ladies' pocket-handkerchiefs, while the only evolutions practised were the intricacies of quadrilles'. Alongside his elegant sarcasm were well-made points about how short-handed *Vanguard* was after disembarking her fleetmen, the inexperience of the two Officers of the Watch who were at the wheel on *Vanguard* and *Iron Duke*, the unanswered questions on speed and signalling, and the way in which the Admiralty Minute contradicted the Court Martial. In concluding he demanded that the First Lord 'must not speak again in that tone of jaunty indulgence about a few blunders having been made. He must show the House that he grasped the full import and appreciated the gravity of those great questions that so vitally affected the nation which had been involved in that sad disaster.'

Ward Hunt rose, and proceeded to justify himself in a speech that went on for half as long again as Goschen's lengthy argument. He said he was glad of the opportunity to address the House on this matter, not least because 'for months he had been assailed with a virulence and a persistency which he thought he hardly ever remembered in his experience to have seen directed against any public man.' He blamed the Press for distorting what he had said 'on a festive occasion' – the very same argument that twenty-first century politicians employ. Taking Goschen's points in turn, he maintained that he had 'acted in that matter as he believed to be right and just'. The Court Martial's findings seemed to him to indicate 'the finding of a divided body', and that when he looked at the evidence it was clear to him that Tarleton and Hickley were blameless. He spoke at length about speeds and signals and Admiralty Instructions. He clearly believed that Murphy had seen a 'phantom ship' because nobody else reported it (this despite the evidence received during the Court Martial). Much as Goschen's speech was larded with sarcasm, Hunt's oozed complacency, the very thing Goschen had warned him against. As he finished, other MPs spoke, including Sir John Hay (not Lord John Hay), a serving Naval officer, who among other things rightly asked 'I should like to know why Captain Hickley was right in being off deck before his ship had regained his station, and why Captain Dawkins was wrong?' Admiral Egerton MP commented that Tarleton had not had the opportunity to explain his actions, and Captain Pim concurred. An Amendment was proposed that would bring Tarleton before a Court Martial in order to clear his name, but after much debate it was with-drawn. Serjeant Sherlock MP thought that 'Captain Dawkins had been treated with great severity – nay, more, with considerable injustice in these proceedings, and trusted that both Captain Dawkins and Lieutenant Evans, who had been condemned, would be speedily restored to the Service'. Joseph Samuda, MP for Tower Hamlets, himself a builder of iron ships, said firmly that even if all the pumps had been set to work, the effect would have only been to keep the ship afloat for an extra three minutes.

Anyone with any interest in Naval matters said his piece, most of them scathing about the Admiralty's performance. The motion was eventually put, and agreed to, and the House went on to other business. And that was that, so far as Parliamentary dis-cussion of the merits of the case was concerned. Much had been said, and in fairness the arguments had been picked over in very fine detail, but little had been achieved other than to let the various parties state their positions. Everything remained exactly the same as it had been.

The debate aroused fierce reaction among Tarleton's correspondents, for varying reasons. One (whose signature is indecipherable) wrote: 'Mr G's speech is a dirty, petty, party speech. Mr W.H. is no less party, but he is bold, + manly, like a gentleman. They are speeches characteristic of the two men …. If you do go *[to sea]* again, I think you will not again make the blunder that you did last year, namely take it for granted that your Captains can be treated any further than you can heave them – it is a mel-ancholy fact that 9 tenths are either incompetent, or careless, or lazy ….'[273] Captain Whyte of *Warrior* similarly castigated Goschen, but had even harder words for *The Times*: 'It never has a good word for the Navy + attacks Mr Hunt whenever they have an opportunity … They write a great deal of nonsense especially about trying you there could be no charges + indeed for your sake if they could have done so it would have shown the Public how clear you were in the business.'[274]

Richard Dawkins redoubled his efforts. He continued to gather evidence, such as this Affidavit sworn by the Pilot at Kingstown:

'I John Tallant residing at Sandycove in the County of Dublin Do solemnly and sincerely Declare that the Master of the Norwegian Barque Uller told me that the *Vanguard* was nearly running over him and would have done so had she not slackboarded her helm, and that he afterwards saw the *Iron Duke* Bowsprit and *[illegible]* over her bows.

Mad and subscriven before me a Justice of the Peace for the said County at Bella Vista Sandycove Kingstown 17th August '76 J Quin JP'

And some information arrived unsolicited, such as a friendly letter from Admiral Tarleton, written in September 1876: 'I called at Kingstown on my way back from Scotland in the 'Hawk' + left it on just such a day as that of the 1st Sept last year. A beautiful bright morning at 10 o'c when we started and at Noon we were in a fog which lasted off and on …'[275].

For months he worked on preparing a Memorial to be presented to the Admiralty, which would be a comprehensive and final protestation of his innocence, incorporating new evidence that the Court Martial had not heard. 'I shall endeavour in my remarks', he wrote in his preparatory notes[276], 'to make them clear both to Landsmen as well as Seamen'. There was the accusation that he had not bothered to ask for a tow. Dawkins wrote 'Since the Court Martial Captain Hickley has written to your Memorialist to say that the Officer who took the message has come forward and stated that he delivered it personally to Captain Hickley, and the Officer has himself written to your Memorialist to the same effect' (no letters from Hickley appear among the Dawkins papers in the National Maritime Museum Library). John Tallant's affidavit was advanced as evidence in support of the real existence of the sailing ship that crossed *Vanguard*'s bows, and added to Dawkins' argument that the real cause of the accident was the 'reckless navigation' of *Iron Duke*. The Memorial spends some time on the capacity of the pumps, and the unsuspected existence of the ventilation holes in 85 bulkhead, which in Dawkins' opinion had introduced 'terrible danger' into the watertight arrangements of the ship. He referred to the shortage of crew. In the Notes he said that he had applied to the Admiralty for two Sub-Lieutenants for signal staff, but they had not been provided; Admiral Tarleton had said 'They have not got them', which seems strange in view of the numbers of officers who were unable to obtain a place on a ship.

In his conclusion Dawkins gave his own list of circumstances that brought about the collision:

'I. The taking of an Iron-clad to sea short-handed.

II. The sudden envelopment of the Squadron in a fog.

III. The suddenly-reported presence of a ship close ahead.

IV. The unexpected and unauthorized sheer of the '*Iron Duke*' out of line.

V. The unwarranted increase of speed of '*Iron Duke*'.

VI. The sudden measures at once taken by the Captain of '*Iron Duke*' to regain his station, at a far greater speed than he was aware of.

VII. The total absence of any Fog Signals from the '*Iron Duke*'.

VIII. The tremendous effect on the '*Vanguard*' of the ram of the '*Iron Duke*', owing to the great speed of the latter.

IX. The ignorance that existed as to the power of flotation of an Iron-clad ship.

X. The inability to use the steam-pumps, owing to–

a. The faulty fitting of the circulating pumps.

b. The objectionable fitting of the suction communication from the pumping engine to the main drain.

c. The immediate flooding of the stoke-hold compartment, and consequent extinguishing of the fires.

XI. The want of efficiency in the watertight compartments, caused by the unauthorized cutting of seven ventilating holes in them by Dockyard Subordinate Officers.'

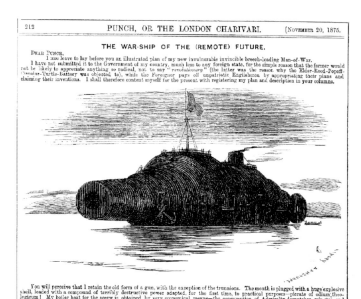

THE WAR-SHIP OF THE (REMOTE) FUTURE.

Dear Punch,
I beg leave to lay before you an illustrated plan of my new invulnerable invincible breech-loading Man-of-War. I have not submitted it to the Government of my country, much less to any foreign state, for the simple reason that the former would not be likely to appreciate anything so radical, not to say "*revolutionary*" (the latter was the reason why the Elder-Reed-Popoff-Circular-Turtle-Battery was objected to), while the Foreigner pays off unpatriotic Englishmen by appropriating their plans and claiming their inventions. I shall therefore content myself for the present with registering my plan and description in your columns.

You will perceive that I retain the old form of a gun, with the exception of the trunnions. The mouth is plugged with a huge explosive shell, loaded with a compound of terribly destructive power adapted, for the first time, to practical purposes—pirate of odium theologicum! My boiler heat for the screw is obtained by very economical means—the consumption of Admiralty despatches, minutes, and old Blue Books. The magazine is situated in the breech of the gun-ship, the remainder of the bore serves for the housing of the crew, stores, &c. The great popularity of the ship is that if the Captain desires to strike a decisive blow, he pipes his men on deck, which is reached through the touch-hole, and at the right moment explodes the magazine!!!

I remain, dear *Punch*, your obedient Servant,
Thorough.

1. *Punch's* view of the development of the ironclad, November 20, 1875. Cartoon by Linley Sambourne.

2. *Pictures above and overleaf:* The first HMS *Vanguard*, 1586. The second HMS *Vanguard*, 1631. The third HMS *Vanguard*, 1678. The fourth HMS *Vanguard*, 1748. The fifth HMS *Vanguard*, 1787 – Nelson's flagship. The sixth HMS *Vanguard*, 1835. Models in the Britannia Royal Naval College, Dartmouth. Photographs by Keith Franks – by kind permission of the College.

3.

4.

5.

A Third Rate of 74 guns, she was built at Deptford in 1787. She was Nelson's flagship while he was in the Mediterranean, leading the British Fleet at the Battle of the Nile in 1798, when 12 out of 14 French ships were captured or destroyed, and later in Sicily. She also took part in Duckworth's action off San Domingo in 1805 and the expedition to Copenhagen in 1807. She was broken up in 1821.

6. *Above.*
7. *Below.*

VANGUARD 6

The last sailing battleship of the name, this Vanguard was built at Pembroke in 1835; she weighed 2609 tons and carried 30 guns. She took part in Stopford's capture of Acre in 1840, and in 1867 was renamed the Ajax. She was broken up at Chatham eight years later.

8. HMS *Vanguard*. The only known photograph, courtesy of the National Maritime Museum, Greenwich (N5239).

9. HMS *Iron Duke*. Courtesy of the National Maritime Museum, Greenwich (N5234).

10. HMS *Vanguard* (1870). Model in the Britannia Royal Naval College, Dartmouth. Photograph by Keith Franks – by kind permission of the College.

11. Kingstown Harbour, around 1900. Photograph by G Clarendon, from *Pictorial Scotland and Ireland* (Cassell 1902).

12. The Coastguard Station at Kingstown (Dún Laoghaire). Photographs by Tony Daly.

13. *Above left:* Admiral Henry Dennis Hickley, Captain of HMS *Iron Duke* in 1875, by courtesy of Guy Hickley Esq.

14. *Above right:* Stoker Charles Boynes, *Iron Duke* Jul–Sep 1875, by courtesy of Mike Boynes.

15. *Above left:* Pte Walter Jewell RMLI and wife Harriet, *Vanguard* Aug 1874-Sep 1875, by courtesy of Shirley Stapley.

16. *Above right:* Ordinary Seaman 2nd Cl Robert Thompson, *Vanguard* Feb-Oct 1874, by courtesy of Derek and Gary Paine.

17 and 18. *Above left and right:* Boatman Elias Rendall and Boatman Thomas Crocker, Coastguards who were aboard *Vanguard* during the Summer Cruise in 1875. By courtesy of Fred Burnett and Paul Hanna.

19. *Above left: Captain Dawkins with Admiral Hastings.* Photograph in the possession of Prof Gianni Lombardi. Printed on the original: *Hermanos Phot. 71 Calle del Palacio Lima (Peru).* HMS *Zealous*, Dawkins' first command, passed through the Straits of Magellan in March 1867. This photograph must date from that time. Hastings is seated on the left, Dawkins on the right. The junior officers standing are not identified.

20. *Above centre:* Mrs Mary Louisa Dawkins (née McGillivray). Photograph in the possession of Prof Gianni Lombardi.

21. *Above right:* Captain Richard Dawkins. Photograph in the possession of Prof Gianni Lombardi.

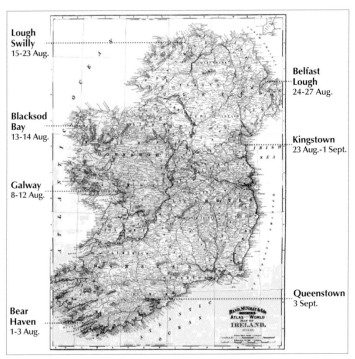

22. The First Reserve Squadron's Summer Cruise round Ireland 1875, showing the dates when the squadron arrived at and left the ports of call. Rand McNally map of Ireland 1897 from the David Rumsey Map Collection. Used with permission.

Lough Swilly
15-23 Aug.

Belfast Lough
24-27 Aug.

Blacksod Bay
13-14 Aug.

Kingstown
23 Aug.-1 Sept.

Galway
8-12 Aug.

Queenstown
3 Sept.

Bear Haven
1-3 Aug.

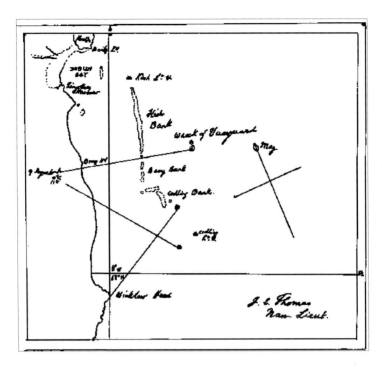

23. *Above:* Tracing of chart drawn by Navigating Lieutenant J C Thomas, inserted into the Captain's Log of HMS *Vanguard*. The National Archives: Public Record Office ADM 53/10409.

24. *Right: Sinking of H.M.S.* Vanguard – from a sketch by one of the Officers, *Illustrated London News*, Saturday September 11 1875, frontispiece.

25. *Illustrated London News* sketches of HMS *Vanguard* and the appearance of the wreck immediately after the sinking, September 1875.

26. 'Court-Martial on
the Officers of H.M.S.
Vanguard', *Illustrated
London News*, Saturday
September 25 1875.
Seated at head of table:
Rear Admiral Lord
John Hay. On his right:
Admiral Chamberlain;
on his left Captain Hope.
Standing: Vice Admiral
Sir Walter Tarleton,
looking down on Mr
Eastlake, Judge-Advocate.
On left at separate table:
Captain Dawkins and
Mr Lishman. On chairs:
Nav Lt Thomas and
Lt Hathorn.

27. *Above left:* Cartoon from *Punch*, September 25 1875, by John Tenniel. The caption reads: 'Vulcan: "It's no fault of mine: I can make a ram; I can make a torpedo; and I can make an iron ship! But I can't teach you to use them!"' One of several cartoons on similar themes published after the loss of *Vanguard*.

28. *Above right:* Sir Edward Reed, naval architect Designer of *Vanguard* (by Ape).

29. *Above left:* The Rt Hon George Ward Hunt MP, First Lord of the Admiralty (by Ape).

30. *Above right:* Rear Admiral Lord John Hay KCB, President of the Court Martial (by Ape).

31. *Above left:* Rear Admiral Richard Dawkins in later life (i), Photograph in the possession of Prof Gianni Lombardi.

32. *Above right:* Rear Admiral Richard Dawkins in later life (ii). Photograph in the possession of Prof Gianni Lombardi.

33. *Above left:* Admiral Algernon C F Heneage, Member of the Court Martial (by Spy). By kind permission of Antique Maps and Prints.

34. *Above right:* The Dawkins family grave in Stoke Gabriel churchyard. Photo by Chris Thomas.

35 and 36. *Above left and right:* Watercolours by Richard Dawkins RN, by courtesy of Gianni Lombardi.

37. Stoke Gabriel House, Stoke Gabriel, Devon where Richard Dawkins and his family lived from 1872 to 1899. Photograph courtesy of Kildare James Esq.

38. *Diving operations at the Wreck of the* Vanguard – *sketched from on board H.M.S.* Amelia *despatch-boat. Illustrated* London News, sketch by Capt S P Oliver RA, Saturday October 2 1875.

39, 40 and 41. *Above and opposite above:* The eighth HMS *Vanguard,* 1909. The ninth HMS *Vanguard,* 1944 – the last British battleship. The tenth HMS *Vanguard,* 1986. Models in the Britannia Royal Naval College, Dartmouth (3) Photographs by Keith Franks - by kind permission of the College.

42. Professor Richard McGillivray Dawkins. Sketch by Osbert Lancaster from With An Eye To The Future (1967) "The Professor happily perched in the higher branches of a large chestnut tree". Reproduced with the agreement of John Murray (Hodder Headline). I have been unsuccessful in locating the copyright holder.

43. *Left:* Professor R McG Dawkins in 1936, Photograph by Elliott & Fry.

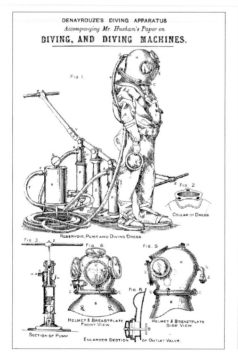

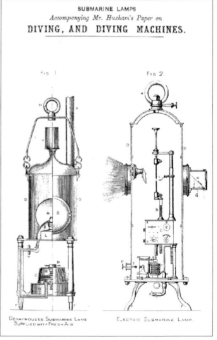

44. *Above left:* Diving apparatus of the 1870's. By courtesy of the Historical Diving Society.

45. *Above right:* Submarine lamps of the 1870's. *Left*: Denayrouze, *Right*: Siebe and Gorman. By courtesy of the Historical Diving Society.

The Memorial was completed by June 1877, and is a solid, well argued piece of work. Its purpose was not just to clear his name, but to restore his financial situation. 'In addition to the sentence of the Court Martial I became a pecuniary looser [*sic*] of between £400 and £500 in personal property, not one farthing of which the Admiralty would allow me although I wrote to their Lordships pointing out my loss.' In the final version this becomes 'your Memorialist … begs Your Lordships to take into most favourable consideration that (without taking into account the pecuniary loss already sustained by him) further compulsory half-pay involves to him the loss of all the professional advancement earned by 36 years of good service, a punishment which he trusts Your Lordships will think wholly disproportionate to the circumstances of the case. In conclusion, your Memorialist again earnestly begs Your Lordships to grant him further active employment. And your Memorialist, as in duty bound, will ever pray.'

On 25 October 1877 Their Lordships responded to the Memorial, stating baldly that they 'do not see any probability of their being able to offer you the command of a ship'. Dawkins wrote to Tarleton 'I must now give up all hopes of ever been [*sic*] employed again, it is of course very hard.'[277] All the work he had done had come to nothing.

Chapter 11

'A good man if ever there was one'

Richard Dawkins after the verdict

Existing photographs of Richard Dawkins show a serious, solidly-built individual, conscious of his Victorian dignity, and give no hint of the passions and enthusiasms and capacity for family love that betray themselves in his journal and correspondence. From adolescence to middle age his life had been aboard ship or waiting for the summons to come aboard. His circle of friends were all in the Queen's uniform, his instincts were conditioned by the ever-changing wind, the smell of salt air and coal-dust and the ever-present tumult of seamen and Marines and fleetmen. Deprived of all that gave shape to his life, what outlets could there be for the energy that seemed undiminished by years of war and weather?

The answer lay in the family. Richard and Mary had married in 1870, and after their eldest, Richard McGillivray Dawkins, was born they settled in Stoke Gabriel near Totnes in Devon in 1872. Stoke Gabriel is one of many lovely villages in that area, an ancient foundation mentioned in Domesday Book in 1073. It stands on a steep-sided inlet of the River Dart, and has for centuries been a little Paradise for salmon fishing and apple growing – apples, of course, for the cider that kept the local inhabitants going in lean times as well as good. In the 1870's life centred on the 900 year old Church of St Mary and St Gabriel. There were at least two mills, one of them tidal, and small businesses thrived. A local guidebook records:'in 1881 it had 642 inhabitants. These included a thatcher, a tailor and draper, a blacksmith, twelve farmers, several fishermen, a Rear-Admiral, and two boot-and-shoe makers. The tenants of the Church House Inn and the Victoria and Albert are described as 'victuallers' – nowadays we should add the word "licensed"!'[278] On the western edge of the village, on the road leading to the mansion called Duncannon, stands a much older house now known as Stoke Gabriel House. Here the Dawkins family lived happily for nearly 30 years.

Stoke Gabriel House was built in the second half of the eighteenth century, and given the name 'Mazonet'. During the Dawkins tenure it carried the improbable name of 'Maisonette', of which Mazonet was quite possibly the Devonian equivalent. By the time of the 1906 Ordnance Survey map and the later Inland Revenue survey it had reverted to the local spelling. Of course, the true locals may always have called it Mazonet, ignoring whatever conceits the grand Naval incomers might have. It was, and still is, a beautiful house with an unsurpassed view across the fields to the Dart, and a wonderful place for a peaceful retirement, however enforced that retirement might be. The present owner, Kildare James, tells me that he has a painting of about 1780 by William Payne called 'Mazonet on the Dart taken from the River', which once belonged to King William IV. There were certainly royal connections. George Wynn (or Wynne or Winne) of Plymouth entertained Prince William Henry, Duke of Clarence, at the house in the late 1780s, and his daughter Sally was one of the Prince's companions. In 1793 Thomas Hicks acquired the house and doubled its size (perhaps before that it deserved to be called 'little house'), but died soon after in 1801. In the nineteenth century the house was successively in the possession of one Madge, then Richard Hume, and Carew Hunt who had it from 1856 until it was sold to Richard Dawkins. After the turn of the century various people owned Mazonet, until Kildare James' father arrived in 1936. He too had a creditable Naval pedigree. Born in 1864, he joined the Navy at the age of 13 and learned his trade on *Britannia* alongside the future King George V, with whom he appears in a college photograph. Kildare James wrote 'He retired at 40 years as a Captain RN, went back in the First World War. Offered his service for 2ⁿᵈ World War, but was refused! He died in 1951 aged 87 years. … At the end of the war my Father got *[the name]* changed to Stoke Gabriel House unfortunately. Said he was tired of it being called a small house.'[279]

Big as it was, the house was full of bustle, but more sadness was to follow. After Richard McGillivray, two daughters had been born: Annie Theodora in 1873 and Mary Katherine in 1874, both baptised in the parish church. On 26 July 1876, when Richard was in the midst of compiling his case for reinstatement, a second son, Frank, was also baptised there, but within six months he was dead, and buried on 30 January 1877 in Stoke Gabriel churchyard. In his draft memoirs Richard McGillivray Dawkins hints that Frank's death might have had some connection with the disaster that had befallen his father, but 'it is possible that my mother's grief and distress would have had results that made this fortunate; my father none the less was overwhelmed by this fresh grief'.[280] The loss was eased by the arrival of Edith Louisa in 1878. Less consolation was afforded by the arrival of a letter in December of that year from the Admiralty, that read:

'Sir,
I am commanded by My Lords Commissioners of the Admiralty to acquaint you that the time having arrived for your advancement to flag rank without your having the necessary qualifying service, you have been this day placed on the list of Rear Admirals on the Retired List, and I am to inclose your Commission accordingly.
I am, Sir,
Your obedient servant'[281]

His retired pay was to be £460 a year; fortunately Mary Louisa had capital and some £800 a year from her earlier marriage. No further communications from his former employers appear among his papers. He was 50 years old.

Richard Dawkins had already begun to direct his energies into local affairs. In 1877 the Totnes Histrionic Society gave a series of Amateur Dramatic Entertainments at the Royal Seven Stars in Totnes under the patronage of Captain Dawkins RN.[282] He supported local industry by joining the Dart Board of Conservators, a body that regulated fishing, boats and all uses of the river. He was also a member of the Dart Fishery Board, and Patron of the Totnes and Bridgetown Regatta. He was Chairman of Stoke Gabriel School Board, and would have been involved in the building of the new village school that opened in 1876, replacing the church schoolroom that had been in use for over 200 years. He was a Justice of the Peace, and at Paignton Petty Sessions after his death the Chairman 'referred to the loss the Bench had sustained by the death of Admiral Dawkins, and expressed the sympathy of the Bench with Mrs Dawkins and family. Mr TW Windeatt, as the senior professional man in the Court, said Admiral Dawkins' decisions were always honest and conscientious, and that he endeavoured to do justice without bias, fear, or affection.'[283]

The 1881 Census return lists the family at Maisonette, occupation of the head of the household 'Rear Admiral RN & JP for Devon'; Mary Louisa is there, with Annie, Mary Katherine and Edith, and a bevy of unmarried female servants. There were Mary Glass from Teignmouth, 22, Parlour Maid; Rose Heskett from Marnhull in Dorset, 15, House Maid; Grace Old from Truro, 26, Nurse Maid; Sarah Ridout from Marnhull, 16, Kitchen Maid; and Caroline Ash from Cornworthy in Devon, 27, the Cook. Listed first among them is the Governess, Mary Ann Bertram, a 25 year old from Jersey. At the time of the next Census in 1891, there were four new servants, and Maria Anna Bertram [sic] is listed as a Visitor. In 1938 Richard McG Dawkins wrote that 'when I was a little over six, the first and perhaps the most hopelessly incompetent of our governesses arrived; three others succeeded her ... This first governess after vain attempts to keep a place remained in the house as a family nuisance till my mother died; we then pensioned her off. Before the first of her successors arrived, I was sent, at the age of just over nine to be a boarder with the headmaster of the Totnes Grammar School.' Indeed Richard (junior)'s name does not appear among those at Maisonette on the night of 3/4 April 1881. He had gone away to school. He was back again at the time of the next Census, ten years later.

The children meant a great deal to Dawkins; writing to his wife he referred to them as 'the chicks', and always sent his love. Young Richard's departure had an effect on him. Their relationship had been loving, but their personalities were poles apart. Richard senior had showed his son as much love as he could, and the letter quoted in Chapter 4 is evidence of his affection. But Richard junior was later to write 'With my father I had no intimate relations. I respected him then and now deeply respect his memory, but our natures were too different for anything more, and I must have been as years went on more and more a disappointment to him.' In fact this son made a great success of his life, as we shall see, but not until after his father had died. His younger brother John commented:

'To his father, the Rear Admiral, a good man if ever there was one, he was a dutiful and affectionate son; but when all was said and done, what closer bond than ordinary family affection could there be between a typical naval officer and this rather odd little boy – red-haired, hot-tempered, left-handed, short-sighted, unable to run or throw a ball properly and of apparently frail physique, while at the same time acutely intelligent and with a thirst for knowledge?'

The departure of his eldest at the age of 9 to boarding school was a milestone in his life, and he returned again, as he must have done many times, to the documents about the loss of his ship. It was time to draw a line under the affair, but not without considerable bitterness. In March 1881 he read through his Notes for the last time, and added, in a more unsteady hand, a further note to the effect that he had not been able to publish anything in his defence during his lifetime, because the Admiralty would have taken away his pension; but that

'I am still of opinion the members of the Court were influenced against me and backed up to it by Rear Admiral Lord Hay ... I am sorry to say the Captains lent themselves to this dreadful plot ... My last wish is if any of my children are ever in a position to publish the whole affair in a book I think it is a duty they owe to themselves to shew their Father acted as a man of judgement and was most unjustly condemned.'[284]

Thus he tried to throw off the shadow of his disgrace, but he was no longer the man he had been before 1875. For a picture of him in the darker times we can turn to the unpublished memoirs of his eldest son: 'My father was of a melancholy temperament and never succeeded in recovering from ... the loss of his ship, which befell him in 1875 when I was just short of four years old. In earlier years he had had the cheerful gaiety which often goes with a fundamental sadness ... of it I saw only faint and passing signs. ... My father's naval service had carried him to all parts of the world; only to Australia and New Zealand he had never been. Of these things, which had been the very centre of his life, he hardly ever spoke and never at any length. From old naval friends he cut himself off almost entirely, though on his rare visits to London he did not avoid his club. ... Through all his years of retirement my father relieved or perhaps fed his melancholy by doing water colour drawings of the sailing ships he loved so much. ... It was after his marriage that at Ryde he took lessons in water colour and acquired some skill in managing his brush. Gardening, looking after a small estate and work as a magistrate and guardian occupied his later days; every few years he went to London for a short visit.'

Some delightful examples of his watercolours are filed with his papers at the National Maritime Museum, and his great-grandson Gianni Lombardi has others. They express his meticulous care for detail and his eye for beauty in the world around him.

When his son moved from Totnes Grammar School to Marlborough, the Rear Admiral found another outlet for his enthusiasms. His obituary notice records that 'the gallant officer was well known all over the Torquay Parliamentary Division, and took a prominent part in the electoral campaign that culminated in the Liberal victory in 1885. Deceased was a staunch Liberal.'[285] Richard Junior saw something more in this than simple interest in politics:

'The disaster of 1875 ... occurred when a Conservative government was in power. That in his own opinion and I believe in that of many of his brother officers he so signally failed to obtain fair treatment was I think the main reason why in later life he followed the Liberal party ... His general frame of mind was orderly and disciplined, tempered by a very strong feeling for what he felt to be the essential rights of all men: in this sense no one could have been more democratic than he showed himself. He had a great dislike for the more advanced members of his own party; like many other people he was much impressed by the character of Mr Gladstone.'

According to Richard junior, this affiliation could have caused problems with Mary Louisa, who was of a different persuasion: 'The political difference with my father appeared most clearly after the Home Rule Bill of 1886, but it did not, I am sure, affect their mutual relations, and indeed my mother had not much in the way of political feeling beyond a sort of cavalier toryism sentimentally derived from her McGillivray ancestry and a tradition that two of her great uncles ... had fallen at Culloden.'

Mary Louisa Dawkins was the great driving force of the family. She is described as very intelligent, competent, and well-read; she taught her eldest son to read before he went to school, having herself learned the skill at the age of three. Like most of her contemporaries she wrote quantities of letters, those to Richard at school showing her lively wit and love for the family. A couple that were preserved by John Dawkins reveal the children's family nicknames: 'Ting' for Annie, the eldest daughter, 'Spid' for Mary Katherine ('a strong character, not always easy to persuade' – John McG Dawkins), 'Nunc' for Edith and 'Jackdaw' for John, the baby of the family. At the time of these letters (1890), Mary Louisa was teaching Mary Katherine: 'Spid's lessons break into my time considerably'.

'Jackdaw', John McGillivray Dawkins, was born in 1887, when his mother was 46 and his father 58, a joyful and again much loved late addition to the family. By this time Richard McG was 15, and in the middle of his time at Marlborough College. Totnes Grammar School had been a hideous experience. 'The food was uneatable; for the first week of each term I could hardly swallow anything. The school hours were long; long hours of boredom and almost complete idleness. The teaching was ridiculous. ... There was no order in the school and nothing was learned. There were no books to read...'– maybe we should draw a veil at this point over young Dawkins' fulminations about the place where his formal education began. At Marlborough he again met mindless bullying and pointless lessons, but revelled in Homer, Rosetti, and Ruskin. In 1890 he left Marlborough, and his father, with the best of motives, thought it best if he learned a useful trade – electrical engineering. Richard junior went to Kings College in the Strand, London, where he lasted two academic years out of the prescribed three. He was apprenticed for five years to Crompton's, a firm of electrical engineers at Chelmsford, a quiet period during which he continued to read the Greek and Latin classics and studied Sanskrit, Icelandic, Irish Gaelic. He was preparing for a very different future from anything his father might have imagined.

The five years might have been many more had not his father, the Rear Admiral, died on 20 March 1896 at the age of 67; Richard was at his bedside. The certificate gave as the cause of death Dropsy (2 months) and pneumonia (10 days). The funeral took place the following Monday afternoon. The cortege was met at Stoke Gabriel church gates by three clergy, the organist played the Dead March from *Saul* and a great crowd of mourners followed the coffin. The local paper listed many of them, but none of the names indicate members of *Vanguard*'s crew, or Admiralty interest, though a Captain Bickford from London might have been their representative. Thus was Richard Dawkins at last released from the shadow of his disgrace. The obituary in *The Times* of 24 March 1896 did at least record that:

'Neither the verdict of the Court-Martial nor the subsequent Minute was received with satisfaction, and Sir Henry James (now Lord James of Hereford) commented severely on the matter in a speech at Taunton. However, Captain Dawkins was not employed again.'

Within less than a year, his wife Mary Louisa died at the age of 56, and the family went their separate ways. For Richard McGillivray Dawkins, the inheritance meant that at last he could follow his own inclinations. At 26 and largely self-taught, he went to Cambridge to read Classics. He was awarded a scholarship at the end of his first year, and became a Fellow of Emmanuel College in 1904. Meanwhile after obtaining his degree he joined the British School of Archaeology in Athens, of which he became Director in 1906, and was responsible for some first class pioneering archaeological research. He remained first of all a linguist, and immersed himself in Greek dialect and folklore, publishing a series of works on these and related subjects. In 1907 he had a stroke of financial luck in the shape of the death of his mother's cousin John Doyle, as a result of which he had no money worries, and acquired a large Victorian house called Plas Dulas in Denbighshire, North Wales, which he filled with his growing library together with icons, embroideries and other relics. During World War I he worked for Naval Intelligence in Crete, and when peace returned he was appointed the first holder of the Bywater and Sotheby Chair of Byzantine and Modern Greek Language and Literature in the University of Oxford. There he remained for twenty years up to his retirement, gaining a reputation for originality, lack of affectation, good humour, and kindness to his young students. Osbert Lancaster wrote of him in *With an Eye to the Future*:

'No eccentric professor of fiction could possibly hold a candle to the reality of Professor Dawkins whose behaviour and appearance placed him, even in an Oxford far richer in striking personalities than it is today, in a class by himself. Ginger-moustached, myopic, stooping, clad in one of a succession of very thick black suits which he ordered by postcard from the general store of a small village in Northern Ireland, he always betrayed his whereabouts by a cackling laugh of great carrying power.'[286]

In May 1955, still at Oxford but hampered by the effects of a broken hip, he died in his eighty-fourth year; Osbert Lancaster wrote 'His end was blissful; one fine June day, having leant down to smell a rose in Wadham College garden, he suddenly drew himself upright, cast aside his crutches and with his face irradiated by a seraphic smile fell back dead at the feet of Maurice Bowra'. The official records say he fell dead in an Oxford street in May, but Lancaster's account is the more entertaining and fitting for the man. Richard M Dawkins never married.

The other Dawkins children, though less unusual in their career paths, were by no means ordinary. The three girls had been educated at Cheltenham Ladies' College, and all three decided to go to Italy, possibly in pursuit of their cultural education. Annie, the eldest, had a First Class degree in languages from Newnham College, Cambridge; she did not marry, and died in Rome in 1933. Edith and Mary Katherine met two Italian brothers, Guelfo and Bruno Mazzarrini, proprietors of a vast estate in Città della Pieve, near Perugia. Edith, who married Bruno, was killed by an Allied bomb in Rome in 1944. Mary Katherine married Guelfo, who died in 1920 of an illness contracted during the First World War. Each couple had a son and a daughter; Edith's son moved to the United States and her daughter married and went to Germany, while Mary's children remained in Italy, where her grandson Gianni Lombardi is now Professor of Geology at University of Rome 'La Sapienza', and has provided me with much invaluable information and photographs of his great-grandparents. Mary clung jealously to her British nationality, which proved useful during the Second World War, as the family could benefit from food parcels at a time of great want.

The youngest son, John, was 9 years old when his mother died. He followed his brother to Emmanuel College Cambridge to study classics, then went into the Consular Service. He spent his career at various posts around the Mediterranean, ending up as Consul in Casablanca, from where he resigned in 1930. He married a Dutch girl and taught languages in Oxford for some years, but had no children. In the 1950's he spent some time editing his brother's papers for presentation to the Taylor Institution in Oxford, adding his own lively comments. Professor Lombardi well remembers him as tall and well built, a quintessentially British Gentleman.

Rear Admiral Dawkins saw none of his children's achievements, but their presence made his life in Stoke Gabriel a good one. By any standards he was comfortable. Besides the joys of the children he had a wonderful marriage, an excellent house, and a reasonable income. But after 1875 he was never at rest. His youngest son John wrote in 1957 about the *Vanguard* incident 'the dossier of which I have left still unexamined – though I saw it years ago. A model of wicked injustice that really shook the nation at the time. That still remains a problem piece for me. I feel I ought to do something more than hand it over to some cold hearted librarian at the Admiralty or the Greenwich Museum. Dick [RM Dawkins] would have been a big enough man to get my poor father's memory vindicated, but he never did anything, since, although he respected his father and loved him when a child, there was a huge gulf between them in character. No wonder I was given a warm welcome, and almost spoilt for life, when I came along!'[287] Later he did read his father's papers, which he found 'absolutely harrowing'[288], but still was unsure what to do about them. He had no children himself, and the Italian branch of the family 'seem uninterested in these papers'. With the help of a very enthusiastic member of the present-day Italian contingent, we can at last publish the full story.

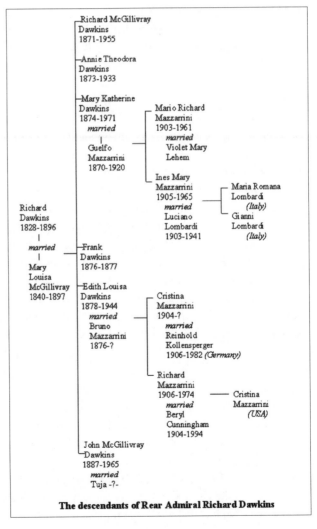

The descendants of Rear Admiral Richard Dawkins

Chapter 12

'Our Service is not at all popular at present'

The consequences for others involved

As Mike Boynes of Southsea wrote of his great-grandfather, Stoker 2nd Class Charles Boynes, the incident 'completely changed his life and therefore ours'[289]. Charles was serving aboard *Iron Duke*, and he and his fellow crew members should have been little affected by what happened, but the momentary encounter in the fog on a Wednesday lunchtime touched many of those involved more than might be expected. Some seemed to press on with little damage done to their careers. Commander Dashwood Tandy, whom the Court had damned as showing 'a great want of energy', and who had been so disgusted by their treatment and lack of compensation that he had said 'I don't feel the slightest interest in going on in the Service', nevertheless earned these notes on his record: 'Nov 76 Captain Rowley speaks of his zeal & tact whilst in *Iron Duke* – 31 Jany 1880 Proceedings against slave trade approved & thanked by Portuguese Governor of Mozambique for co-operation (see Capt Earle's letter 11 Dec 79) – 18 May 80 Very good report of inspection of *Vestal*'[290]. Still a Commander, he left *Vestal* to join the Coastguard in December 1882, but within 10 months he had died. The *Kildare Observer* carried this report of his death: 'The deceased gentleman was on a visit to his brother-in-law, T.J.de Burgh, Esq., High Sheriff of the County, and was driving in company with Mrs de Burgh and Captain Slaney to Baron de Robeck's residence at Gowan Grange, when he suddenly took ill on the way and expired in the course of a few minutes. The principal evidence taken at the inquest was that of Captain Slaney, who deposed – I was in company with the deceased this day (Wednesday) driving from Oldtown to Gowran Grange. When we started the deceased was in perfect health as far as I could see. On the way we got out of the trap to walk up the hill. On top of the hill we got again into the trap, and after we had gone a short distance I noticed deceased's head fall down on his chest, as I thought in a fainting fit. I took him into my arms, and, with the assistance of a man, carried him into a neighbouring house. He never spoke. I believe he died in my arms before I took him out of the trap. Just before he got ill he complained of being unwell, and said that since he was in the East Indies the exertion of walking up a hill always told upon him. Dr Gormly …said … that in his opinion death resulted from heart disease.'[291]

He was just 43. His widow was awarded a pension of £80 a year.

Chief Engineer Robert Brown, who had survived an official reprimand three years earlier, also carried on as Chief aboard various ships until his retirement in 1883 at the age of 52. After 30 years service he received a pension of £400 a year. Another 'guilty party' nearing the end of his service was David Tiddy, the 'old carpenter … of considerable experience'. After a spell on *Indus*, much of it at Plymouth, he retired in September 1880 to his little place in Home Park Buildings, Stoke Damerel (Devonport) with his Pembrokeshire-born wife Ann, to look after their young niece Elizabeth while she was at school. He had served for more years than Brown, but his pension was just £108.16s.6d.

The other senior technical officer, Navigating Lieutenant James C Thomas, had longer to serve but did not stay the course. He had married an Australian girl, Ellen, 12 years younger than himself, and a daughter (also Ellen) was born while *Vanguard* was on duty at Kingstown. After a time on half pay he joined *Terror* on promotion to Staff Commander, but had to retire 'unfit' at the age of 42 in 1881. He too settled in Plymouth, at 32 Headland Park, on £200 a year. Thus the five *Vanguard* officers who had suffered reprimands all continued to serve, apart from Captain Dawkins.

The impact of the Court Martial – or more precisely, of the Admiralty Minute – on those sentenced was most tragic for Lieutenant Pierre Gervais Evans of *Iron Duke*. At 26, he had spent half his life at sea, and was not as lacking in experience as the Court Martial had assumed. He had spent time on watch before, sextant in hand, alone in charge of the wheel. 'I have been officer of the watch at sea in a square-rigged ship as sub-lieutenant and midshipman, about two years and a half, and about three months at lieutenant. I had kept officer's watch on a ship forming part of a squadron nearly all the time.'[292] On that day in the sudden fog, with his Captain below, he had done what seemed the most sensible thing – change course slightly so as not to run into the ship ahead. Immediately the Captain had appeared and told him sternly to get back on course. He had spoken up boldly before the Court, and was mightily relieved when, despite the sheering out of line being adduced as a reason for the accident, his name did not appear in the Court's verdict or sentences. Then out of the blue, came the blow from the Admiralty: 'Their Lordships are pleased to approve the several sentences passed upon Captain Dawkins and certain officers of the *Vanguard* and they order Lieutenant Evans to be dismissed from HMS *Iron Duke*.'

Evans had already left *Iron Duke*, and was spending a fortnight on *Black Prince*, then acting as a depot ship. He was sent 'to College to study', then in May 1876 embarked on *Raleigh*, serving on the Mediterranean station. Eighteen months later the ship was in 'Bashika Bay', otherwise written as 'Beseika'– presumably Besikion, an alternative name for Lake Volvi to the north of the Halkidiki peninsula in Greece. On the weekend of 16 July Pierre Evans had been ashore, exploring the area, obviously in a disturbed state of mind. 'He exposed himself to much fatigue in the marshes of the neighbourhood, taking little food, and also drinking of the marsh water. The weather was exceedingly hot and sultry at the time.'[293] Lake Volvi is an area rich in wildlife, and the marshes have since been drained to some extent, but the environment must have been inhospitable for Evans' wanderings. Little wonder that the following Tuesday he reported sick with a headache and 'general malaise', and a temperature of 104°. By the twenty-third he was much better but had not recovered his appetite. A few days later he began to take milk and soup regularly and went on to a regime of quinine. But this was a false dawn; the fever returned, and the ship's surgeon, John Messer, continued to ply him with medicines including 'Port Wine after dinner'. While most ships' Surgeons had qualified at one of the Royal Colleges, the standard of medical knowledge was not always as high as it might be. Padfield says that 'it is probable they killed rather more than they helped'[294]. In 1870 William Hathorn writes about a participant in a 'Hare and Hounds' chase who 'could not keep his speed up on account of a bad <u>heel</u> from which he had been suffering previously & even had leeches applied the day before'[295]. And so the treatment went on through the early days of August. The Surgeon's log covers four pages of meticulous record of every temperature and bowel movement and close observations on trembling hands and an 'excited and anxious expression'. The account makes for very painful reading. Messer was especially interested in the illnesses he encountered in the Eastern Mediterranean, and subtitled his log for 1877 'Fevers in the Levant'.

At 8 in the evening on 9 August Evans became 'vociferously delirious'. Sedated, he seemed to sleep peacefully, and woke to take a little beef tea, but on 10 August 'he continued to sink and died at 7.10 pm'. The Captain entered in his log 'Departed this life Lieut P G Evans aged 27 – Irish – New Town Donevail Co Cork of remittent fever'. At 9.45 a funeral party rowed away to HMS *Torch*, and made their way aboard her to 'Chanak' (the port of Çannakale on the Dardanelles in Turkey). Evans was unmarried, and left nothing behind except a persistent legend, retailed by the estimable Admiral Ballard thus: 'The end of this unfortunate young officer was not long in following. After a spell on half pay he was appointed abroad and died of fever. In his final delirium he imagined himself once more on deck in a fog and the very last words that passed his lips were "*Vanguard* ahead!"'[296] Unfortunately, the phrase does not appear in Surgeon John Messer's meticulous record, but then no other utterances of the dying Evans were noted either.

Pierre Evans was not the only one of the young Lieutenants to suffer problems within a short time of the incident. Some of those who had not been censured fared little better. Edward Noble, the senior Lieutenant on *Vanguard*, swapped postings with another officer, the reason being revealed in one of William Hathorn's letters:

'Noble is likely to leave us before this day week by exchanging with Lieut Harding of the *Aurora* stationed at Greenock – Noble will be a great loss to our Mess – he leaves us in consequence of some little <u>amour</u> difficulty in Kingstown'[297].

The move was little help to him. A few months later he was hospitalised in Greenock, and transferred to Haslar Hospital 'where he was under observation for Melancolia'[298].

He was given permission to take one year's leave in South America, then changed his mind and retired from the Service in June 1876 on 5 shillings (25p) a day. He did go to South America, and the official record states baldly 'Died, on or about 17 March 1877, from an accident at Charcomus, Buenos Ayres'. He was barely 30.

His fellow Lieutenant Edmund Speck took a different route to escape the stress. In September 1876 he was court-martialled for drunkenness when at Zanzibar 'whilst borne in *London* for passage to *Undaunted* – Severely reprimanded – D*[ismissed]* ship & to lose 2 yrs, Sen'ty.'[299] Sixteen months later he too retired at his own request, and in 1892 his name was removed from the List, 'not having been heard of, nor drawn his Retired Pay, since March 1886'

Of the eager and able young Lieutenants, only William Hathorn seems to have come through relatively unscathed. He continued in the Navy for another nine years, but his letters home betray an increasing disillusionment. As early as 1873, commenting on the introduction of a new retirement scheme, he wrote that 'All the Lieuts are taking the bait and I think very 'wizely' too … our Service is not at all popular at present & I am confident that if so much humbug & inconsistency is permitted to live as at present – the little 'esprit de corps' which we still possess will be a thing of the past.'[300] The Court Martial verdict did not improve his opinion. At first he stayed on *Iron Duke* as she replaced *Vanguard* at Kingstown. The following year his father died after a lengthy period of ill health. William continued to write as fully as ever, albeit on black-edged paper. In February 1876 he tells how he 'jumped overboard (before breakfast) to save the life of a boy, who was drowning … being very fat he was naturally pretty buoyant'[301] He started lessons in Hindustani from an Indian living in Dublin. Then in December 1876 he joined HMS *Danae*, and was off to warmer parts again. The next few years took him to Australia and New Zealand, where he found more relatives and family friends, and achieved some measure of immortality: 'Hathorn Sound is named after me. The landing party that you will read about included W.H. in charge of half the company. We landed 80 men'[302] Back again and on to HMS *Impregnable*, whose Captain Bradshaw noted: 'Most attentive and zealous – possesses high qualifications coupled with zeal and judgment' Bradshaw's successor Captain Wilson added 'Very zealous attentive and trustworthy' and Admiral Stewart 'concurs & adds that he is an excellent boat sailor'.[303] Nevertheless, despite the verve of his letters, he was still discontented. At the height of his reputation and aged only 35, he retired with the rank of Commander, probably disenchanted by Naval life. In search of something more exciting, he went first to South Africa and took up ostrich farming. By the end of 1885, only ten months out of the Navy, he was already deeply into the feather market: 'Our Birds are doing very well … fortunately the birds are very stupid, & clumsy in turning round sharply – otherwise they would be very difficult creatures to manage'[304] Eventually however ostrich economics proved unsatisfactory, and WCSH, the man who always asserted that he performed best in really hot places, decamped to western Canada in the late 1890's, accompanied by his nephew 'Thornie' (R H Greaves, Lady Turton-Hart's father), to try his hand at gold mining. He followed the tracks of other prospectors to the Klondyke, and settled there very happily, to the extent (in 1906) of being licensed as a Lay Reader at the church in the little town of Atlin. The Admiralty lost contact with him around the age of 60, as they had with his colleague Speck, and he was removed from the Navy List – but was restored four years later. In 1931 his health betrayed him and he returned to England, to be with his family in Folkestone, where he died of heart failure in 1932, in his eighty-third year.

Vanguard's engineer officers were not to be in the Navy for very much longer. Valentine Horne never achieved promotion and retired in 1881 'unfit' at the age of 44. James Redgrave served on various ships until in 1884, in his early 40's, he too became 'unfit' and was retired with the rank of Chief Engineer ('Retired Pay £150 per annum – maximum'). William Vivyan similarly went from ship to ship, finally joining *Defence* in June 1880, but later that year after a couple of weeks in Plymouth Hospital he died in service. William George Paige, whose evidence at the Court Martial had been so graphic, displaying sound common sense and dedication to his task, blotted his copybook drastically only two years later when he was aboard *Simoom*. The register of Court Martials for 1877[305] records: '1877, July 18, Paige, W G, Engineer 'Simoom' Stealing a Parrot Dismissed the Service.'

Whatever possessed him spelt disaster for his family; dismissal meant no pension entitlement. William came from generations of Portsmouth folk, and had married Eliza Whitefield in Portsea in 1864. Their first child Annie was born in Queenstown, Ireland, that same year. There followed another daughter and three sons, all Portsmouth born except for William junior, who saw the light of day in Constantinople (his father was serving on HMS *Asia* at the time). Reginald had been born just a month before William senior was court-martialled, and Frank arrived the following year; soon afterwards the father died. His great grandson, Robert Paige, passed on a note made by his aunt, William George's granddaughter, about a memory that Frank Paige recorded. He said the TV live recording of Sir Francis Chichester receiving accolade from H M Queen reminded him of his father's death – Greenwich College reminded him that his eldest brother (Uncle Will) had been allowed to go there when his mother was left with five children to support and no pension or means to enable her to do so. His grandfather *[William George Paige's father, another William, born 1814]* helped and 'Ma kept a boarding house (15? Hampshire Terrace), the other boys could go to Greenwich when old enough. Father's father caught yellow fever in Jamaica and was brought home to Haslar (RN Hospital) where he died.'[306] The parrot must have been desirable, but the cost was far too great.

Even those with walk-on parts in the drama seem to have been affected. The Chaplain, the Rev. Spencer Musson, disappears from the Navy List after 1875, but turns up in the 1881 Census return under the guise of Schoolmaster, Unmarried, age 39, born in Bermuda, at Addlestone Hill Iris Lodge School, Chertsey, Surrey. This appears to have been what used to be called a 'dame school' for young ladies run by a Mrs Eliza Lewis; the six scholars range in age from 9 to 16 and come from two families. Musson was the only man in the house apart from Albert Green, Manservant. The Church of England, like the Royal Navy, was an overcrowded profession, and Geoffrey Best comments that 'Clergymen who could not get a footing on the ecclesiastical escalator made livings by teaching (a business for which a clerical character was a conventional selling-point).'[307] Nevertheless Musson did have a position on the Chaplain's list, and it is fair to assume that the events of September 1875 may well have repelled him to such an extent that he decided not to go to sea again. *Alumni Cantabrigiensis* records that he was admitted at the Inner Temple in 1880, so he must have decided to apply his learning to the service of the law.

Captain Henry Hickley of *Iron Duke* came out of the affair unstained, as we have seen, despite great pressure to transfer some of the blame to him. He went on quietly, making no waves, and received the customary rewards. Nevertheless he was 55 before receiving promotion to Rear Admiral in 1880, at which rank he was appointed as Senior Officer on the Coasts of Ireland in 1885, three months later becoming Vice Admiral. All of Hickley's later service was recorded as 'Harbour' rather than 'Sea', but he made good use of it. In 1880 he received the following commendation:

'I am commanded by my Lords Commissioners of the Admiralty to express to you their sense of the zeal and ability, which you have shown in superintending the training of the Boys for the Royal Navy, and their appreciation of the various reports and suggestions which from time to time you have submitted, to insure the special instructions for this service being carried out on a uniform system in all the Training Ships.'[308]

Unlike Richard Dawkins, he had, as his obituary recorded, 'seen no war service'[309], but like his counterpart lived in some comfort in the West Country, on a very respectable pension of £740 a year. His 1881 Census entry shows the family at 25 Ker Street, Stoke Damerel, the Head of the House listed as 'Harry D Hickley', a more informal form of address than one might expect. Like Dawkins, he had married a girl 14 years younger than himself, Mary Jane (née Rundle), born in Devonport. In 1881 there were five children at home: Laura Fanny (13), Lily (11), Elizabeth (8), Charles (7) and Esther (4), and of course the household required four domestic servants, all women and all but one born locally. The oldest child, John Dennis Hickley, was by that time well established in the Navy, having signed on at the age of 12½. Earlier that year he had passed his Lieutenant's certificate while at sea off Lisbon, and appeared to be set for as successful a career as his father's – the words 'very steady' and 'promising' appear in the record. Meanwhile, like Dawkins, his father became a Justice of the Peace and involved in the community, but was able to do so while still a serving officer. In 1890 the Committee of Plymouth Life Boat expressed their deep regret that he was moving away from the area, having given them 'valuable services over more than 9 years … [with] unfailing courtesy'[310] The move coincided with his retirement in January 1891, and he was made full Admiral in April of the following year. He took the family to Oxford, to 7 Fyfield Road. Then in 1895 came tragic news: John Dennis had been drowned in a lagoon while on a shooting expedition near Lourenço Marques. Two years later Mary Jane died, but Laura, Lily and Esther, maiden ladies in their 20's and 30's, were still living with Henry at the time of the 1901 Census. Henry's papers at the National Maritime Museum are few and give no such glimpses of his family life as do those of Richard Dawkins. It is interesting that 'Mrs Hickley's Address Book' for 1885–86 has no entry for Dawkins![311] Henry's own Diary for 1878 is full of mundane references to fishing, obviously a favourite pastime, and health problems ('Bronchial and a little sign of gout' on 19 April) and tantalising notes such as, for 12 January: 'Unpleasant letter on the conduct of the Boys at Bristol – young scamps.' The 'young scamps' went on to useful careers. John Dennis and Spencer Allen both joined the Navy. The former, as we have seen, died in 1895, and the latter in action in 1914 (he is buried in Tunbridge Wells cemetery). Alfred Charles joined the Gurkha Rifles, as did his son, another Henry Dennis, who died in Mesopotamia in 1916. Of the girls, Laura and Elizabeth did not marry, while Lily and Esther did, within a couple of years of their father's death; Esther married a naval man. According to my correspondent Elizabeth Edwards, who has spent some years researching various branches of the Hickley family, there are no living descendants of Admiral Henry Dennis Hickley. Spencer was with his father when he died of 'failure of Heart' in Fyfield Road at the age of 77 in 1903. His body was taken by train to Exeter and buried in Heavitree churchyard. All the family were there, Hickleys in profusion, along with (in contrast to Dawkins' funeral) Admirals and Generals. His estate was valued at £882.5s.3d.

Of Hickley's officers aboard *Iron Duke*, apart from Pierre Evans, the one most remarkable is Lieutenant Stephen Thompson, whose career record makes him seem all the more like A A Milne's Tigger, thus:

'See report of gallantry in saving life from drowning – Bronze RHS medal Oct 78. Egyptian campaign 1882. Employed on Sweet water Canal. Worked day and night getting provisions [?] up to front. Capt Rawson strongly recommends also for work at disembarkation at Ismailia … granted Egyptian Medal 1883 … Satisfaction expressed with the judicious manner in which the drills and exercises practised by the RN Art^y Volunteers – London Brigade – when embarked in Avon were selected by him. *Hector* 3 Apl 85. VG. Good Channel Pilot, handles his Command and navigates her very well. 21 Sep 86 Inspect^n of *Foxhound* … ship efficient and in good order, company clean and active, exercises satisfactorily performed. 30 Aug 89 Commodore Markham reports his zeal in obtaining information about hostile movements during the manoeuvres.'[312]

Rarely in any service record is there so much comment and so many recommendations for promotion; yet Thompson remained a Lieutenant until his retirement at the age of 45 in 1894, with the rank of Commander. Perhaps his superiors found such enthusiasm hard to handle; how he tolerated his last five years of service in the

Coastguard it is hard to imagine. Even after retirement he kept on coming back for odd spells of duty, and in 1903 he was given command of the Bristol Division of the RN Volunteer Reserve.

Staff Captain Batt, who played an important part in the efforts to salvage the wreck, was the most senior of all the Navy's Staff Captains, and strictly at the end of his career. In June of 1875 he had written to the Admiralty pleading not to be compulsorily retired after seven years in his current rank. He was an asset to the dockyard, as the supporting comments show: 'There appears to be no doubt that Staff Captain Batt is a very efficient officer...' 'In my opinion Staff Captain Batt is the ablest Master Attendant now employed.'[313] The Admiralty of course refused, but he did stay on, having moved to Chatham, until 1882. On retirement he was ranked Captain, and awarded almost the same pension as Richard Dawkins, but he died within 18 months.

There remains the unfortunate Captain Samuel Travers Collins RMLI, the only person whose conduct was criticised by Captain Dawkins, though 'Captain Dawkins hoped the Court would understand that he did not wish to cast any reflection whatever on the gallantry of Captain Collins.'[314] But Collins' name had been mentioned, and the wheels of Naval justice ground on. The Admiralty considered his case, and on 20 October 1875 issued a severe reprimand, delivered in public in the presence of the officers of the ship. Thereafter he spent most of his time at the Plymouth Headquarters, save for a brief spell in the Mediterranean. The only thing considered noteworthy by the naval scribes was that he 'passed Equitation at Canterbury, Feby 1880.'[315] He retired 'on account of age' in May of that year with the honorary rank of Major (he was 42). About that time he married the 20-year-old Edith Annie, and settled in Herefordshire, at White Lodge near Leominster. At the turn of the century he moved to spend a few years on the banks of the Wye in Monmouthshire, but five years later returned to Laburnum Cottage in Luston. One Friday morning about a month later he decided to take the train to Leominster, and walked the mile and a half to Berrington and Eye railway station, aiming to catch the 10.21 am train. He arrived in good time to buy his ticket, and went through to the platform. A moment later the Stationmaster heard a commotion, and left his office to find Major Collins on his back and dying. He had had almost 30 years of quiet retirement. Perhaps railway stations should carry a health warning for seagoing folk; Captain Hickley's elder brother, Admiral Victor Grant Hickley, had also collapsed and died on Taunton railway station in 1888.

Chapter 13

'A magnificent and unique shipwreck'

The attempts to raise the wreck, and today's recreational diving

One of the more surprising aspects of this story for me, researching it 130 years after the event, is that *Vanguard* is still there on the seabed, very largely intact. Indeed at one time she had the distinction of being one of the very few wrecks that are named on Admiralty charts. When I made contact with the late Philip Oglesby, Regional Diving Officer for Dublin West and a member of the Marlin Sub Aqua Club, almost his first words were 'Why didn't they raise the guns?' His colleague Roy Stokes commented that 'the true "modern" value of this battleship did not seem to be thoroughly explained at the time'. Half a million pounds worth of public money had been unceremoniously sunk, and from a twenty-first century perspective very little seems to have been done to recover the country's investment. But this belittles a considerable amount of work that was done, and conceals a certain amount of official incompetence.

It was late summer, and at first it seemed conditions in the Irish Sea were as good as they would ever be for a salvage operation that year. That is to say, there had been decent weather but as the season advanced wind and waves, and the Spring tides, could sabotage plans at a moment's notice. Indeed the weather in this stretch of water can hardly ever be depended upon, a factor that would weigh heavily with any calculation of the possibility of salvaging a wreck. On the Saturday evening after the accident, the steam tender *Vivid* arrived at the site of the wreck, where *Warrior* was standing watch. She carried some workmen, Dockyard technical experts, and two divers who started work on the Sunday morning. The operations 'require to be conducted with the utmost caution, as the vessel is scarcely accessible on account of the rigging, with which she is literally covered. This will have to be to a great extent removed before it will be possible to get into the interior of the *Vanguard* or to make a proper inspection of her condition.'[316] *Warrior* left the scene on Monday morning, and meanwhile Staff Captain Batt, Master Attendant at Devonport Dockyard and in charge of the operations, had been to the Admiralty to report on the possibilities. Their decision was not to raise the hull of the ship during the winter. 'The divers will, however, at once proceed to remove her masts and guns. The hull will remain where it is, lying on a sandy bottom. To prevent the sand from getting into her the hold will be covered over. Attempts will be made next spring to raise her.' At this stage she was lying at an angle to starboard, with her maintopmast head projecting 24 feet (7.3 metres) above the surface of the sea, the foretopmast about 15ft (4.5m), and the mainmast 10ft 10in (about 3m) below the surface, a significant hazard to other shipping. The mizentopmast and the topgallant mast had been snapped off, but the former just reached the surface. The difficulty of negotiating the rigging was no less: 'Her topsails are loose, and with the loose ropes streaming out with the tide form the great danger at present to the divers ... The strong tides running are a great hindrance, and will only allow about four or five hours' work per day, and then only about two and a half hours at one interval. Could fine weather be insured, there is no doubt she might be floated into shallow water by stages ... but the year is so advanced that much fine weather can hardly be expected; and as all appliances must be on the heaviest scale to be of the slightest use in raising her, some considerable delay must be experienced before they could be got ready, and when ready the Winter will be upon us, and the Winter season in the Irish Channel is a wild time.' The team were beginning to understand the problem of lifting a huge mass of iron.

To the twenty-first century salvage operator it seems odd that no attempt was apparently made to 'bump' her into shallower water, a technique in which the Royal Navy and its contractors became very proficient in the Great War. Nevertheless they kept trying in other ways. On the Monday as *Warrior* steamed away the divers were below trying to recover some of the stores that Charles Dawson had so meticulously listed, and they managed to clear the foretopsail yard and sail yard, which the tender *Amelia* towed to Kingstown. 'Great difficulty was met from ropes and gear floating under water, preventing access to the deck.' What was worse was that their equipment was not up to the job. 'One reason why so little has been done up to this time [8 September] is in consequence of the rigging being made of iron and the divers not having any tools for cutting through it.'[317] A couple of days later reinforcements arrived in the shape of about 100 divers and others from Devonport aboard a steam tug with two lighters in tow. More rigging was brought up, and at last the weather improved. On Saturday 11 the sea was 'as smooth as glass', and they successfully shifted the mainyard, which the tug *Carron* towed to the mainland. 'This huge piece of timber will be lifted out of the water early to-morrow and placed alongside the smaller one, brought up a few days ago, and which is an object of great curiosity to visitors.' The favourable conditions did not last; on the Monday and Tuesday there was a heavy swell. 'There is every prospect of stormy weather prevailing for some days, and little progress will be made.'

And so it went on. On 17 September *The Times* reported that diving operations had been completely suspended. The next day the divers went below at high water but could stay no longer than 15 minutes. By now they had heavy lifting equipment, two vessels known as 'lumps' carrying steam machinery capable of lifting 80 tons each, with which they aimed to raise the iron mizenmast. 'Before this can be safely attempted, however, the sea must be perfectly calm. In the gale of last night the men on board the lumps kept their cork jackets on for a considerable time, ready to jump into the sea if anything happened to the lumps, which are anything but safe in a rough sea.' It was gradually becoming clearer that this was to be no easy task. Even the optimistic *Times* feared that 'The conviction begins to be entertained on all hands … that any attempt to raise the hull would be futile.'

While the professionals became increasingly pessimistic about raising *Vanguard*, the amateurs who wrote to the newspapers had no such inhibitions. As early as 6 September *The Times* carried a letter from 'Naval Architect' specifying four large ships, specially strengthened, and 40 iron chain or steel rope cables (a proven technique of long standing) – but admitting that 'the success or failure of the whole would depend most materially on the weather in so large a channel'. Less down to earth were two letters in *The Daily Telegraph* the same day. One was from 'F.B.C.', who confidently offered the following: 'It struck me that the *Great Eastern* might raise her. Instead of wasting valuable time in taking out the stores, &c, if she was merely dismasted, the *Great Eastern* anchored over her, and by means of cables passed over the decks at short intervals … the *Great Eastern* when she had lifted her could take her where she liked.' This was juxtaposed to a proposal from one A S Menier, who wrote that 'Through a peculiar combination of my own, I think it is really practicable – in fact rather easy – without requiring the aid of divers, and with but a small amount of work.' He was cagey about exactly how this was to be achieved – 'it would be too long to detail in a letter' – but some clue might be found in his closing remark:

> 'There is no doubt at all as to the feasibility of rescuing the *Vanguard*, and I should be very happy indeed if my suggestions could be of some utility to the country which has given so much aid to my several inventions for ballooning, especially with hot air – with that hope, I remain, Sir, yours very obediently …'

Menier's helpful suggestion was followed by another three days later in the same newspaper, from 'A.H.D.', who suggested 'the introduction by divers into all accessible parts of the vessel – under the decks, in cabins, hold &c – of a large number of empty India-rubber bags, such as are commonly used as gasholders. These being connected by small wire-lined flexible tubes with the surface could be easily filled with air by the same pumps that supply the divers, or preferably by hydrogen gas (easily made on the spot).' AHD admitted this probably would not be enough to float the ship, but the weight would be reduced enough to make lifting her 'a comparatively simple matter.' When *Punch* jumped on this bandwagon early in October, it was hard to distinguish their bizarre proposals from those already offered:

> 'Dear P.,
> Concerning the proposed floating of the *Vanguard,* could not the experiment be tried of attaching to her, at low tide, a number of those gentlemen who are so clever in floating Public Companies? ….

Sir,

I have given intense thought to the problem of raising the hull of the *Vanguard*, and, up to the present time, I have come to the firm conclusion that one of the obstacles to successfully floating it is its great weight; and another may be found in the fact that there is a large hole in the vessel's side

Dear Sir,

I have a firm belief that successive shocks, from seaward, produced by a huge battery charged with a sufficient number of Electric Eels, would have the effect of driving the *Vanguard* into shallow water ….

I am, Your galvanic servant, ELECTRICIAN.

Sir,

I have a splendid idea for floating the *Vanguard*, which I mean to keep to myself. Yours sincerely, AUT FACE UT TACE.

My Dear Punch,

Of course, long before this, you have come to the same conclusion as myself with respect to raising the *Vanguard*.

You may just as well try to raise the Devil.

Nothing can be done except to censure the *Iron Duke* and give the *Vanguard* what the Court Martial has already given her Captain and principal Officers, Admiral Tarleton and the Captain of the *Iron Duke,* in other words, everybody concerned in her loss – a good 'blowing up'.

Yours, sternly, COMMON SENSE.'[318]

At the same time, commercial companies were sniffing around the wreck and making their expertise known, quietly but firmly. A letter appeared in *The Times* on 8 September and another in *The Daily Telegraph* the next day, over the name of Siebe and Gorman, Submarine Engineers to the Admiralty, 5 Denmark Street, WC (Denmark Street in London's Soho later became known as 'Tin Pan Alley', centre of the music industry, and no. 5 is now a music shop). Oddly, the letters contradict each other. On 8 September the company stated firmly 'Sir, – there is not the slightest doubt that you will be inundated with correspondence from various wild schemers offering plans for the recovery of the *Vanguard*. Will you allow us, as practical men, to say that her recovery is hopeless; there is not the least chance of bringing a body with sufficient power in position to obtain a lift.' They foresaw no problem about divers working at a depth of 20 or even 25 fathoms, but 'we contend that diving is not the difficulty, but the being able to keep sufficient power over the wreck – a matter at this season impossible.' On the following day in the rival newspaper they reaffirmed that divers could work at the required depth, and the Admiralty had the means to do the job: and 'we would venture to say that if the necessary power can be obtained there is a probability of her being floated, the main difficulties being the weight, the weather, and the current.' Thus in their view the hull could definitely be raised, or not, as the case might be.

Augustus Siebe was born in Germany in 1788, and emigrated to England after the battle of Waterloo to settle in London as a precision engineer. In 1828 he obtained a patent on a rotating water pump, and sales went so well that he was able to acquire the Denmark Street premises, marry and proceed to father nine children. Around 1830 the Deane brothers (who had considerable success in salvaging vessels from Irish waters) asked him to convert their 'smoke helmet' into a proper diver's helmet, which Siebe attached to a watertight rubber suit filled with air; his pump supplied the air from the surface. At last divers had equipment that allowed them to move around under water without the danger of being flooded and with enough air to breathe. Augustus Siebe was dubbed the 'father of diving'. He took his son-in-law, William Gorman, into partnership and the business was thereafter known as Siebe, Gorman and Company. The factory moved to Lambeth in 1876, and to Chessington after being destroyed by a German bomb in 1941, at which location they went on producing the Standard Diver Dress until 1955, after which they went into production of aqualungs. In 1975 they moved to Cwmbran in Wales and gave up making diving equipment, returning instead to breathing equipment for fire-fighters.[319] The company closed down in the 1990's, and their surviving archives and memorabilia are now held by the Science Museum in London. In 1875 the company was certainly the foremost British authority on what the successful diver should be wearing.

But Siebe and Gorman were not to have the field to themselves. On 11 September *The Times* reported that 'in addition to the increased staff of divers from the Government Dockyard at Devonport, a small staff sent over by a private firm, Messrs. Ronquerel and Denayrouse, submarine engineers, London and Paris, arrived at Kingstown this morning by the Holyhead mail steamer, and were subsequently conveyed to the scene of the wreck of the *Vanguard* by the steam tender Amelia. They bring with them a peculiar kind of lamp patented by the firm, which can be lit under water and kept lit for a considerable time.' The sub-editor had badly misread his correspondent's handwriting, since the people concerned were Benoit Rouquayrol (1826-1875) and Auguste Denayrouze (1837-1883), whose supporters regard them as the *real* progenitors of the suit in which a diver could operate independently of a surface air supply. Rouquayrol was a mining engineer from Espalion, Aveyron, France, who in 1860 patented a self-contained breathing system for use in flooded mine shafts. It was welcomed, but he made little profit from it until he was joined by Denayrouze, a naval Lieutenant whose career had come to a premature end as a result of a chest ailment, and who suggested they should work on its application in diving. Their invention became gradually more sophisticated (1865, addition of a whistle to warn of the impending end of the air supply; 1866, inclusion of a metal filter 'destined to stop any small alien items').[320] At first they envisaged divers wearing nothing but a breathing mask and a canister of compressed air, but belatedly realised that eyes and body also needed protection. Thus they also worked on perfecting the rubber diving suit with the help of Auguste's brother Louis Denayrouze, together adding improvements year on year. The system was virtually re-invented in the twentieth century by Jacques Cousteau, but Rouquayrol and the Denayrouze brothers deserve credit for an invention well ahead of its time, and the foundation of modern scuba.

The sinking of such a large ship as *Vanguard* in relatively shallow water was an irresistible magnet for manufacturers wanting to show off their latest products. The French turned up early on in the affair, apparently with the specific intention of testing their new underwater lamp. It was a petroleum lamp, supplied with fresh air by a separate supply pipe from the surface, either from the diver's reservoir or a special pump. It cost about £20. Siebe's lamp was electric, burning in a vacuum, powered from a battery on the surface. Its cost was some £85, including the dynamo.[321] Denayrouze wrote smugly to *The Times* on 30 October:

> 'A few days after the wreck of the *Vanguard* the Admiralty entered into a contract with us for the use of our submarine lamps for the operations on the wreck, and the competitive trial on Saturday was for the purpose of testing the merits of our lamps as compared with an electric lamp which had been lent to the Admiralty. At 12.45 pm orders were given for the electric light to be prepared, and by the aid of four men it was got ready in four and a half hours. Our lamp was made ready in ten minutes. Both lamps ... remained submerged for an hour and a half ... our lamp was burning brilliantly ... The divers also reported [that] the electric light "winked and blinked like a gaslight that had water in it" ... The last diver who went down, named Woollicott, reported that the electric light was out, and on pulling up the lamp this was found to be the case, and the glass broken by the intense heat. Captain Batt, RN, then ordered the Denayrouze lamp to be hauled up, and on being brought to the surface it was seen to be burning as brilliantly as ever.'

Staff Captain Batt had indeed been set the task of testing their lamp. Admiralty Board General Minutes record on 24 September 'Messrs Siebe and Gorman's Sub-marine Lamp to be sent to Kingstown to-night in charge of two Petty Officers from the *Vernon*. Staff Captain Batt to make trials with this Lamp against Messrs. Denayrouze's.'[322] And there was a contract with the French firm. In November the Admiralty authorised payment of £113.13s.1d to Messrs Denayrouze 'for the use of their Lamps, in operations on *Vanguard*, services of attendant, etc.'[323] But neither company seemed particularly interested in actually raising the wreck. In fact in a Parliamentary debate in 1877 it was stated that 'The French divers under M Denayrouze who were consulted would not have anything to do with the ship, as they said she was so deep in the water, and the pressure was so great as to render it all but impossible for divers to work.' It was certainly dangerous work. A book published in the 1920's has the following description:[324]

> 'At the wreck of the foundered *Vanguard* in the Irish Channel in 1875, when divers went down they found such strong currents prevailing that they had to cling to the rigging to prevent themselves from being swept away. Moreover, the depth was 150 feet, and there was also the danger of entanglement of the life-lines and air pipes.

Clinging to the rigging the divers had to cut away the masts which formed a danger to navigation. One diver slipped from the bridge to the deck, and was so stunned that he was drawn up apparently dead, and two hours elapsed before he recovered.

Another diver lost consciousness through the rapid increase of pressure, as he descended quickly to the 150 feet, and in that unconscious state he became entangled in the rigging. The attendant signalled as usual, asking if he were all right, and obtaining no reply, ordered him to be hauled up. But because of the entanglement, it was not until seven or eight men made desperate efforts together, that the unfortunate man was rescued. He was black in the face, and in a minute or so more he would probably have died.

In short, work at the *Vanguard* was so dangerous that some divers would not descend a second time, though the fees were £7 per day, with all expenses paid, and also two guineas *[£2.10]* for each descent.'

Staff Captain Batt's report of 14 October[325] named the man as 'C Ingledon, Rigger Diver ... happily the Surgeon considers him out of danger, yet will require medical care for a few days.' The *Annual Register* for 30 November 1875 added 'Notwithstanding all these difficulties, the divers ... White and M'Culloch successfully reached the hull which lies in deep darkness and measured the hole in the side by means of notching a wooden lath carried down for the purpose and placing against the aperture.' But Batt thought it was time to suspend attempts for the winter. He went on 'I also consider it my duty to remark, although reluctantly, that the tone of the Divers is becoming dispirited from the amount of disappointment, weather and continual failures that they have been exposed to'.

By December the Admiralty had just about given up, and it was decided to invite tenders for raising the ship and delivering her in dock. There were various conditions, including:

Those tendering should provide evidence of their financial ability to do the job
Delivery would be complete only when the ship was in dock
No payment until delivery completed
The ship is to be raised whole, and not in pieces and 'Their Lordships state that they will not bind themselves to accept any tender'[326]

(On the same day, *The Times* reported the first use of the Plimsoll mark on the hull of a naval storeship.) *Punch* of course could not resist this. In its Christmas Day issue appeared a selection of letters supposed to have been received by the Admiralty. One 'Jeremy Diddler, Knight Commander of the Golden Fleece of Costa Rica' cited personal friendship with Baron Munchausen as evidence of his financial probity.'Lunar Fisk' shared his recipe:'Take half-a-pound of common salt, a little salad oil, and a few ounces of gunpowder, and mix them well together over a slow fire, being careful to remove the scum as it rises to the surface. Now get your steam-engine and balloon, and proceed as in ordinary cases of hair-cutting by machinery. You will now find you have an enormous lever-power at your command, and the heaviest weights may be lifted with ease, and even impunity.' He besought their Lordships to keep his ideas secret. And so on, and so forth.

It was reported that there were some 450 responses to the advertisement, and some may not have been unlike *Punch's* wildest dreams ('Some of them being of the wildest and most insane description' according to A F Egerton MP). They kept on coming. The Digest of Admiralty In-Letters for 1876[327] painstakingly records the number of 'Plans and Suggestions for raising *Vanguard*', 20 from people or firms whose names all began with A, 21 from B, and so on, totalling 507. After the great debate in the House of Commons in February 1876, *The Times* quoted the *Army and Navy Gazette*: 'There is yet some hope of the *Vanguard* being restored to the list of Her Majesty's ships, as we hear of a scheme for carrying out the great work of raising the vessel being nearly ripe for execution. If success should crown these efforts, we believe the honour will belong to France.' A few days later it looked even more certain: 'The tender of a French firm has been accepted … the work … will commence in earnest in the first week of May.' But nothing much seemed to happen. By August Ward Hunt, First Lord of the Admiralty, answering a question in the House about whether the Admiralty would subsidise any plan by a Naval officer to raise the ship (naturally they would not), admitted that 'Every negotiation for a contract for the raising of the *Vanguard* has fallen through, and we now propose to advertise for tenders for the selling of the ship.'[328]

Meanwhile complaints about the wreck kept coming in. At the end of September 1876, more than a year after the sinking, 'The captain of the *Leona*, a timber ship from Nova Scotia, which was beating up the Channel in a gale on Friday night, mistook the light over the sunken ship for the Kish Light … in the morning he discovered his error, and becoming alarmed, as there was a heavy sea with a strong tide running, he cast anchor and made signals of distress.'[329] A lifeboat was sent to help and took off the crew of 19, but was struck by huge waves and capsized. Four men, three of them from *Leona*, were lost. Time and time again fishermen complained of their drift nets and other tackle becoming snagged in the standing rigging, even though *Vanguard* was gradually sinking into the sandy bottom. Video footage of the wreck taken in 2000 clearly shows how much is still cosily wrapped in fishing nets. By February 1877 *The Times* could report that 'The prevailing opinion is that she is now too far embedded in the sand for it to be possible to raise her, and that if it is attempted by inflation her decks will give way.' As it happens she does not seem to have sunk any further since that time. The seabed in the area is composed of hard sand and shale.

Another St Elmo's fire of hope appeared that month. The Admiralty were reported to have taken out a contract with one Captain Coppin of Glasgow, who was issuing shares at £10 each to raise funds for the exercise. He intended to build four huge pontoons and pass steel wires under the hull, but recognised that since divers could not work at such depths (now 22 fathoms from surface to keelson) for more than 20 minutes at a time, the task presented great difficulties. However Captain Coppin 'has had a large experience in endeavouring to raise sunken vessels' – not, one might note, in succeeding to raise them. At the end of February the widely experienced Captain wrote to *The Times*, bravely specifying the various weights and dimensions necessary, even including 'a new deep-diving dress, the invention of Messrs. Tylor and myself, enabling the divers to remain with safety several hours under water at a greater depth than where the *Vanguard* lies.'

But still nothing happened. It was not until a year later that the full story emerged, in the course of an acidulous speech by a Dr Cameron in the House of Commons on 12 March 1877. First, he castigated the Admiralty for using their own dockyard divers instead of those specially trained in deep water work, who would have to have been paid 'as high as £5 per dive to induce them to undertake such a task'. He went on to talk about the mysterious Frenchman with whom a contract had apparently first been made. 'The plan on which the vessel was to be raised was described as being a combination of air balloons, inflated in the interior of the vessel, and caissons attached to her externally', and the engineer in question was a M. Louis Othon. Dr Cameron said M Othon 'knew nothing whatever about salvage operations, and … had adopted the plan … from one of the numberless specifications of inventions connected with the raising of ships procurable from the Patent Office'. What Othon did know about was money. He had recently set up a company under another name to obtain a large supply of corks from Bordeaux, and cited his contract with the Admiralty as collateral for the supply of yet more corks, in a way which was so obviously fraudulent that the cork merchant had taken steps to have him arrested. The Admiralty had apparently not even taken up the financial references supplied by M Othon.

Again according to Dr Cameron, within a few months the Othon negotiations had collapsed, and the Admiralty had taken up with a Dr Rutherford of Newcastle. Over several months Rutherford went to some pains to produce working drawings, and financial back-up, but later wrote despairingly to Cameron 'To this hour I do not know why the negotiations fell through … the entire history reveals the utmost infirmity of purpose'. The Admiralty advertised for tenders for purchase in August 1876, this time asking for two-thirds of the purchase money up front, and the handing over of all guns and certain other equipment at fixed prices that seem to have been well below market value – ten 9-inch guns for £2500 sounds like a bargain. Then in January 1877 Captain Coppin appeared on the horizon. The Admiralty liked what they saw, and negotiations went a long way, up to the point when they presented him with a draft contract full of conditions 'exposing the contractors to constant Admiralty interference, and providing that valuations, by whatever official they might appoint, should be taken as final – conditions which were never contemplated by the contractors, and to which no prudent man would submit.' The whole affair displayed 'utter business incapacity'. A.F. Egerton, replying for the Admiralty, naturally disagreed, saying that Othon had not provided proof of solvency, and neither Rutherford or Sowerbutts (the third short listed contractor) had been able to agree conditions. He said he would be disappointed if a contract were not soon entered into with

Captain Coppin. Siebe and Gorman were irritated by the constant talk of divers not being able to operate at *Vanguard*'s depth, and wrote sharply to *The Times* about it. But like Denayrouze they were not going to get drawn into the actual salvage operation.

On into 1878 the affair dragged. In April in answer to a parliamentary question W H Smith MP said 'Hopes of raising the *Vanguard* are not abandoned. A contract was entered into with Captain Coppin more than a year ago, and he has until the 31ˢᵗ of October to raise the ship. We are told that he has made preparations for that purpose, and great hopes are entertained that something will be done; but, until after October, it will not be possible for us to take any further steps.'[330] In August Smith had to report that the contractor had made no progress. 'It was to be feared that when the 31ˢᵗ of October came the *Vanguard* would be found remaining where she was at the present moment.'[331] By the Spring of 1879 the Admiralty sounded exhausted. 'It is intended to remove the masts of the *Vanguard* as soon as the weather is sufficiently fine to enable us to do so; but there is no intention at present to remove or destroy the wreck of the ship, being advised that the wreck will not be dangerous to navigation.'[332] The final reference in *The Times* index is to an item published on 24 July 1879:

'The light-vessel and indicating buoys which have been employed to mark the wreck of the *Vanguard* will be removed on the 1ˢᵗ of August. The masts, etc., of the *Vanguard* have been destroyed sufficiently to prevent any obstruction to navigation, and there is now a clear depth of 10 fathoms at low water spring tides over all portions of the wreck.'

Three years and eleven months after she sank, the unequal struggle against weather, tides, and human ineptitude had been given up, and *Vanguard* was to be allowed to rest in her sandy bed. In 1987 she was sold to a Mr Houlihun, ostensibly for salvage, but nobody attempted to violate her peaceful state. Ownership passed in 2002 to Mr John Hartnett, who has discussed the possibility of raising some items with the Irish Government.

There she lies still, remarkably untouched by time, but now an object of great interest to recreational divers. For many years she was left alone until in 1999 the Marlin Sub Aqua Club of Dublin, the only such group to have surveyed the wreck under licence, decided to make her the subject of a special project for the year 2000. The project leader was Philip Oglesby, the local Regional Diving officer, for whom *Vanguard* became a consuming passion. His daughter has written 'My dad devoted all of his spare time doing research on the *Vanguard*, it was his total passion, and when he wasn't doing research he was diving his "socks off".'

This project was something special for the Marlin SAC. The depth now ranges from 30 to 52 metres, unusual for the Irish Sea, and careful planning and training were paramount. It was decided to conduct the survey by video. Filming began at the end of June 2000, and 40 decompression dives, at least two divers on each, were completed in ten weeks. Roy Stokes of Marlin SAC subsequently wrote an article in the Irish diving magazine *SubSea* from which the following passages are taken[333]:

'A detailed study of the ship's main wheel assembly from the main deck was carried out ... the bosses of the Mangin propellers are at 46 metres and were visited three times in order to confirm the make-up of the assembly, which some sceptics say was not possible.

It also quickly became the view of the Marlin dive team that Captain Dawkins knew exactly what became of 'tin junks' with big holes in their bottom and made the correct decision when he abandoned his ship to save all of her crew. We can confirm from observations made of the collision damage to the ship that the reports by divers of the day on the huge vertical gash behind the battery box were indeed correct. Receiving no mention in reports researched, and situated below an area of intact hull under the obvious collision area, there is another huge hole in the hull. Extending to the seabed, this is the damage that was quite likely caused by the ram which was said not to have penetrated the inner hull, but out of which we made an exit during a dive in the lower deck!

Our main enemies were poor light, depth and time, weather, bad water clarity and disappearing marker buoys. The project was a true adventure and the results were so pleasing that they have spurred us on to initiate the making of a full documentary film in 2001.

Diving on the HMS *Vanguard* has to be one of the most exciting in the British Isles ... she contains all of her fittings, armament, winches, capstans and screws ... a magnificent and unique shipwreck.'

The video was completed and is a fascinating record of *Vanguard* in her present state. In 2002 the Irish television company Nemeton produced a series of programmes on wrecks around the Irish coast under the title of *Éire Fo-Thoinn*, of which episode 5 was devoted to *Vanguard* and featured much of Marlin SAC's video work, as well as commentary by Philip Oglesby and Roy Stokes.

For those who might like to visit her, *Vanguard* now lies 14.2 miles south-east of Dún Laoghaire harbour at latitude 053.12.810 and longitude 05.46.000, and the best time to dive is one hour before high or low water, though these times might alter with certain tidal conditions. The waters of Dublin Bay are becoming clearer each year, especially in July and August. But Roy Stokes makes this plea: 'The range of depth and the extent to which this shipwreck can be penetrated does give cause for careful planning and leaves no room for a lack of discipline or messers ... It is important that we should recognise that this shipwreck is "different". It is, in fact, unique and that while visiting the wreck you should temper your visit to recover souvenirs with the view of leaving it for others as others have left it for you. Its future, which is by no means clear, is of course in the hands of the authorities.'

Perhaps Richard Dawkins' correspondent was right when he wrote 'I shall address this to the *Vanguard* altho' she lies 15 Fms deep'. She still exerts influence from down there, a permanent memorial to the casual cruelty and judicial ineptitude of the Naval authorities in the late nineteenth century, and to the dedication of a loyal Captain and his shattered crew.

Postscript: Philip Oglesby

As I was writing these final chapters in the late summer of 2003, Philip Oglesby of Marlin SAC died very suddenly of a brain haemorrhage. Happily he had just completed one of the best dives of the season in crystal clear water. To me in writing this book he was an inspiration and a great help; he will be a considerable loss to his family and to the Irish diving community. Philip Lecane, great-grandson of AB Philip Lequesne of HMS *Vanguard,* wrote:

'Roy Stokes had very kindly invited me to go to the site of the *Vanguard* with the Marlin SubAqua Club on one of their trips. One evening, as I was having my tea, Roy phoned my house. The lads from the club were in Dún Laoghaire harbour, about to go to the wreck. If I could get there within half an hour I could go with them. I would stay with Roy on the "rubber" while the rest of the team dived on the wreck. I drove to the harbour and was introduced to the lads as they were getting into their gear. I was mildly apprehensive sitting in the 'rubber' as it sped out of the harbour en route for the wreck site. Part of my apprehension came from a belief that the lads were probably a bunch of 'macho men' who would be contemptuous of their green-horn passenger. I couldn't have been more wrong. They treated me with amazing kindness. Philip in particular was anxious to ensure that I was comfortable. He chatted and joked and said that all Philips should stick together. He really made me feel included. At one point he took off his woollen hat. It had "Phil" embroidered on one side and the club badge on the other. He put it on my head saying "Now you have your own hat. Welcome to the Marlin SubAqua Club." It was a kindness I will never forget, from a man I had met only minutes before. Later at the wreck site Roy Stokes took my photo wearing Philip's hat. At the time Philip and the rest of the team were diving on the wreck.'[334]

Diving operations were naturally suspended at the loss of their driving force, but the SAC are determined that Philip's work will continue. Discussions are proceeding with Dúchas, the Irish Heritage Service, about the lifting of the ship's wheel and its conservation. To have it on display in the National Museum will be a fitting tribute to the passion and dedication of Philip Oglesby.

Chapter 14

'But this is Vanguard, bless her!'

'I've been in better, been in worse, I've sailed in large and small.
Though most of 'em had failings, I'd affection for 'em all....
But, this is Vanguard, bless her! and I'm proud I've worn her name
and I'll bet you, if you're honest, that you're thinking just the same.'
(collected by Shirley North, who served on HMS *Vanguard* 1952–54)

Vanguard today

It would be a satisfying 'closure' (as current terminology has it) to list positive lessons that were learned from the loss of *Vanguard*, but any such list would be woefully short. KC Barnaby has a few:

'It was very undesirable to have all the boilers in one compartment, since its flooding deprived the ship of all steam power.

Watertight doors and their fastenings were unsatisfactory and took too long to close.

It was most essential for watertight bulkheads to be kept intact and not pierced for openings.

For armoured warships, it was very desirable to provide further wing bulkheads in the wake of the armour. The old wooden warships always had a 'wing passage' at the 'wind and water' position between the orlop and the lower deck. This was kept free from all obstructions and in action patrolled by the carpenter's crew who were provided with shot plugs of wood and oakum and sail cloth with which to close any shot holes in the wooden sides.'[335]

Clearly this is how the old 'Why didn't you stop the leak with sailcloth?' canard arose. These were important design factors, but the overall design of warships was moving so quickly that one suspects they were lost in the detail of more obvious changes – dispensing with sails, ever-bigger armament housed in turrets, steel construction, and so on, culminating in the *Dreadnought* of 1906, signalling a complete change in naval strategy, designed to deliver a knock-out blow rather than gradually wear the enemy down.

The most obvious lesson was the one in citing which George Ward Hunt made himself a laughing-stock – the deadly effectiveness of the ram bow on an iron hull. In 1866 the fleets of Austria and Italy had clashed in the Adriatic, in what became known as the Battle of Lissa. The Austrian ironclad *Ferdinand Max* had steamed straight into the side of the Italian flagship *Re d'Italia*, also an ironclad, at some 10 knots, sending her to the bottom in a few minutes, after continuous pounding by artillery had failed to cripple her. Here, much closer to home, was more splendid evidence of the value of the ram. In 1860 Nathaniel Barnaby had written 'One of the ancient modes of fighting was by the use of rams ... so long as vessels of war were propelled by oars ... Sailing vessels are not under command in this way, and therefore such a mode of fighting has been, for the last 500 years, impracticable. But steam has again given us this control over our ships, and the opinion is growing that we shall revert to this most ancient mode of warfare.'[336] Enthusiasm for the ram among naval architects and administrators generally was great. As *Punch* put it, 'Seeing that the *Iron Duke* poked her ram through the mail of the *Vanguard*, we now clearly discern that all our Ironclads of the future must be of the *Punch* type.'[337]. After 1875, when Barnaby had taken over from Reed, he remained cautious. Quoting four recent cases of ramming, he wrote 'In all four cases the blow was unexpected and the ship unprepared ... In the last *[i.e. Vanguard]*, the ship was struck with a force as great as is ever likely to be attained in action and in the most fatal place ... she nevertheless floated more than an hour.'[338] Of course ramming meant getting very close to your target, in most cases undesirably close, and in doing so breaking up carefully planned battle formation. As guns got bigger and more accurate, there was less need to get in amongst the enemy, and ramming, once thought to be the future of naval warfare, simply faded away.

So it was that *Vanguard*'s sister ships were already obsolescent as they trundled round Ireland, and Coastguard support work was the best they could hope for. *Iron Duke*, after discharging *Vanguard*'s crew to the hulk *Canopus* and returning her own fleet-men to Hull, found herself transferred to Kingstown to take over *Vanguard*'s duties there. Perhaps as a result of running into *Vanguard* she acquired a reputation for being accident-prone. In October a Press Association telegram reported 'On Saturday, as the *Iron Duke* was being taken out of Devonport Dock, she ran foul of the *Black Prince*. The latter lost her davits in the collision, but little other damage was done.'[339] In 1878 she saw sea service again on the China station as Admiral Coote's flagship, but managed to ground herself on the Woosung Bar at the mouth of the Shanghai River, and stuck fast for five days. A year later she struck a rock off the Japanese coast, as a result of which she had to spend a month in dock in Hong Kong. No wonder that *Punch*, on reading in the Press that 'the *Iron Duke*, on her way to Kingstown, would afford relief to homeward-bound merchant ships in the Channel', commented 'the sailors, and, indeed, all hands on board the homeward-bound merchant ships which the *Iron Duke* was appointed to afford relief to, would, perhaps, if they had known, have been somewhat apprehensive about that arrangement. However, all is well that ends well.

The homeward-bound vessels have got safe home. The *Iron Duke* has happily contrived to steer clear of them.'[340] She returned to British waters and guardship duties in the 1890's, and in 1906 was sold to a breaker's yard.

Warrior, once 'Monarch of the Seas', was already a forlorn sight, emerging from port on only a couple of occasions each year. In May 1883 she entered Portsmouth for the last time under her own power. She was stripped of engines and armament and sat in Fareham Creek for many years, and by the end of the century she was a mastless hulk, bereft even of her figurehead which had been installed at the Dockyard gates. Within a couple of years however she had been refitted, and in 1904 formed part of HMS *Vernon*, the Royal Navy torpedo school. This lasted until 1923, when *Vernon* became a shore-based institution. The Admiralty tried to sell her off, but there were no takers; instead she went to Pembroke Dock (where *Iron Duke* had been built) as a floating oil jetty, and stayed there for half a century. In the 1970's a movement gathered momentum to have her restored, and the Maritime Trust was established to raise the money. The huge task was completed in 1987, when *Warrior* at last came home, beautifully recreated in her former glory, to her present berth in Portsmouth Historic Dockyard.

In 1906 a correspondent wrote to *The Times* to call attention to the 'persistent ignoring of the grand old name *Vanguard* in the naming of our battleships. Against the Armada she took a distinguished part, and at the Nile she was Nelson's flagship. It is true the last *Vanguard* was lost 31 years ago after a collision, but no lives were lost, and there are no painful or ill-omened associations connected with the disaster.'[341] There will have been many with longer memories who would have disputed his assertion. But very soon the name *Vanguard* reappeared, this time attached to a *St Vincent*-class Dreadnought of 19,250 tons built in Barrow-in-Furness and launched in 1909. From 1913 to 1916 she was captained by Cecil Spencer Hickley, son of Victor Grant Hickley and thus nephew of Captain Henry Hickley of *Iron Duke*. It was her lot to be with the Grand Fleet at Scapa Flow, and involved in the Battle of Jutland in May 1916 as a member of the Fourth Battle Squadron. The British and German navies proved to be equally matched, and both returned home to lick their wounds. The end came suddenly and terribly for the eighth *Vanguard*. She was at anchor in Scapa Flow on 9 July 1917 when one of her magazines apparently became overheated and blew up. She sank quickly, with the loss of 804 lives. This time there was certainly a 'painful and ill-omened association' with the name, and it was more than 20 years before its next appearance.

John Brown's yard at Clydebank received an order in March 1941 for the building of a splendid new battleship of 42,500 tons, to be christened HMS *Vanguard*. 'It is a small coincidence that this *Vanguard* is as broad as the first was long,'[342] wrote her first Commander. The largest British warship ever built, she was proudly handed over to the Admiralty in 1946 as the jewel in their crown. In February 1947 she was chosen to carry King George VI, Queen Elizabeth and the Princesses Elizabeth and Margaret Rose on the first royal visit to South Africa. But the days of the battleship were over, and the ninth *Vanguard* spent her days as a training vessel and what one writer described as Portsmouth Dockyard's 'most useful luncheon club'. She was towed away for scrap in 1960, the last of her breed.

Command of the seas now belongs to aircraft carriers and submarines. The tenth vessel to bear the name *Vanguard* is a very different beast from her predecessors. She is a nuclear powered ballistic missile submarine, launched in 1986, and built by Vickers at Barrow-in-Furness. She and the others in her class (*Victorious, Vigilant* and *Vengeance)* are, at 16,000 tons, by far the largest submarines ever manufactured in the United Kingdom. Indeed (according to the informative guide at the Britannia Royal Naval College) she is 'to the inch' the same length as the frontage of that august building. Her size was influenced by the need to accommodate the Trident D5 missile, but the complement is no more than 132 officers and men. The way of life for today's submariner is very different from that of the ironclad rating; the Royal Navy's official website describes it thus:'The messes in *Vanguard* are comfortable and well appointed, fulfilling the role of dining room, lecture hall, lounge, games area and venue for church services. The food on board is good and there is plenty of it. The routine of working, eating and sleeping is broken up by the many forms of recreational activity. These range from watching newly released films to participating in an assortment of games and quizzes, sometimes even a variety show. Alternatively crew members may prefer just to relax and do some reading, whilst a few may opt to use their well stocked library to study for a degree.'[343]

On 25 November 1994 *Vanguard* prepared to leave the Faslane naval base on her first active patrol, to find that the Greenpeace organisation had sunk cement-filled barrels, from which protruded lengths of steel cable, in the Rhu Narrows. Thus the latest in the *Vanguard* line provokes an utterly different reaction from the honour given to her forebears – not perhaps surprising since (according to a Greenpeace press release) she is 'capable of firing the equivalent of 640 Hiroshima size bombs at almost any country in the world'. It is to be hoped that this awesome capability will never be needed, and that for many reasons she will be free of the unglamorous side of *Vanguard* history – sudden explosion, dismasting, collision and foundering.

Anyone interested in visualising the series of ships bearing the name *Vanguard* should certainly take the opportunity to join a guided tour of the Britannia Royal Naval College in Dartmouth, Devon, UK. The building itself is very fine. Designed by Aston Webb, whose work on Buckingham Palace and Admiralty Arch is well known to Londoners, its foundation stone was laid in 1902 by King Edward VII (hitherto the same Prince of Wales whose Indian excursion pushed the loss of the seventh *Vanguard* out of the public eye), as a shore based replacement for the hulk *Britannia* on which Captain Dawkins' young Lieutenants had learned the essentials of their profession. Only in recent years has the public been invited to see the splendours of the College interior. Towards the end of the tour visitors are guided to the Poopdeck, the gallery overlooking the magnificent Quarter Deck, where are displayed models of all ten of the Royal Navy ships that have borne the name *Vanguard*.

The story of the loss of *Vanguard* appears in almost every potted history of the Royal Navy or of the development of warship design, but only a few devote much space to the detail of what happened. As to lessons to be drawn, the incident is cited almost invariably as one among many instances of the power of the ram: 'a formidable instrument indeed – unfortunately for sinking one's own side'.[344] Otherwise its main effect was to raise doubts about the vulnerability of ironclads, especially those designs in which wing passages were not present. The injustice of the Court Martial sentence is usually noted, occasionally categorised as a political act 'to preserve the credibility of ironclads with a scapegoat'.[345] Rather more often accounts of the disaster (or '*Great Naval Blunder*' as one book title has it) mention the alleged demise of the Captain's dog – but then most of these were written for British audiences, and the Anglo-Saxon love of animals is notorious. The best available analyses of what happened are all out of print: those of Admiral Ballard, KC Barnaby, and John Marriott (see Bibliography for details). The loss of one ironclad became a footnote in Naval history, an awful warning of what could happen to an experienced Captain on a relaxed peacetime cruise, in command of a massive iron ship furnished with the latest equipment and fearsome armament, when faced with a sudden change in the weather and a need to resort to signalling procedures that were not in use every day and thus easily forgotten – a situation compounded by the appearance out of nowhere of a Norwegian barque, and the split-second decision of the Officer of the Watch on the other ship to sheer off course momentarily. Such a combination of circumstances could not happen in just that way again. None of the crew lost their lives (thanks to the efficiency of their Captain, but who remembers that?), and all that was to show for it were the two missing fingers on John Marshall's hand, and a space where a small dog might have been.

For many in the upper echelons of the Service the whole thing was an embarrassment to be forgotten as soon as possible. Even the banishment of a Captain of impeccable record and some seniority was not to be dwelt on. An ageing relative of one of the officers in our story, when asked what was known of him, is reported to have said 'Oh him, he was the one who had the Incident'. My correspondent added 'perhaps in a seafaring family it was and still is bad form to have "incidents" even if vindicated.'[346] Certainly Richard Dawkins seems to have been shunned by his colleagues. After the flurry of correspondence from his crew and well-wishers around the time of the Court Martial, only one Naval friend is mentioned in his son's memoirs: 'the one friend he saw something of was an Admiral who lived in his retirement for some time not far from us in Devonshire. He had been with Joe, as he was always called, … in their first ship together.'[347] Of course this isolation may have been at Dawkins' own instigation, such was his disgust at his treatment.

We have seen how some of the officers closely involved were affected strikingly by the sinking and its aftermath. For the majority of the crew, life went on as usual. They served their time, albeit on different ships, and few if any seem to have felt the need to leave an account of the mishap for future generations. Perhaps it was just not dramatic enough. Thus the many folk in Britain and Ireland with whom I have made contact and who are related to members of the ships' crews involved mostly have no more than a sketchy knowledge of 'the Incident' and the sudden change in their ancestors' careers that resulted. Professor Gianni Lombardi of Rome has benefited in a particular way from the *Vanguard* connection. Through his great-grandmother, Richard Dawkins' wife Mary Louisa, he is a welcome and honoured member of the Clan Chattan Association in Scotland (proving that Italians can look good in the kilt) and has made contact with Canadian members of the family of Simon McGillivray.

My own life has been immeasurably enriched by what happened on 1 September 1875. In any other circumstance it seems very unlikely that a 28-year-old Leading Seaman from Devon and a 19-year-old Ordinary Seaman (2nd Class) from Liverpool should have become close companions, but I suspect that an unexpected encounter with the tepid waters of the Irish Sea on that day may well have brought Henry Gaden and Francis Norton together. The son of one married the daughter of the other, and as a result I have enjoyed many happy years of marriage to the great-grand-daughter of Henry and Francis.

She was never a beautiful ship. Frightening, maybe, as a mass of iron in black livery with a surprising turn of speed, but at first sight not in any way endearing. In life she was always in the second rank, a scaled-down version of the really great iron battleships, *Warrior, Black Prince, Achilles, Northumberland.* But *Vanguard* inspired loyalty, and in her foundering showed the toughness that her designer and constructors had laboured to build into her. In the twenty-first century she has become a wreck like no other; 'a magnificent and unique shipwreck, unappreciated and, apart from noble but hollow sentiments in law, unprotected'.[348] It is time that the reputation of her Captain was similarly restored. As he wrote: 'My last wish is if any of my children are ever in a position to publish the whole affair in a book I think it is a duty they owe themselves to shew their Father acted as a man of judgement and was most unjustly condemned.' His children and grandchildren had other things to occupy them, but I hope that by telling the story in this way I have, through my own tenuous connection to his crew on that day of fog and confusion, been able to remind a new generation of the injustice he suffered, and honour the name of Captain Richard Dawkins.

Annex 1

HMS Vanguard Facts and Figures

AUDACIOUS CLASS CENTRAL BATTERY IRONCLAD

Building began at Laird's Birkenhead:	2 November 1867
Undocked (launched):	3 January 1870
Delivered by contractors to Devonport:	9 March 1870
Completed:	28 September 1870

DIMENSIONS

Length 280', breadth 54 ', draught 22'7" (85.34m x 16.46m x 6.88m), central battery 59' (18m) long

MASTS

As constructed:	Foremast	Mainmast	Mizen
Lower	79'0" (24m)	84'6" (25.8m)	67'6" (20.6m)
Topmasts	65'0" (19.8m)	65'0" (19.8m)	46'6" (14.2m)
Topgallants	49'0" (15m)	49'0" (15m)	36'0" (11m)

- Topmast lengths on *Vanguard* were later shortened by 10' (3m)

SAILS

Barque-rigged, area 23,700 sq ft (2,204 sq m)
- But *Vanguard* was described as almost unmanageable under sail.

TONNAGE

6,034 tons (3,774 old)

COMPLEMENT

450 (actual number on board on 1 September 1875: 351)

COSTS

1867-68	£15,882
1868-69	£160,417
1869-70	£80,264
Total	£256,563

ARMOUR

Belt 8" to 6", bulkheads 5"to 4", battery 6" to 4", 10" teak backing. Weight of armour 924 tons.

ARMAMENT

6 x 9" MLR (muzzle loading rifled, each weighing 12 tons) on main battery deck firing through broadside ports 8' above waterline

4 x 9" MLR in embrasure ports in upper battery, 16'6" above waterline

4 x 6" MLR (40-pounders) at extreme forward and aft ends of upper deck

6 x 20-pounder breech-loading for saluting

ENGINES

Two sets of 2 cylinders horizontal return connecting-rod engines, 72" cylinder, 3'stroke, 6 rectangular boilers of 30 lb pressure. 5,812 indicated horsepower. Twin two-bladed Mangin propellers set in tandem with blades behind each other, diameter 16'2", pitch 20'9".

COAL

460 tons – equivalent to 3 days at full power.

SPEED

10 knots under sail

13 knots under steam

- *Vanguard* reached 14½ knots on the Plymouth Mile in 1870.

TURNING CIRCLE

318 to 423 yards (291 to 387 metres) with balanced rudder.

Iron Duke with conventional rudder needed 505 yards.

Annex 2

Ballads and Verses

I

Publications of the Navy Records Society, vol. XXXIII, Naval Songs and Ballads (NRS 1908), "from the Madden collection".

THE *VANGUARD*

Come, all you seamen, stout and bold, and listen to my song,
It's worth your whole attention, I'll not detain you long.

CHORUS

Then let us sing the *Vanguard*'s praise, proclaim her valiant name,
Cruel usage I have met with since I sail'd in the same.

Concerning of the *Vanguard*, a ship of noble fame,
With her r-------- commander, Mickey Walker call'd by name.

At four o'clock you must turn out, the decks to holystone;
One and all you must go down upon your marrow bones.

Then Mr Croycraft comes on deck, and he'll begin to curse and swear;
Both watches of gunners send up on deck to see your lashings are all square.

At eight o'clock it's up top-gallant yards, to the mast-head you must run,
And if you are not the first ship, your name is taken down.

Then down from the mast-head to the gangway you must repair,
And there is the gratings rigged ready to punish you there.

And when on shore by leave you go, if beyond your time you stay,
Then you are put on the stage party for the space of sixty days.

Then next you're put in chokey, boys, you get both thin and white;
And if you break your liberty, scrub copper from morning till night.

But if you are in the black list, as true as I'm a sinner,
Then you must polish brass-work while the crew are at their dinner.

But if a fighting you do go, you'll never get any rest;
They will drive you off the lower deck, in the galley for to mess.

And when you are in the galley mess, your heart is fill'd with woe;
Your monthly money it is stopt, on shore you must not go.

Now, you seamen of the *Vanguard*, you had better not get drunk;
You will be laid upon your back, and they'll use the stomach pump.

If your hammock is dirty, and you know no reason why,
Then you must scrub it in the head, carry it on a boat-hook to dry.

There's a man on our lower deck, he is called Jondy Cross;
If I had my will of him, I'd overboard him toss.

But when on shore the bully comes, if with him you should fall in,
The w-----e that gives to him a drubbing shall have a gown and a gallon of gin.

So now to conclude, and finish my song;
I am a saucy mizen-top man, to the *Vanguard* does belong.

But if to sea I go again, I'd sooner swing in a halter,
Before I'd sail in any ship commanded by Mickey Walker.
Then let us sing the *Vanguard*'s praise, proclaim her valiant name,
Cruel usage I have met with since I sail'd in the same.

NOTES:

Mickey Walker: Baldwin Wake Walker was Commander of the 6th *Vanguard* from September 1836, so this may be a reference to him – but I have not been able to confirm the date of this ballad.
Jondy: the Master at Arms.

II

Bodleian Ballads Catalogue Harding B 13(246)

LOSS OF H.M.S. *VANGUARD*

On Tuesday, Sep. 2nd, 1875, the Iron
Duke, Ironclad, came into collision
with the Vangaurd [sic] off Bray Head, in
The Irish Sea, the latter ship was nearly cut in two, and altho' in consequence
of the nature of her build, all her crew
was saved, yet her loss will cost the country nearly a half million of money.

TUNE – THE MISER

Come listen to my story
Of the dangers of the sea,
It has been Britain's glory
The ocean's queen to be;
For many generations,
We have proudly ruled the main,
But unless things quickly alter,
We shall not do so again.

For that noble ship the *Vanguard*,
She was our nation's pride,
By the '*Iron Duke*' she has been laid
Beneath the ocean's tide.
She was a splendid vessel,
And half a million cost,

It show's the way the nation's
Hard earned money's lost;
Of our gallant-hearted sailors,
Our praise we'll give so free,
But our officers are gentlemen,
Who lose their ships at sea.

It was on a Thursday morning,
When off the Irish coast,
And in a dreadful fog
The *Iron Duke* was lost:
They were cruising altogether,
The Channel Fleet so brave,
When the *Vanguard* was ran into,
And sank beneath the wave.

Altho' the day was foggy,
There must be something wrong,
For one to run another down,
When they were sailing along;
They were so close together,
That mischief they must do,
There's not a sailor in the fleet,
But knows that this is true.

A cable's length had parted
The gallant ship we find,
With a thousand lion-hearted
Sailors there confined;
The *Iron Duke* rushed on them,
And smash'd the *Vanguard's* sides,
It is God's mercy that our men,
Are not beneath the tide.

They saved our gallant sailors,
Five hundred men or more,
Their hearts were sad and heavy,
As they landed on the shore;
Their clothes and cherish'd letters,
They had no time to save,
And many a mother's parting gift,
Has sank beneath the wave.

The world will say that England
Is going down the hill,
When officers make such blunders
That shows their want of skill:
They ought to sack the dandies,
Who strut about so fine,
And wear a sword and epaulettes,
Tho' they never cross'd the Line.

III

This ballad appears in various forms, and seems to have been very popular in the aftermath of the sinking. The version reproduced here is that included in K C Barnaby: Some Ship Disasters and Their Causes (Hutchinson 1968), page 86. Another version appears in The Mariner's Mirror, Vol 22 (1935), page 211, "sent by Admiral Sir Richard Phillimore as the one sung in the gun-room of HMS Minotaur when he first went to sea in 1886". The content of the verses is similar to the above, though the wording is different, and verses 2 and 3 were additional to Admiral Phillimore's text, and sent in by the Earl of Glasgow.

THE LORDS OF THE ADMIRALTEE

Heave-to jolly messmates, I'll spin you a yarn,
you landlubbers listen to me,
and we'll sing you a song of a big ironclad
which went down in the Irish Sea.
Run into and sunk by another tin junk,
t'was very good sport d'ye see.
"For it clearly showed what a fine ram she had got"
Said the Lords of the Admiraltee.

Now the Captain we're told was a mariner bold,
who had sailed ev'ry ocean and sea,
He'd oft been as far as Madagascar
America, Cape and Chinee.
He knowed all the stars and he knowed all the spars,
a very fine officer he,
"So we think he's the lad for this big ironclad"
Said the Lords of the Admiraltee.

So the Captain summons his first lieut down
and stands him a champagne grog,
"Oh bust my boilers and engines" says he
"If I know what to do in a fog.
For it can't be a crime to have served all my time
in big sailing ships d'ye see"
"So of course he's the lad for this big ironclad"
Said the Lords of the Admiraltee.

So we steered nor'east and we steered nor'west
and we steamed both fast and slow.
Till into our ship another one ran
and quickly we went below.
So a ship that had cost half a million or more
went down in the Irish Sea.
"Good gracious how now won't there just be a row"
Said the Lords of the Admiraltee.

"For we can't punish adm'rals because they're like us,
and of course all our duties we know.
But a lieutenant's diff'rent, he can't answer back
so into the jug he must go.
"In steering" says he, "to avoid a big smash
I used common sense d'ye see".
"We know nothing at all about that at Whitehall"
Said the Lords of the Admiraltee.

Now messmates I tell you in Jack Tar's plain way
these things didn't ought for to be
for our ships are not built and our men are not shipped
to go down in the Irish Sea.
For the Adm'rals all who just sit in Whitehall
should know about ships d'ye see.
We must clear out those frauds who proclaim
themselves Lords
from out of the Adm'raltee.

IV

Satirical verses from "Punch"

(i) 25 September 1875, page 120

JOHN'S GROWL

(In re Aries v. Taurus.)
JOHN BULL he stood, in no merry mood,
O'erlooking his silver streak.
Sighed he, "I have prided myself on my JACKS,
As a set-off to Red Tape and Sealing-Wax;
I never yet thought my Sea-doctors were quacks;
If they are, a new lot I must seek.
With my rivals in reg'ments I may not compete,
But, by Jingo, I did pin my faith in my Fleet!

"And when wooden walls and white wings were no more,
Done to death by the Iron-ribbed Demon,
I sighed, but submitted. Thinks I, while my shore
Is guarded by seaworthy ships as of yore,
I must bow to the change, though it's rather a bore,
For at least it has left me my Seamen!
Trim hulk or black bulk, all is one; I've no fear,
While my Blue Jackets know how to fight and to steer.

"But now, by St George, it is pitiful quite!
When the cannon-balls volley and hurtle,
What chance will my Iron-clads have in the fight,
If in peace – and a fog – JACK can't steer them aright,
But they ram one another – go down in my sight,
Run blindly ashore, or 'turn turtle'?
I've a nice show of ships, if on paper I tot 'em,
But they won't serve me much if they're half at the bottom!

"I have paid for them, too, at a pretty stiff rate,
These lumbering mountains of metal:
If matters go on as they have gone of late,
These lubbers of mine, high or low in the State,
Who can't build a seaworthy ship, or steer straight,
With me will accounts have to settle.
What with Public Opinion and Purse, 'twill be funny
If I do not get value received for my money!"

Lamentable Intelligence from the Admiralty

(ii) 23 October 1875, page 159 (extract)

"OUR BULWARKS ON THE BRINE"

ON Seamanship when Sailors disagree
How can JOHN BULL expect to fare at sea?
Fault sinks a ship; on whom should censure fall?
Chiefs judging Chiefs, are snubbed by Chiefs of all.

But where will Admirals, conflicting, end?
How far does "unseaworthiness" extend?
Our iron walls are 'gainst teredo good;
But has that insect not bored heads of wood?

Now *Vanguards* can no longer guard our van.
But Seamen, as to seamanship at sea,
In one particular at least agree;
"My Lords", and the Court-Martial, all the same,
A culprit both condemn to bear the blame.
To whom "My Lords", not erring on the side
Of legal usage, add a man untried.
For half a million sunk the waves below,
Two ruined officers we have to show –
No single scapegoat his superiors saves:
Long may we sing, "BRITANNIA rules the waves".

(i) 11 December 1875, page 240

YOU MUST NOT SPEAK TO THE MAN AT THE WHEEL
(Respectfully Dedicated to the First Lord of the Admiralty)

England is proud of her Iron-clad Fleet,
That all the rest of the world can beat;

What if an Iron-clad sink its twin?
'Tis just that way that fights begin.
Whitehall is pleased that it ended so:
The enemy now our power will know.
What if after, the iron monster tried,
In remorse perchance, a suicide?
It failed, and intelligent folk must feel
'Tis wrong to Speak to the Man at the Wheel.

On the *Iron Duke* an "investigation
Strictly private," must please the nation:
England, of course, don't care to know
Why to DAVY JONES her Iron-clads go;
So an Admiral and Captains three
A confidential Court will be:
And their verdict will that axiom seal –
You mustn't Speak to the Man at the Wheel.

Are we land-lubbers all, who contrive to catch
For the head of our Navy the worst of the batch?
Put a Seaman there with the duffers to deal –
Then you may talk to the Man at the Wheel.

V

National Maritime Museum, Greenwich, Manuscript DAW/15. These and other verses (including "The Lords of the Admiraltee") are among Captain Dawkins' personal papers, but it is not clear whether they were written by him or by someone else.

(i)

I had a little ironclad, I called it *Iron Duke*,
I got it in a little fog, and saved it – by a fluke,
It rammed another vessel down, I took her crew away,
To nearly sink 'em somewhere else, so hollo boys, hooray!

I thought my little ironclad was in a little mess,
And finding I'd no powder hung out signals of distress.
But the little danger over, we all vowed to keep it "dark"
And said we'd only done it for a jolly little lark.

(ii)

"Leiningen, Leiningen, where have you been?"
"I've been to Osborne, a-fetching the Queen."
"Leiningen, Leiningen, what did you then?"
"Ran down a schooner and did for her men."
"Leiningen, Leiningen, what did she say?"
"She said as they ought to get out of the way."
"Leiningen, Leiningen, what did she do?"
"She gave me a present and doubled my screw."

NOTE: This refers to the collision between the royal yacht Alberta and the Mistletoe in August 1875. The Queen, Prince Leopold and Princess Beatrix were on board at the time. Mistletoe sank and her Master and two passengers died.

Paper annexed to the Report of the 'Vanguard' Court Martial,

PRO ADM 1/6369

Statement of Mr C T Dawson, Paymaster, late "Vanguard", of estimated Quantity and Weight of Provisions &c on board at the time of collision

1st September 1875

SPECIES		QUANTITY	WEIGHT		WHERE STOWED
			TON	CWT	
Biscuit	lbs	26,417	12	1	Bread Rm
Spirits	galls	831	4	6	Spirit Rm
Sugar	lbs	4,356	2	8	Dry Provision Rm Port Side
Chocolate	lbs	2,973	1	12	Spirit Rm
Tea	lbs	581		7	Spirit Rm
Salt Pork	lbs	7,258	5	8	Wet Provision Rm
Split Peas	lbs	3,368	1	18	Dry Provision Rm Stard Side
Salt Beef	lbs	6,986	6	0	Wet Provision Rm
Flour	lbs	5,484	2	16	Dry Provision Rm Stard Side
Suet	lbs	553		11	Wet Provision Rm
Rasins	lbs	1,105		14	In Tunnels
Oatmeal	lbs	1,221		12	Dry Provision Rm Port Side
Mustard	lbs	470		6	In Tunnels
Pepper	lbs	219		3	– do – do –
Vinegar	galls	516	2	18	Dry Provision Rm Port Side
Lemon Juice	lbs	145		4	– do – do – do –
Medical comforts					
Wine	bottles	90			Spirit Rm
Pred. Meats	lbs	280		9	Dry Provision Rm Port Side
Candles	lbs	4,949	2	15	In Tunnels
Fresh Beef &	lbs	529			
Vegetables	lbs	287		7	Upper Battery
Clothing Ullages		–	1	10	Slop Rm, Provision Rm Flat
Bedding Sets		300	2	15	Stokers Flat & Chest Rm
Tobacco	lbs	1,100	1	5	Dry Provision Rm Stard Side
Soap	lbs	11,900	6	10	– do – do – do – Port Side

Muster Lists for September 1875: Officers

Transcribed from the Navy List for 1875 and the relevant Ledgers: PRO ADM 117/994 (*Vanguard*) and ADM 117/562 (*Iron Duke*)

HMS *VANGUARD*

Captain	Richard Dawkins	Chief Engineer	Robert Brown
Commanders	Dashwood Goldie Tandy	Assistant	James G Gordon
	Gordon Charles Young	Paymasters	William H W Markham
	(of HMS *Achilles*)		
			Valentine Horne
Lieutenants	Edward Rothwell Wheelock Noble	Engineers	William George Paige
	Edmund W Speck		James Redgrave
	William Crichton Stuart Hathorn		William A M Vivyan
	Alexander Allen (of HMS *Achilles*)		Angus Leitch
			(supernumerary)
Navigating			
Lieutenant	James Cambridge Thomas	Assistant Engineer	Charles H Pellow
		2nd Class	(supernumerary)
Captain RMLI	Samuel Travers Collins		
		Gunners 2nd Class	Edward Jones
Lieutenant RMA	William Miller		Alfred Smith
			George Wheeler
Lieutenant RMLI	William H McCheane		
		Boatswain 1st Class	Arthur Truscott
Chaplain	Rev Spencer Musson BA		
		Boatswains 2nd Class	John Humphries
Staff Surgeons	Dr Constantine Keenan		Richard Hurrell
	Dr James William Fisher		
		Carpenter 1st Class	David Tiddy
Paymaster	Charles T Dawson		

HMS *IRON DUKE*

Captain	Henry Dennis Hickley	Chief Engineer	Richard L Canney
Commander	Arthur C H Paget	Assistant Paymasters	Robert J M Macleod
			Reginald C Hodder
Lieutenants	Philip B Aitkens		
	Pierre Gervais Evans	Engineers	Richard T Rundle
	Stephen H Thompson		John A Lemon
	(supernumerary)		James D Chater
	E B Van Koughnet		
		Gunners 2nd Class	George Large
Navigating			William Reeve
Lieutenant	Heaver Sugden		
		Boatswain 1st Class	John W Ford
Captain RMLI	John Cairncross		
		Boatswains 2nd Class	George F Gartrell
Lieutenant RMA	Arthur B Shakespeare		William Doyle
Lieutenant RMLI	Ringrose W Tully	Carpenter 2nd Class	Frederick Sale
Chaplain	Rev Bartholomew Ring LLD	Assistant Engineer 1st Class	James C Oare
Fleet Surgeon	Dr Charles D Shephard		
		Chief Officers of Coastguard	Henry Latters
Staff Surgeon	Dr John Buckley		William Mains
Paymaster	Charles Barrs		

Muster Lists: Ratings aboard HMS Vanguard on 1 September 1875

Transcribed from PRO ADM 117/994, *Vanguard* Ledger, Michaelmas quarter 1875, and arranged in alphabetical order.

NOTE: Spellings and ranks are as they appear in the Ledger; some ranks are difficult to identify from the handwriting.

Surname	Forenames	Rank	Royal Marines &c	Alias
Abram	Richard	Boy 1 C		
Adams	Joseph J	Stoker		
Ahern	James	PO 1Cl		
Anderson	David	Ldg Smn		
Appleby	George	Gunner	RMA	
Ashley	William	Cpl	RMLI	
Askew	James	S Berth Stwd		
Axworthy	Frederick	Stoker 2 Cl		
Aze	Thomas	Stoker 2 Cl		
Badcock	Isaac	Stoker 2 Cl		
Baker	Samuel	Barber		
Barber	William	D 3 C		
Barlow	James	Pte	RMLI	Jesse Barrow
Barnett	Richard	PO 1 C		
Barry	John	AB		
Bath	John P	Carp Crew		
Bear	Thomas	Gunner	RMA	
Bearder	Joseph	Cpl	RMA	
Bearne	William	Pte	RMLI	
Bell	Samuel	Pte	RMLI	
Bennett	Henry	Car Mate		
Best	William	Pte	RMLI	
Bigmore	William J	Ordy		
Boniface	William	AB		
Borlace	James W H	Eng Rm Artif		
Boughton	Fredk StJ	AB		
Brennan	John	Pte	RMLI	
Broughton	Albert	Boy 1 C		
Brown	Nathaniel	PO 1 C		
Browning	John	Ordy		
Budgen	William	Ordy		
Burgess	George	Sgt	RMA	
Butler	John	Gunner	RMA	

Surname	Forenames	Rank	Royal Marines &c	Alias
Callaway	Henry	Sh Steward 2C		
Camp	William	Sh Cpl 1 C		
Cannon	William	PO 1 C		
Carron	Thomas H	Ord 2 C		
Carter	Edward R	Stoker		
Carter	John	Pte	RMLI	
Cauvin	Joseph	Cook's Mate		
Chambers	Thomas	Pte	RMLI	
Chapman	Daniel H	D 1 C		
Chapman	Donald	Pte	RMLI	
Chapple	Samuel	Pte	RMLI	
Clapson	George	Ordy		
Clubb	James	Gunner	RMA	
Cock	Richard	Pte	RMLI	
Coleman	Joseph	Pte	RMLI	
Coles	Thomas	Pte	RMLI	
Coles	William	Boy 1 C		
Collings	John	AB		
Collins	John	Gunner	RMA	
Connor	Will	AB	Supernumerary	
Cooper	George	Ord 2 C		
Courtis	Benjamin S	Ldg Seaman		
Crabb	John	Sergeant	RMLI	
Cronan	Thomas	AB		
Crothers	Will Jno	B 1 C	Supernumerary	
Cruze	Henry	Painter 1 C		
Damby	Henry	Pte	RMLI	
Danehy	Timothy	Shipwright	Supernumerary	
Daniels	Peter	Plumber		
Dargan	James	D 2 C		
Davenport	Thomas	Pte	RMLI	
Davies	John	A Eng Rm Artif	Supernumerary	
Davis	John	Signalman		
Davis	John B	Ordy		
Davis	William	Pte	RMLI	
Deary	Samuel	AB		
Dewhurst	William	Gunner	RMA	
Dibble	Clifford W	Ordy		
Dickens	William C	Ordy		
Dimmock	Thomas	Pte	RMLI	
Dineford	William	Corporal	RMLI	
Donovan	Richard	Stoker		
Dorset	Joshua	Pte	RMLI	
Dower	Nicholas	B 1 C	Supernumerary	
Doyle	James	D 3 C		
Doyle	Richard	D 3 C		
Drew	John C	Ord 2 C		
Dudding	Thomas	Pte	RMLI	
Duffin	Chas		Cap Hold	
Duggan	Patrick	Caulker		
Edmunds	Joshua	Pte	RMLI	

Surname	Forenames	Rank	Royal Marines &c	Alias
Elliott	James A	Ordy		
Ellis	Edward	Pte	RMLI	Edward Elkis
Evans	Francis	Pte	RMLI	
Ezekiel	Samuel	Boy 1 C		
Fegan	John	AB		
Fellingham		Pte	RMLI	W G Shaw
Fenton	Henry	2 Cap Lr Deck	Supernumerary	
Fidler	Reuben	Gunner	RMA	
Fisher	Abraham	Pte	RMLI	
Fitzgerald		Pte	RMLI	
Flaherty	Sylvester	Arm Crew		
Fletcher	William	Pte	RMLI	
Flood	Samuel	Pte	RMLI	
Foreman	Henry	Musician		
Forester	William L	AB		
Foster	George	Pte	RMLI	
Fox	Joseph	Stoker		Joseph Scraton
Francis	Henry	Pte	RMLI	
Gaden	Henry	Ldg Seaman		
Gallagher	Patrick	AB		
Gardiner	Henry	Boy 1 C		
Gawdon	Frederick G	AB		
George	Richard	Ldg Stoker		
Gibby	John	Pte	RMLI	
Glennie	Max	Ldg Seaman	Supernumerary	
Godfrey	Alfred	Boy 1 C		
Godfrey	John	Pte	RMLI	
Golby	William G	Pte	RMLI	
Good	Richard	AB		
Goodden	Thomas	Stoker		
Gower	Ebenezer	Yeo of Signals		
Graves	William	Ordy		
Green	James C	Ordy		
Gribbell	Simon A	Stoker 2 C		
Griffiths	Robert	Gunner	RMA	
Gully	John	Pte	RMLI	
Haggarty	James	AB		
Hall	William	Gunner	RMA	
Hammond	Edward H	Boy 1 C		
Harding	Benjamin	Boy 1 C		
Harkin	Edward	Pte	RMLI	
Harris	William	Boy 1 C		
Harrold	James	Stoker		
Hawkins	William H	AB		
Hayden	James	Drummer	RMLI	
Hefron	Luke	Ldg Stoker		
Helps	Charles	Pte	RMLI	
Helson	Richard	Stoker		
Henderson	William	PO 1 C		
Hicks	John	Pte	RMLI	
Hill	John	Pte	RMLI	

Surname	Forenames	Rank	Royal Marines &c	Alias
Hill	Samuel	Blacksmith		
Hill	William	Ordy		
Hiscock	Charles	Pte	RMLI	
Hiscocks	Frank H	AB		
Hoit	David R	S Cook		
Holmes	John	AB		
Hooper	James C	Yeo of Sto		
Hosford	Thomas	Sailmaker		
James	George	Ordy		
Jeffery	Thomas	Gunner	RMA	
Jewell	Walter	Pte	RMLI	
Jones	Alfred	Pte	RMLI	
Jones	William	D 1 C		
Jordan	Henry J	PO 1 C		
Kearns	Thomas	D 2 C		
Kellond	George	PO 2 C		
Kent	John	D 2 C		
Keohane	Michael	AB		
Kid	Peter	Ldg Stoker		
Knight	Oliver	Gunner	RMA	
Knight	Thomas	Gunner	RMA	
Lancastle	Sidney	Pte	RMLI	
Lane	Patrick	PO 2 C		
Langler	George	AB		
Langley	Mathew	Pte	RMLI	
Leaman	John E	Ordy		
Leatherbarrow	George	Pte	RMLI	
Lequesne	Philip	AB		
Liddle	James	Ldg Stoker		
Linscott	Simon	Ordy		
Little	William J	Nl Schoolmaster		
Lloyd	John	Pte	RMLI	
Long	James	PO 1 C		
Loveday	Thomas	Corporal	RMA	
Maguire	Daniel	AB		
Mahoney	Cornls	Laneptr		
Malier	Michael	Pte	RMLI	
Malpass	Thomas	Gunner	RMA	
Mann	Henry	Pte	RMLI	
Mann	Thomas	Pte	RMLI	
Mannerings	William	Stoker 2 C		
Marks	Joseph	PO 1 C		
Marriott	George	Pte	RMLI	
Marriott	James W	Drummer	RMLI	
Marshall	John	Ldg Seaman		
Martin	Edward	Gunner	RMA	
Martin	Thomas	PO 1 C		
Martin	Thomas	Pte	RMLI	
Martins	Robert	Yeo of Signals		
Maunder	William	Ordy		
May	John	Ordy		

Surname	Forenames	Rank	Royal Marines &c	Alias
May	William	Pte	RMLI	
McCallion	Daniel	AB		
McCarthy	Eugene	AB		
McConnell	Moses	Ord 2 C		
McGuinness	Nicholas	Ordy		
Meekins	Robert H	Boy 1 C		
Merrett	James	Pte	RMLI	
Metyard	Edward	Pte	RMLI	
Miller	William T	Pte	RMLI	
Milward	James	Pte	RMLI	
Mitchell	George	Gunner	RMA	
Moiest	Hubert F	Ordy		
Moore	John	Gunner	RMA	
Moore	William	Boy 1 C		
Morgans	James	Ordy		
Morley	James P	Ldg Seaman		
Morrish	Robert	Ord 2 C		
Mugford	William	D 1 C		
Mumford	Jno	Cooper		
Murdoch	James	AB		
Murphy	Denis		PO 2 C	
Murphy	Michael	Ordy		
Murphy	Timothy	Stoker		
Mutch	William H	Ordy		
Newcombe	Jno	Pte	RMLI	
Norman	William	Ord 2 C		
Norton	Francis	Ord 2 C		
Nowlan	Edward	Ordy		
O'Grady	Will	B 1 C	Supernumerary	
Oliver	William H	AB		
Oman	John	Pte	RMLI	
Osborne	Charles F	Boy 1 C		
Osborne	James A	Sk Berth Att		
Osborne	William J	Sh Stewards Boy		
Oxford	Christopher	Stoker 2 C		
Page	Abraham	Gunner	RMA	
Palk	John	PO 1 C		
Palmer	Hugh C	Boy 1 C		
Parish	Thomas	Ord 2 C		
Parry	William	AB		
Paston	James	Gunner	RMA	
Peace	Ralph	Pte	RMLI	
Peaty	William	Ord 2 C		
Pengelly	Thomas	Ordy		
Percy	William	Armr		
Perkins	Ernest	Ordy		
Perry	Thomas W J	Pte	RMLI	
Pettifer	James	Gunner	RMA	
Phillott	John	Pte	RMLI	
Pleass	Thomas	Ordy		
Porter	Thomas	Signalman 2 C		

Surname	Forenames	Rank	Royal Marines &c	Alias
Potter	Alfred	Ordy		
Price	Joseph	PO 1 C		
Rae	John	Ropemaker		
Rawlings	Thomas	Armr		
Raymond	John	Pte	RMLI	
Rayner	George	Pte	RMLI (of HMS *Achilles*)	
Redmond	James	D 2 C		
Reeve	Charles	AB	Supernumerary	
Reeves	Mark	Pte	RMLI	
Richards	Henry	Ordy		
Richards	John	Pte	RMLI	
Ridout	Alexander	Sergeant	RMLI	
Roberts	John M	Ord 2 C		
Robjohns	Henry	Stoker		
Roch	Richard	Pte	RMLI	Richard Roach
Rodgers	John	Pte	RMLI	
Roger	Charles	Pte	RMLI	
Rooney	Daniel	Ordy		
Rose	Henry A	Eng Rm Artif	Supernumerary	
Rusholme	Thomas	Writer 3 C		
Ryan	James	Gunner	RMA	
Salsbury	Henry	Pte	RMLI	
Salter	Thomas	Pte	RMLI	
Sarahs	Henry	Pte	RMLI	
Sargeant	Richard	Sh Steward 1 C		
Sargeant	William J	PO 1 C		
Screech	William	PO 1 C		
Selley	Robert	Pte	RMLI	
Shepherd	John	Boy 1 C		
Simmonds	William H	Blksths Crew		
Skeats	Tom	Pte	RMLI	
Skinner	Edward A	Shipwright		
Smale	Richard	Stoker		
Smith	George H	Gunner	RMA	Henry Garrett
Smith	John	Pte	RMLI	
Smith	John	Sh Stewards Ast		
Smith	William	Pte	RMLI	
Smither	Daniel B	Ord 2 C		
Sparks	George	Pte	RMLI	
Stacey	James A	Cap Coun		
Staddon	George H	Writer 3 C		
Staden	Frederick	D 2 C		
Steer	James W	Ldg Seaman		
Stephen	Frederick	Pte	RMLI	
Stevens	Richard	AB		
Stewart	Will	PO 1 C	Supernumerary	
Strachen	James	Gunner	RMA	
Swinfin	William	Pte	RMLI	
Symons	Thomas	Ordy		

Surname	Forenames	Rank	Royal Marines &c	Alias
Tamlin	Aaron	Boy 1 C		
Taylor	Richard	Gunner	RMA	
Taylor	Thomas	Ord 2 C	Supernumerary	
Toms	Anthony J	D 3 C		
Toogood	Richard	Pte	RMLI	
Toomey	Daniel	AB		
Toop	Alfred	Pte	RMLI	
Townsend	John	Pte	RMLI	
Turner	George	Boy 1 C		
Vince	George	Ordy		
Vosper	John	Cat Crew		
Voss	Charles	Ord 2 C		
Wakefield	Thomas	Gunner	RMA	
Wakeham	William	D 3 C		
Waldren	James	Master At Arms		
Waldron	George	D 1 C		
Wallis	John	Car Crew		
Walmsley	Richard	Ord 2 C	Supernumerary.	
Ward	John	AB		
Ware	George	Ordy		
Warren	Will Hy	Ord 2 C	Supernumerary	
Warren	William	Ord 2 C		
Watson	Simon	PO 2 C	Supernumerary	
Watts	William	Pte	RMLI	
Webb	Charles	Boy Writer		
Webb	Charles	Writer 3 C		
Webb	Josiah	Pte	RMLI	
Webber	James	Ldg Stoker		
Webber	William	Sh Cpl 2 C		
Weekes	Alfred	Ordy		
White	Charles	D 3 C		
White	William	Stoker 2 C		
Williams	Edward	PO 1 C		
Williams	George	Ordy		
Williams	George	Pte	RMLI	
Williams	Henry	Gunner	RMA	
Williams	Samuel	Stoker		
Williams	Samuel H	Ord 2 C		
Wills	Samuel S	Ldg Stoker		
Wilson	John	AB		
Wilton	Joseph	Stoker		
Wise	Samuel	Butcher		
Woodman	Henry	Corporal	RMLI	
Worrell	William H	Ordy		

Crews of the Vanguard tenders on 1 September 1875

Surname	Forenames	Rank	Tender
Abell	Robert	CPO	Amelia
Ashplant	Richd	Ord	Victoria
Bennett	Dan W	AB	Victoria
Briscoe	Jas	D3Cl	Amelia
Burrell	Geo	Ord	Victoria
Cain	John	D3Cl	Amelia
Carter	Michael	Second Mate	Amelia
Cassidy	Willm	Stoker	Amelia
Cleave	Francis	CPO	Amelia
Coatsworth	William E	AB	Amelia
Coghlan	Jas	Sq.Sn.	Victoria
Dew	Fredk	Ship's Steward's Asst	Amelia
Driscoll	Jas	CPO	Victoria
Earl	Willm	AB	Victoria
Gibbs	Willm J	B1C	Amelia
Greenwood	John	Ord 2C	Victoria
Gunn	John	AB	Victoria
Harris	Arthur	Ord	Amelia
Harvey	Geo M	AB	Victoria
Hawker	Jas	AB	Amelia
John	Willm G	AB	Victoria
Johns	Edward	AB	Victoria
Kain	Chas	Senior Mate	Amelia
Lewis	Lewis P	Engr	Amelia
Long	Alfd	Engr	Amelia
McCullen	Geo R	AB	Victoria
McCullen	Josh	Chief Officer in Command	Victoria
McGowan	Dan	Sq.Sn.	Victoria
McGregor	Jas	Sq.Sn.	Amelia
Morrow	Thos	AB	Victoria
Read	Hy W	Sq.Sn.	Amelia
Roach	Ja	Ord	Amelia
Roach	Jas	AB	Victoria
Ryan	Christr J	AB	Victoria
Simpson	Willm	Ldg Sto	Amelia
Sugar	Willm	Chief Officer in Command	Amelia
Tucker	Thos	AB	Amelia
Wallis	Richard J	AB	Victoria
Webster	Alfd	AB	Amelia
Williams	Thos	AB	Victoria
Young	John	Shipwt	Victoria

Notes

1 GM Trevelyan, *A Shortened History of England* (Penguin Books 1959) p 461. Every effort has been made to trace the copyright holder of this work, without success.

2 GM Trevelyan, *A Shortened History of England* (Pelican Books 1959) p.451.

3 Quoted in Geoffrey Best, *Mid-Victorian Britain 1851-75* p309. This and further quotations from this work reprinted by permission of Harper Collins Publishers Ltd.

4 John Beeler: *Birth of the Battleship* p 27.

5 For a fuller description of these trials, see DK Brown: *Before the Ironclad: Development of Ship Design, Propulsion and Armament in the Royal Navy, 1815-60.*

6 Sir John Rennie, quoted in Burns: *The Devonport Dockyard Story* p.42.

7 KC Barnaby: *Some Ship Disasters and their Causes* p.18. This and further quotations from this work reprinted by permission of The Random House Group Ltd.

8 Beeler, op cit p 48.

9 Admiral GA Ballard: *The Black Battlefleet* p 17.

10 Barnaby, op cit p 15.

11 Website www.netmarine.net/tradi/celebres/dupuy/, 2002.

12 EHH Archibald: *The Metal Fighting Ship* p 5. This and further quotations from this work by kind permission of Blandford Press, division of The Orion Publishing Group (London).

13 Parliamentary papers 1861 v No.438, p.231

14 Archibald, op cit p 8.

15 Ballard, p 50.

16 Beeler, p 41.

17 Ballard, p 19.

18 Ballard, p 172.

19 De Guiche, *Memoirs* (pub 1743), quoted in Padfield: *The Battleship Era.*

20 Beeler, p 87.

21 *The Times* 2 January 1873 p 9.

22 John F Beeler, *British Naval Policy in the Gladstone-Disraeli Era* p105.

23 Quoted in Beeler *Birth of the Battleship* p 49.

24 Quoted in Barnaby, p 29.

25 WCS Hathorn, letter to his mother 30 April 1870 (private collection).

26 DK Brown, *Warrior to Dreadnought.*

27 Hathorn letter to his parents, 9 September 1870.

28 Quoted in AJ Watts: *The Royal Navy, and Illustrated History* p 37, by kind permission of Continuum.

29 Brown, p 74.

30 Peter Padfield: *The Battleship Era* p 34. This and later quotations from this work by kind permission of peter Padfield..

31 Quoted in Padfield, p 69.

32 *Illustrated London News,* 8 April 1865, quoted in Best: *Mid-Victorian Britain 1851-75.*

33 Best, p 283.

34 Richard Hill, *War at Sea in the Ironclad Age* p 75. This and further quotations from this work by kind permission of Continuum.

35 Peter Padfield, *Rule Britannia!* p55. This and further quotations from this work reprinted by permission of The Random House Group Ltd.

36 *The Guardian* 25 February 2003.

37 WCS Hathorn: Letter to his parents, July 1869.

38 Hathorn letter, 21 July 1869.

39 Hathorn letter, 28 July 1869.

40 Hathorn letter, 31 October 1869.

41 John Winton, *Hurrah for the life of a sailor!* p 190. This and further quotations from this work reproduced by kind permission of the Executors of the estate of John Winton.

42 GA Ballard, *The Black Battlefleet* p173.

43 Padfield, *op cit* p 57.

44 Quoted in John Winton, *op cit* p195.

45 Quoted in Padfield, *The Battleship Era* p87.

46 DK Brown, *Before the Ironclad* p60.

47 Capper, *Aft – from the Hawsehole* p74.

48 Padfield, *op cit* p64.

49 W Laird Clowes, *History of the Royal Navy Vol VII* p17.

50 http://www.royalmarinesofficialsite.co.uk.

[51] Quoted in William Webb: *Coastguard! An official history of HM Coastguard* (HMSO 1976). Crown copyright material is reproduced with the permission of the Controller of HMSO.

[52] Winton, *op cit* p 215.

[53] The National Archives (TNA): Public Record Office (PRO) ADM 139/638

[54] The following quotations are taken from Derek Paine, *A Pictorial History of Greystones, Bray and Enniskerry.*

[55] Information included in an email to the author from Gary Paine, 12 January 2004; see *The HMS Ganges Association, Cornwall Division: Extracts from the Falmouth Packet Newspaper 1866-1899.* (April 2002).

[56] Letter to the author, 28 November 2001.

[57] *The Times* 17 September 1875.

[58] Taken from John McIlwain, *HMS Warrior* p21.

[59] WCS Hathorn, letter to his parents, 1 March 1871.

[60] Rick Jolly, *The Pussers Rum Guide to Royal Navy Slanguage* p26.

[61] Padfield, *Rule Britannia!* p29.

[62] Winton, *op cit* p184.

[63] Clowes, *op cit* p17.

[64] 'Martello Tower', *At School and At Sea,* quoted in Winton, *op cit* p309 .

[65] *Punch* 23 October 1875.

[66] Quoted in Commander W J Lamb OBE MVO: *HMS Vanguard 1586-1946.*

[67] Lamb, p 10.

[68] *Maritime South West, No.18 [2005]* (published by the South West Maritime History Society) p142.

[69] *Naval Songs and Ballads,* Publications of the Navy Records Society Vol XXXIII, p 320.

[70] Lamb, p 32.

[71] GA Ballard, *The Black Battlefleet,* p 173.

[72] Admiral Houston Stewart, quoted in DK Brown, *Warrior to Dreadnought.*

[73] Letter from Tarleton to Sir Alexander Milne, 7 August 1875, National Maritime Museum Greenwich manuscript MLN/164/10.

[74] W H Davenport Adams, *Famous Ships of the British Navy,* Appendix p 281.

[75] 1871 Committee on Designs, quoted in D K Brown, *Warrior to Dreadnought.*

[76] Ballard, p 174.

[77] Ballard, p 183.

[78] See Ship's Book, PRO ADM 135/488.

[79] William Webb, *Coastguard!* , p 37.

[80] Hansard vol. 227 column 1030.

[81] H F Whitfield, *Plymouth and Devonport,* p 148.

[82] Quoted in K V Burns: *The Devonport Dockyard Story,* p 13.

[83] W G Hoskins, *Old Devon,* p 120.

[84] Whitfield, p 345.

[85] Quoted in Whitfield, p 360.

[86] Whitfield, p 361.

[87] Quoted in Whitfield, p 402.

[88] Peter Pearson, *Dun Laoghaire – Kingstown* p 9. Published by the O'Brien Press, Dublin, copyright Peter Pearson.

[89] Pearson, p 26.

[90] Pearson, p 98.

[91] Pearson, p 63.

[92] Quoted in *Dublin's Riviera in the Mid 19th Century,* comp. Hall and O'Reilly, p 19 ff , reproduced by kind permission of the Genealogical Society of Ireland.

[93] Notice reproduced in Pearson, p 38.

[94] Ship's Log, 21 April 1875 to 30 September 1875, PRO ADM 53/10409.

[95] National Maritime Museum Greenwich manuscript DAW/11a.

[96] NMM DAW/11c.

[97] WCS Hathorn, letter to his parents, 27 July 1875. In the event *Favorite* and *Defence* do not appear to have accompanied the Squadron on the cruise.

[98] TNA: PRO ADM 196/15 p287.

[99] Letter to the author from Linda Johnson, 24 March 2002.

[100] GA Ballard, *The Black Battlefleet* p184.

[101] *Naval and Military Record* 31 December 1903 p10.

[102] Letter to the author from Elizabeth Edwards, 16 November 2001.

[103] Email from Guy Hickley, 14 March 2002.

[104] Email to the author from Guy Hickley, 13 March 2002.

[105] PRO ADM 196/36 p631.

[106] PRO ADM 196/17 p517.

[107] Letter to the author from Mike Boynes, November 2001.

[108] Court Martial proceedings, first day, reported in *The Times,* 11 September 1875.

[109] PRO ADM 167/8.

[110] Letter dated 14 February 1865 to his parents.

[111] PRO ADM 196/17 p173.

[112] Letter from WCS Hathorn to 'G ', 27 September 1866..

[113] Letter, ditto, 25 February 1869.

[114] Letter to his parents, 3 January 1869.

[115] Letter from Mary Fordyce to 'Aunt Bella' from Government House, Madras, 21 February 1871.

[116] PRO ADM 196/38 p575.

[117] PRO ADM 196/60.

[118] PRO ADM 196/23 p273.

[119] PRO ADM 194/43.

[120] *The Times* 29 September 1875.

[121] *The Times* 28 September 1875.

[122] Parliamentary Papers 1876 Vol XLVIII.

[123] Email to the author from Shirley Stapley, 23 July 2001.

[124] Email to the author from Philip Lecane, 21 August 2001.

[125] Enclosure dated March 1993 with letter to the author from Maureen Selley.

[126] Portsmouth City Records Office ref. CHU 3/1b/15.

[127] Draft autobiographical notes by Richard McGillivray Dawkins, Taylor Institution, Oxford ref. F.Arch.Z Dawk.6(1-6).

[128] As note 2.

[129] National Maritime Museum, Greenwich, manuscript DAW/1.

[130] NMM manuscript DAW/1.

[131] DAW/1.

[132] DAW/1.

[133] TNA: PRO ADM 196/36 page 297.

[134] DAW/1.

[135] Griffiths, Lambert and Walker: *Brunel's Ships* p126.

[136] DAW/1.

[137] DAW/1.

[138] DAW/1.

[139] NMM manuscript DAW/2

[140] Letter to the author from the Library and Museum of Freemasonry, London, 16 August 2002.

[141] DAW/1.

[142] DAW/1.

[143] NMM Manuscript DAW/3.

[144] Taylor Institution ref f.Arch.Z Dawk. 6(1-6).

[145] DAW/1.

[146] This and following quotations all from NMM manuscript DAW/4.

[147] George Malcolm Thomson, *The North-West Passage* p241, reproduced by kind permission of David Higham Associates.

[148] NMM manuscript DAW/1.

[149] Taylor Institution. F.Arch.Z.Dawk.

[150] DAW/1.

[151] DAW/1.

[152] Peter Padfield, *Rule Britannia!* p62.

[153] Taylor Institution, as note 149.

[154] As note 20.

[155] Journal of the Clan Chattan Association, Vol X No.3, 1997.

[156] Roger Hall: *An Imperial Businessman In The Age Of Improvement: Simon McGillivray After The Fur Trade* in *Dalhousie Review*, September 1980.

[157] NMM DAW/3.

[158] From *Up and Down the River Dart,* by Robert Crabford, pub. about 1900, courtesy of Totnes Museum.

[159] DAW/4.

[160] DAW/4.

[161] NMM manuscript DAW/11a.

[162] Parliamentary Papers 1876 Vol XLVII.

[163] Hansard vol 227 col 1049.

[164] K C Barnaby, *Some Ship Disasters and their Causes* (Hutchinson 1968).

[165] WCS Hathorn: letter to 'Flo and Theo' from *Vanguard* at Galway, 9 August 1875.

[166] Evidence given by Captain Dawkins at the Court Martial, reported in *The Times*, 11 September 1875. In this and other chapters, quotations from the Court Martial proceedings are, for ease of reference, taken from the *Times* reports. E.g., 'CM, *The Times,* 16 September 1875 ' denotes a quotation from evidence given by the witness named unless otherwise stated.

[167] Letter from Richard Dawkins to Mrs Mary Dawkins, 6 August 1875; National Maritime Museum, Greenwich manuscript DAW/11a.

[168] Hathorn letter, 9 August 1875.

[169] Letter from Richard Dawkins to Mrs Mary Dawkins, 28 August 1875; NMM manuscript DAW/11a.

[170] TNA: PRO ADM 50/343.

[171] PRO ADM 117/994.

[172] Milne to Tarleton, 28 August 1875, Tarleton Deeds (in the care of the Tarleton Fagan family), bundle 173.

[173] *The Daily Telegraph* 3 September 1875.

[174] From Signals Log of *Warrior,* bound into Court Martial proceedings PRO ADM 1/6369.

[175] Captain's log, HMS *Vanguard* PRO 53/10409.

[176] Record of observations from the Royal Engineers Meteorological Observatory at O.S.O. Dublin for September 1875, provided by Met Éireann (The Irish Meteorological Service) in April 2001.

[177] CM, *The Times,* 17 September 1875.

[178] CM, evidence of Admiral Tarleton, *The Times,* 14 September 1875.

[179] CM, evidence of Robert Martins, *The Times* 16 September 1875.

[180] CM, *The Times* 17 September 1875.

[181] CM, evidence of Captain Hickley, *The Times* 18 September 1875.

[182] CM, *The Times* 21 September 1875.

[183] CM, *The Times* 17 September 1875.

[184] CM, *The Times* 21 September 1875.

[185] CM, *The Times* 21 September 1875.

[186] CM, *The Times* 20 September 1875.

[187] CM, *The Times* 18 September 1875.

[188] CM, *The Times* 20 September 1875.

[189] CM, *The Times* 23 September 1875.

[190] CM, *The Times* 23 September 1875.

[191] CM, *The Times* 23 September 1875.

[192] CM, *The Times* 23 September 1875.

[193] CM, *The Times* 23 September 1875.

[194] CM, *The Times* 22 September 1875.

[195] CM, *The Times* 22 September 1875.

[196] 'An officer on board the *Vanguard* at the time of the late collision has written the following letter to a friend in Maidstone ' *The Times* and *The Daily Telegraph* 8 September 1875.

[197] CM, *The Times* 24 September 1875.

[198] CM, *The Times* 23 September 1875.

[199] Mrs Saxby, *Breakers Ahead* p 115.

[200] 'An officer... to a friend in Maidstone ' *The Times* and *The Daily Telegraph* 8 September 1875.

[201] WCS Hathorn, letter to his parents, 2 September 1875 and copy of his report to the Captain with a further note for his parents, 1 September 1875.

[202] *The Times* 25 September 1875.

[203] *The Devonport Independent, and Plymouth and Stonehouse Gazette,* September 4 1875.

[204] CM, *The Times* 14 September 1875.

[205] CM, *The Times* 15 September 1875.

[206] CM, *The Times* 14 September 1875.

[207] *The Daily Telegraph* 4 September 1875.

[208] *The Western Times,* Exeter, 7 September 1875.

[209] 'An officer ... to a friend in Maidstone ' *The Times* and *The Daily Telegraph* 8 September 1875.

[210] CM, *The Times* 18 September 1875.

[211] National Maritime Museum, Greenwich manuscript DAW/11a.

[212] *The Times,* September 3, 1875.

[213] WCS Hathorn, letter to his parents 9 September 1875.

[214] *The Daily Telegraph,* September 3 1875.

[215] National Maritime Museum, Greenwich, manuscript MLN/164/10.

[216] *The Daily Telegraph,* September 7 1875.

[217] *The Times,* September 4 1875.

[218] NNM MLN/164/10.

[219] *The Times,* September 6 1875.

[220] *The Times,* September 7 1875.

[221] NMM manuscript DAW/11a.

[222] Hathorn, letters to his parents, 2 and 4 September 1875.

[223] *Who Was Who, 1916-1928.*

[224] NMM manuscript DAW/11c.

[225] KC Barnaby, *Some Ship Disasters and their Causes* p 73.

[226] Peter Padfield, *Rule Britannia* p187.

[227] Richard Hill, *War at Sea in the Ironclad Age* p 85.

[228] Geoffrey Regan, *Naval Blunders* p 90 by permission of Carlton Books.

[229] *Illustrated London News,* September 25 1875, p 306. The illustration appears in the same issue.

[230] Court Martial Report, PRO ADM 1/6369.

[231] NMM manuscript DAW/11c.

[232] This and subsequent quotations, unless otherwise noted, come either from the transcript in PRO ADM 1/6369, or from the reports in *The Times,* which appear to be generally accurate.

[233] TNA: PRO ADM 167/8, entry dated 20 October 1875.

[234] KC Barnaby p 79.

[235] KC Barnaby p 80.

[236] This and most following quotes from correspondence may be found in National Maritime Museum, Greenwich manuscripts DAW/11c.

237 R Dawkins letter to Admiral Hathorn, 7 October 1875 (Hathorn papers).

238 NMM DAW/11b.

239 NMM DAW/11a.

240 WCS Hathorn, letter to his parents 30 September 1875.

241 *Punch* October 9 1875, p144.

242 Admiral G A Ballard, *The Black Battlefleet* p187.

243 KC Barnaby, *Some Ship Disasters and their Causes* p79.

244 *The Times* October 4 1875.

245 *Western Daily Mercury* October 6 1875.

246 NMM DAW/11b.

247 NMM MLN/164/10.

248 NMM MLN/164/10.

249 4 November 1875, Tarleton Deeds (in the care of the Tarleton Fagan family), bundle 173.

250 20 May 1876, Tarleton Deeds bundle 173.

251 23 February 1876, Tarleton Deeds bundle 173.

252 *The Times* October 13 1875.

253 NMM DAW/11a.

254 Hathorn letter to his parents 24 October 1875.

255 NMM DAW/15.

256 NMM DAW/11a.

257 *Punch*, October 23 1875 p159.

258 Quoted in http://homepage.ntlworld.com/pernod/5.html.

259 *Kilvert's Diary, 1870-1879*, entry for 19 August 1875 (Penguin edition 1977, page 313).

260 Hansard vol 227 28 February 1876 column 1026.

261 *Punch* November 20 1875 p207.

262 Tarleton Deeds bundle 173.

263 Hathorn letter to his parents 24 October 1875.

264 TNA: PRO ADM 167/8.

265 Hathorn letter 7 November 1875.

266 Hansard Vol 233 23 April 1877 column 1671.

267 NMM DAW/11c.

268 The following extracts are from NMM DAW/9b.

269 *Western Morning News* November 18 1876.

270 NMM DAW/10.

271 Letter of 20 January 1876, NMM DAW/10.

272 Hansard Vol 227 28 February 1876 columns 1026 to 1098.

273 Tarleton Deeds, as above.

274 Tarleton Deeds, as above.

275 NMM DAW/12.

276 NMM DAW/9a. The Memorial itself is at NMM DAW/8.

277 Tarleton Deeds, as above.

278 Brian Hamment-Arnold and others, *Stoke Gabriel*, p15.

279 Letter to the author from Kildare James, July 2003.

280 This and subsequent quotes from the Dawkins sons Richard and John are taken from the Papers of R McG Dawkins, Taylor Institution F.Arch.Z Dawk.6.

281 National Maritime Museum, Greenwich manuscript DAW/1.

282 *Totnes Times* 20 January 1877.

283 *Totnes Times* 28 March 1896.

284 NMM DAW/9a.

285 *Totnes Times* 28 March 1876.

286 Osbert Lancaster, *With an Eye to the Future* p77. Reproduced with the agreement of John Murray, part of Hodder Headline, but I have been unsuccessful in locating the copyright holder. A fuller account of the life of RM Dawkins may be found in *Richard McGillivray Dawkins 1871-1955* by RJH Jenkins (Proceedings of the British Academy Vol XLI).

287 Taylor Institution.

288 NMM DAW/14.

289 Letter to the author, November 2001.

290 TNA: PRO ADM 196/37 p1315.

291 *The Kildare Observer* Saturday October 6th 1883, by courtesy of David Hope.

292 *The Times* Court Martial report, September 18 1875.

293 Surgeon's Log, HMS *Raleigh* PRO ADM 101/212.

294 Peter Padfield, *Rule Britannia* p69.

295 WCS Hathorn, letter to his brother George, 24 February 1870.

296 GA Ballard, *The Black Battlefleet* p188.

297 W Hathorn: letter to his parents, 24 October 1875.

298 PRO ADM 196/39 p960.

299 PRO ADM 196/39 p1224.

300 Letter to his parents, 9 October 1873.

301 Letter to his mother, 28 February 1876.

302 Letter to his mother, 28 October 1879.

303 PRO ADM 196/38 p575.

304 Letter to his mother, 1 November 1885.

305 PRO ADM 194/44.

306 Letter to the author from Robert Paige, 25 September 2002.

307 Geoffrey Best, *Mid-Victorian Britain 1851-75* p97.

[308] National Maritime Museum, Greenwich manuscripts MSS 82/093.

[309] *Naval and Military Record,* 31 December 1903, p10.

[310] Letter, 9 October 1873.

[311] NMM Manuscript MSS 85/011.

[312] PRO ADM 196/39 p1302.

[313] PRO ADM 1/6361, Devonport Yard correspondence.

[314] *The Times* Court Martial report, September 16 1875.

[315] PRO ADM 196/60.

[316] *The Times,* September 6 1875. All quotations about salvage operations in this chapter are taken from reports or letters published in *The Times* unless otherwise noted.

[317] *The Daily Telegraph,* September 9 1875.

[318] *Punch* October 9 1875 p139.

[319] Much of this information from www.divingheritage.com.

[320] www.iro.umontreal.ca; author's translation from French original.

[321] Information from contemporary accounts supplied by the Historical Diving Society.

[322] TNA: PRO ADM 167/7.

[323] PRO Admiralty Board General Minutes 1875, ADM 167/8.

[324] FM Holmes, *Celebrated Mechanics and their Achievements* p 90 (London, ca. 1920). Information supplied by the Historical Diving Society.

[325] PRO ADM 1/6361.

[326] *The Times* December 9 1875.

[327] PRO ADM 12/982.

[328] *Hansard* vol 231 p276 11 August 1876.

[329] *The Times* October 2 1876 and *Hansard* Vol 232 20 Feb 1877.

[330] *Hansard* 8 April 1878.

[331] *Hansard* 16 August 1878.

[332] *Hansard* 17 March 1879.

[333] *SubSea* No.102, Winter 2000.

[334] Email to the author, 2 September 2003.

[335] KC Barnaby, *Some Ship Disasters and their Causes* p85.

[336] From a paper read before the Institution of Naval Architects, quoted in WH Davenport Adams, *Famous Ships of the British Navy,* p290.

[337] *Punch* September 11 1875 p105.

[338] Quoted in KC Barnaby, *op cit* p85.

[339] *Punch* October 30 1875 p182.

[340] *Punch* December 18 1875 p266.

[341] *The Times,* 25 December 1906.

[342] Commander W J Lamb: *Vanguard 1586-1946,* p37.

[343] www.royal-navy.mod.uk (January 2002) Crown copyright; used with permission.

[344] Richard Hill, *War at Sea in the Ironclad Age* p35.

[345] Peter Padfield, *The Battleship Era* p93.

[346] For obvious reasons the source of this quotation is withheld!

[347] Autobiographical Notes by R M Dawkins, Taylor Institution f.Arch.Z.Dawk 6.

[348] Roy Stokes, article in *SubSea* Winter 2000.

Bibliography

1 HMS *VANGUARD* AND HER LOSS IN 1875

Admiral G Ballard: The Black Battlefleet (Nautical Publishing Company Ltd and Society for Nautical Research, 1980)

K C Barnaby: Some Ship Disasters and their Causes (Hutchinson 1968)

John Harris: Lost at Sea (Guild Publishing 1990)

P K Kemp: Nine *Vanguards* (Hutchinson 1951)

Commander W J Lamb OBE MVO: HMS *Vanguard* 1586-1946 (no publisher, 1946?)

John Marriott: Disaster at Sea (Ian Allan 1987)

Geoffrey Regan: Naval Blunders (Carlton Books Ltd, 2001)

Mrs J M Saxby: Breakers Ahead, or, Uncle Jack's Stories of Great Shipwrecks of Recent Times: 1869 to 1880 (Nelson 1891)

2 THE DEVELOPMENT OF THE IRONCLAD

W H Davenport Adams: Famous Ships of the British Navy; or, Stories of Enterprise and Daring Collected from Our Naval Chronicles, ... and an Appendix on Iron-Clad Ships by N Barnaby (James Hogg & Sons, 1863)

E Archibald: The Metal Fighting Ship 1860-1970 (Blandford 1971)

Admiral G Ballard: The Black Battlefleet (Nautical Publishing Company Ltd and Society for Nautical Research, 1980)

John Beeler: Birth of the Battleship, British capital ship design 1870-1881 (Chatham Publishing, 2001)

D K Brown: Before the Ironclad, Development of Ship Design, Propulsion and Armament in the Royal Navy, 1815-60 (Conway Maritime Press 1990)

D K Brown: Warrior to Dreadnought, Warship Development 1860-1905 (Chatham Publishing 1997)

Denis Griffiths, Andrew Lambert & Fred Walker: Brunel's Ships (Chatham Publishing 1999)

Richard Hill: War at Sea in the Ironclad Age (Cassell, 2000)

Andrew Lambert: Battleships in Transition, The Creation of the Steam Battlefleet 1815-1860 (Conway Maritime Press 1984)

Oscar Parkes: British Battleships (Seeley Service 1966)

3 MORE GENERAL NAVAL HISTORY

John F Beeler: British Naval Policy in the Gladstone-Disraeli Era, 1866-1880 (Stanford University Press 1997)

W Laird Clowes: History of the Royal Navy, 1857-1900 (Sampson Low 1903)

J J Colledge: Ships of the Royal Navy (Greenhill Books 1969 – edition of 1987)

Conrad Dixon: Ships of the Victorian Navy (Ashford Press Publishing 1987)

David Howarth: Sovereign of the Seas, the story of British Sea Power (Collins 1974)

Peter Padfield: The Battleship Era (Pan Books, Grand Strategy series, 1972)

Peter Padfield: Rule Britannia, The Victorian and Edwardian Navy (Pimlico, 2002)

Anthony J Watts: The Royal Navy, an illustrated history (Brockhampton Press 1999)

4 HMS *WARRIOR*

Robin Dulake and Ian Robinson: HMS *Warrior*, Britain's First Ironclad (*Warrior* Preservation Trust 1987)

John McIlwain: HMS *Warrior* (Pitkin Pictorials 1991)

5 SHIPBOARD LIFE

Lieutenant-Commander Henry D Capper OBE RN: Aft – from the Hawsehole, sixty-two years of sailors' evolution (Faber & Gwyer, 1927)

David Marcombe: The Victorian Sailor (Shire Publications 1995)

Navy Records Society, Vol XXXIII: Naval Songs and Ballads (NRS 1908)

John Winton: Hurrah for the Life of a Sailor! Life in the lower-deck of the Victorian Navy (Michael Joseph 1977)

6 THE COASTGUARD SERVICE

William Webb: Coastguard! An official history of HM Coastguard (HMSO 1976)

7 REFERENCE WORKS

A List of Her Majesty's Ships in Commission, August 1875 (Eyre & Spottiswoode for HMSO, 1875)

R Gardiner (Ed): Conway's All The World's Fighting Ships 1860-1905 (Conway Maritime Press 1979)

Charles Hocking: Dictionary of Disasters at Sea During the Age of Steam 1824-1962 (London Stamp Exchange 1990)

Rick Jolly & Tug Willson: Jackspeak, the Pusser's Rum guide to Royal Navy Slanguage (Palamanando Press, 1989)

8 ABOUT DEVONPORT AND DÚN LAOGHAIRE

Sally Birch (Ed): Stoke Gabriel (1991?)

Lt Cdr K V Burns DSM RN: The Devonport Dockyard Story (Maritime Books 1984)

Brendan Hall & G H O'Reilly (compilers): Dublin's Riviera in the Mid 19th Century (Irish Genealogical Sources No 18, Genealogical Society of Ireland 2000)

John de Courcy Ireland: History of Dún Laoghaire Harbour (Pub.? 2001)

Derek Paine: A Pictorial History of Greystones, Bray and Enniskerry 1835-1980 (Pub? 2001)

Peter Pearson: Dún Laoghaire – Kingstown (Urban Heritage Series 2, O'Brien Press 1981)

Henry Francis Whitfeld: Plymouth and Devonport: In Times of War and Peace (privately published, 1900)

TODAY'S DESCENDANTS (OR OTHER RELATIVES) OF THE OFFICERS AND CREW OF HMS *VANGUARD*, HMS *IRON DUKE* AND THEIR FLAGSHIP HMS *WARRIOR* IN 1875

Mrs Ann Bogdanovic (Devon, UK), great-granddaughter of Private Walter Jewell RMLI, *Vanguard* (1874–Sep 1875)

Michael Boynes (Hampshire, UK), great-grandson of Stoker Charles Boynes, *Iron Duke* (Jul 1875–Sep 1875)

Fred W Burnett (Devon, UK), great-grandson of Boatman Elias Rendell, *Vanguard* (Summer Cruise, Jul-Aug 1875)

Mrs June Cangey (UK) (and her daughter Cathy), great-great-great-granddaughter of the first cousin of Lieutenant Pierre Gervais Evans, *Iron Duke* (Jul-Sep 1875)

William Casey (Cork City, Ireland) Distant cousin by marriage of Boatman Charles Harcourt, *Vanguard* (Summer Cruise, Jul-Aug 1875)

Janette Courtney (Australia) Great-granddaughter of Commissioned Boatman John Sweet, *Vanguard* (Summer Cruise, Jul-Aug 1875)

John Deering (New York State, USA), whose wife is a distant cousin of Lieutenant Ringrose Tully RMLI, *Iron Duke* (On strength of Endymion Jan 1875-Mar 1877)

Sqn Ldr Tony Douglas-Beveridge RAF(retd) (UK) Great-grandson of Commissioned Boatman George Boiling, *Vanguard* (Summer Cruise, Jul-Aug 1875)

Captain Christopher Fagan DL (Hampshire, UK), great-grandson of Vice Admiral Sir Walter Tarleton, *Warrior* (Flagship Jul 1875-1876)

Stuart Fegan (UK), great-grandson of Boatman Daniel Fegan, *Vanguard* (Summer Cruise, Jul-Aug 1875)

Paul Hanna (Arlington Heights, Illinois, USA) great-grandson of Boatman Thomas Crocker, *Vanguard* (Summer Cruise, Jul-Aug 1875)

Guy Hickley (Somerset, UK), whose great-grandfather was brother to Captain Henry Hickley, *Iron Duke* (Jul-Sep 1875)

David M Hope (Kent, UK) Whose wife is the great-granddaughter of a first cousin of Commander Dashwood G Tandy, *Vanguard* (Oct 1873-Sep 1875)

John Hussey (Dublin, Ireland), Whose wife is great-granddaughter of Ordinary Seaman Michael Cavanagh, *Iron Duke* (Dec 1875-Jul 1877)

Linda Johnson (Surrey, UK), Great-granddaughter of Steward Charles Burridge, *Warrior* (Jul 1875-Jul 1877)

Philip Lecane (Co. Antrim, Ireland), Great-grandson of Able Seaman Philip LeQuesne, *Vanguard* (Feb 1874-Sep 1875)

Prof. Dr. Gianni Lombardi (Rome, Italy), Great-grandson of Captain Richard Dawkins, *Vanguard* (Oct 1873-Sep 1875)

Quentin J Morgan (S. Wales, UK), Whose wife is great-granddaughter of Boatman Richard T Edgcombe, *Vanguard* (Summer Cruise, Jul-Aug 1875)

Robert Paige (Hampshire, UK), Great-grandson of Engineer William G Paige, *Vanguard* (Aug 1874-Sep 1875)

Derek Paine (Co. Wicklow, Ireland), Grandson of Ordinary Seaman 2nd Class Robert Thompson, *Vanguard* (Apr-Oct 1874) - and whose aunt's grandfather was Thomas Curling, *Vanguard*

Gary Paine (Surrey, UK), Great-grandson of Ordinary Seaman 2nd Class Robert Thompson, *Vanguard*

George Paul (Berkshire, UK), Grandson of Boatman John Henry Paul, *Vanguard* (Summer Cruise, Jul-Aug 1875)

Mrs Marjorie Penn (Cornwall, UK), Granddaughter of Engine Room Artificer John Davies, *Vanguard* (Jun-Sep 1875)

Mrs Maureen Selley (Devon, UK), Whose late husband was great-grandson of Pte Robert Selley RMLI, *Vanguard* (May-Sep 1875)

Mrs Ann Smith (Prince Edward Island, Canada), Whose husband is great-grandson of Commissioned Boatman Florence Sullivan, *Vanguard* (Summer Cruise, Jul 1875)

Mrs Shirley Stapley (Devon, UK), Granddaughter of Private Walter Jewell RMLI, *Vanguard* (1874-Sep 1875)

Mrs Kaye Tully Steele (Oregon, USA), Great-great-niece of Lieutenant Ringrose Tully RMLI, *Iron Duke* (On strength of Endymion Jan 1875-Mar 1877)

John Tarleton, (New York State, USA), Distant cousin of Vice Admiral Sir J Walter Tarleton, *Warrior* (Flagship Jul 1875-1876)

Mrs Vivien Teasdale (Yorkshire, UK), Great-granddaughter of Stoker Henry Farrow, *Warrior* (Jul-Sep 1875)

Mrs Daphne Thomas (Warwickshire, UK), Great-granddaughter of Leading Seaman Henry Gaden, *Vanguard* (Feb-Sep 1875), and Ordinary Seaman 2nd Class Francis Norton, *Vanguard* (May-Sep 1875)

(The late) Lady Margaret Turton-Hart (Devon, UK) Great-granddaughter of the sister of Lieutenant William C S Hathorn, *Vanguard* (Jul-Sep 1875)

Acknowledgements

Any piece of research involves seeking the aid of a lot of people, and in listing those who have been especially helpful to me I risk omitting many whose contributions have been significant. To those whose names do not appear here, my heartfelt apologies. First of all, my thanks go to the descendants and other relatives of the officers and crew of *Vanguard* and the other ships involved, who have not only been generous in providing information about their ancestors but have also given enthusiastic support to the project. Their names are listed at the end of this note. Special gratitude is due to Maureen Selley, currently Chairman of the Devon Family History Society, who gave me the initial impetus to write this story.

I am greatly indebted to Dr Andrew Lambert, Laughton Professor of Naval History at King's College London, for having read through my typescript, corrected the inevitable errors, and given me much encouragement and advice, as well as for providing such a generous foreword.

On a range of maritime subjects I am grateful to David Clement of the South West Maritime History Society, to John Bevan of the Historical Diving Society, to Roy Stokes and the late Philip Oglesby of the Marlin Sub Aqua Club of Dublin, and to Tony Daly of Coastguards of Yesteryear; and in the field of *Vanguard* history, Bill Schleihauf (the eighth *Vanguard*) and Shirley North, who served aboard the ninth *Vanguard*. Others who have helped in many ways have been Elizabeth Edwards, historian of the Hickley family, Brian Hamment-Arnold and Kildare James of Stoke Gabriel, and Denis Metherall, past Master of the United Grand Lodge of England.

Libraries and museums to whom I owe much include the Britannia Royal Naval College, Dartmouth (Dr Richard Porter); the Caird Library at the National Maritime Museum, Greenwich; the Library and Museum of Freemasonry; the National Archives, including the Public Record Office at Kew and the Family Records Centre; the Royal Naval Museum, Portsmouth (Allison Wareham); the Taylor Institution, Oxford; Totnes Museum (Sue King); and my local Kenilworth branch of Warwickshire County Library.

Finally, my family. My son-in-law Mark Evans, who among other things is Secretary to the British Aviation Archaeology Council, has been invaluable in asking awkward questions and checking the text minutely. My daughter Candida, granddaughter Sabrina and above all my wife Daphne (the only "*Vanguard* descendant" to have two relatives on board on that day in 1875) have encouraged and tolerated and supported me throughout, and I am eternally grateful.

Chris Thomas
Kenilworth, Warwickshire
November 2005